**THE GOOD NEWS IS:**
Men want intimacy, too

**THE BAD NEWS IS:**
What a man considers intimacy is
*not at all* what a woman thinks it
is. This is a basic law of male
psychology.

Dr. Connell Cowan and Dr. Melvyn Kinder,
authors of the celebrated bestseller *Smart
Women, Foolish Choices*, now unravel the
puzzling patterns of a man's attraction
and—yes!—committment, telling exactly
what goes on inside his heart and mind
when he relates to a woman.

# WOMEN
# MEN LOVE
## WOMEN
## MEN LEAVE

Dr. Connell Cowan and Dr. Melvyn Kinder are
clinical psychologists. Their innovative work,
using videotape techniques in the treatment of
marital and family crises, has been featured in
many national magazines and on television.
Their first book together, the bestselling *Smart
Women, Foolish Choices*, is available in a Signet
paperback edition.

# WOMEN MEN LOVE WOMEN MEN LEAVE

## What Makes Men Want to Commit

by

### Dr. Connell Cowan &
### Dr. Melvyn Kinder

A SIGNET BOOK

**NEW AMERICAN LIBRARY**

The cases and voices heard throughout this book are real, but names and identities have been changed for the purpose of confidentiality.

This edition published by arrangement with
Clarkson N. Potter, Inc.

First Signet Printing, May, 1988

1 2 3 4 5 6 7 8 9

To Casey, the woman I love, and to Sean, Coby, and Joey, and the women they will someday love.

C.C.


For Sara, wise confidante and caring wife, for whom my love grows stronger with the years, and for our children, Eric and Alexandra.

M.K.

# CONTENTS

# ACKNOWLEDGMENTS

We wish to thank Robert Gottlieb, our literary agent, for his enthusiastic encouragement, professionalism, and his ever thoughtful advice.

Our deepest thanks to Carol Southern at Clarkson N. Potter and Elaine Koster and the editorial staff at New American Library for their perceptive and enormously beneficial reactions and suggestions about the manuscript.

Our appreciation to Carol Lacey and Linda Shulman for their help in preparing the manuscript and to Laura Daltry for her editorial assistance, insightful feedback, and advice.

We especially wish to thank our tireless editor, Carolyn Hart. Once again, her intuitive and astute observations, as well as her skillful shaping and guidance, were invaluable to the final form of this book.

And to our wives, Casey and Sara, for their warm and generous support, their willingness to be tireless and resourceful sounding boards, and for tolerating our preoccupation with the project—our love.

# PART ONE

# Women Men Leave

# CHAPTER ONE

# Why Love Seems So Elusive

For so many women today, men are confusing, even incomprehensible. They seem to operate according to a murky set of rules women have never quite learned.

Victoria, 30, is a nurse at a big-city general hospital. She's ready to get married and start a family, but, like so many women today, she's baffled by men's behavior. "I help male patients of all ages through all kinds of medical crises, but when it comes to relationships, I don't have a clue to what's going on in a man's head. What do they want? What does it take to make them want to call back? How do you turn a few dates into a relationship, how do you make it work? I am so tired of going home aching with loneliness and secretly feeling that things will never change."

Donna is a 41-year-old attorney who has been married for nine years. "I'm so different now than when Tom and I first got married, but he doesn't seem to appreciate that. I don't know whether he's threatened or what, but I wish he would talk to me . . . I wish he cared about what's going on inside of me!" Donna wants to be more intimate with her husband but has no idea how to make that happen.

Arlene, 28, a department store buyer, is always going out yet never gets beyond three or four dates with the same man. "I end up making excuses for myself. Sometimes I put the guy down, or I make a joke out of it. Now that I'm nearly 30, I'm afraid I'll never get a man to fall in love with me. All my friends are in relationships, and I can't figure out why I'm not." Arlene knows there is something about her behavior that makes men leave, but she doesn't know how to change the self-defeating patterns that may be set in motion even on the first date.

Cecile, a 36-year-old graphics designer who's been living with a man for eighteen months, describes a growing anxiety. "Even though I know Rusty loves me and eventually wants to get married, I'm still worried. I keep hearing about friends who separated right before they were going to announce their engagement. I feel so conflicted. I'm afraid to push him, but at the same time, I can't just be passive and say nothing." If Cecile understood why and how men eventually commit themselves to a woman, she would not be so apprehensive. In the absence of that kind of insight, she feels enveloped by fear.

The common thread running through the lives of all these women is their compelling wish to understand the nature of a man's love. Whether it is the first date or a marriage of many years, they want to feel they can change the course of love, that they can heighten a man's attraction and strengthen his commitment. But, sadly, they feel powerless to transform that need into a reality.

\* \* \*

## Why Is Love So Puzzling?

We all want to find and nourish warm, rich, and fulfilling relationships. Why, when we all have the same hopeful intentions, does love become so easily diminished; why do couples drift away from each other? Why does love blossom into an enduring bond for some people, but never seem to develop roots for others?

Relationships do not typically unravel because of major conflicts—surprisingly, those are often handled in constructive ways. Most relationships die slowly and without the conscious awareness of either party. There is a fine line between a relationship that moves in a positive direction and one that slips silently into apathy or the slow accumulation of disappointments and resentment. Most of us do not know where that line is and do not have the specific guideposts to track it over a period of time.

When we know what affects relationships, we are then able to change them. Although some women and men believe that love is too special, fragile, and wondrous to tamper with, the reality is that love is governed not by quirks of fate, but by particular psychologies—ways of understanding and predicting how people will behave in certain situations. The person who is in love feels out of control, may feel "swept away" with infatuation, yet secretly may be pessimistic and helpless when love mysteriously goes awry. Isn't it better to have a sound understanding of the dynamics of love? Hope and optimism are never misguided when grounded in knowledge and certainty.

The voices you heard at the beginning of this chapter essentially are asking, "How do I make love happen, and how do I keep it alive?" There are answers. It *is* possible to influence this most wonderful, delightful, and necessary of life's experiences. You *can* learn to have an effect on a man's feelings of trust, friendship, and passion.

The ability to effect change is not an accident of fate, nor is it an instinctive trait possessed by only a few women. The first step is understanding that learning and information can alter love's path.

In the past twenty years much has been written concerning women's hopes, dreams, and secret fears. Unfortunately, there has not been a comparable source of information about the evolving nature of male psychology, particularly as it relates to women. In addition to this gap in information, there is another more basic reason why men seem so incomprehensible to women. The fact is, men have generally never been all that eager to be known in depth by women. The "male mystique" has served men well in disguising the truth about their fears and insecurities; it has protected them from being a disappointment to women. But despite this need to feel strong and invincible, men have an even more compelling need to be known by the woman they love.

## The Need for Love

The desire to know more about the opposite sex seems to be stronger than ever before, and there are some specific reasons for this. In recent years, men and women have begun to re-embrace the concept of marriage and family and value it as part of a general return to traditional values that has occurred in the eighties. Spurred on by a disenchantment with the pleasures of single life, a growing concern with social diseases, and the resulting end of the sexual revolution, men and women are again favoring a more conservative and monogamous life-style.

For some women, there are some special and rather poignant urgencies. Women of the baby-boom generation—women ranging in age from 25 to 40—are, in increasing numbers, eager to marry and begin families while they still can. Moreover, many of these same women have found a fast-track career life not as fulfilling as they had expected. So, somewhat disillusioned, and painfully cognizant of their biological clocks, many single women of this generation want to find men and establish firm bonds with them.

The wish for commitment has given rise to a new set of concerns. Women clearly desire commitment, and think that most men today don't. We do not believe this to be the case, and throughout this book we will be presenting information about just what it is in a woman that makes a man *want* to commit to her. We will also discuss the basic difference between men and women with respect to the timing of commitment and marriage, which is a very real source of tension. It is this difference that contributes to the myth that men do not wish to commit themselves.

Men under the age of 35 often appear to avoid commitment because they are consumed with work and career. In the eighties especially, with the intense new work ethic and the rise of a new "yuppie" materialistic philosophy, men are choosing to put marriage aside for more years than they did in the past. That is not to say that men do not ultimately want to commit themselves to a relationship. What it means is that their highly focused emotional investment in work predominates. Unlike women, men do not have biological clocks that force them to reorder their priorities.

The need for love is a pressing issue not only for

single women but for married women as well. They too have concerns about the quality of their relationships with men. While the basic structure of her marriage may seem stable, a woman often senses tensions, feels she is disappointing her husband as well as being disappointed herself, and she may not know how to change things or even know if it is possible to do so.

Some basic but poorly understood differences between the sexes account for many of the confusions and tensions that arise in love relationships. When the reasons for these differences are known and the ways such differences affect relationships are understood, exchanges between men and women become far more comprehensible and less frustrating.

## Tensions Between the Sexes

Like most people, you may assume that women willingly embrace love, while men are more ambivalent—they can take it or leave it; that women innately are more monogamous and faithful, while men are polygamous, more prone to roam even when they seemingly have been given everything by the woman they love; that men are less capable of and less comfortable with intimacy, while women easily give full expression to love; that men are romantic only when in pursuit, and that their amorous gestures are mere "tricks," which are discarded the moment they feel certain of a woman's love; that women are love addicts, and men are love holdouts; that women like to be swept off their feet and men like to be babied in a relationship.

The fact is, there are elements of truth in all of these statements. These are the ingredients in the age-old tension and misunderstanding between men and women—the battle of the sexes. You undoubtedly have experienced these curious tensions in your own life. You are not alone—we all struggle with them. Men and women have always been fascinated, intrigued, suspicious, frustrated, and mystified by each other.

The term *battle of the sexes* came about because as men and women are drawn to each other, feelings of wariness and suspicion are heightened. Why should this be so? What causes men and women to need and desire each other and yet be so cautious, so easily disappointed and frustrated? There is a simple reason for this complex dilemma. Men and women are different. We delight in some of these differences yet absolutely fail to understand, much less appreciate, many others.

Perhaps the most basic conflict between men and women comes from the fundamental difference in how they view intimacy—what it means, its priority in their lives, and the comfort it gives them. This does not mean one sex loves more fully. It means the sexes view love and experience closeness differently. Our disappointments with love result from our not taking these primitive differences into account.

## Moving Toward Intimacy

Women and men approach love in different ways because of one terribly important fact: boys form their identity and unique sense of self by separating from their mothers and modeling themselves after their fathers, while girls develop their sense of self by continued affiliation with their mothers and by modeling themselves after them. This single variation between boys and girls is responsible for the myriad confusions and misunderstandings that occur when men and women love.

Intimacy occurs when we reveal our innermost thoughts and feelings, and our partner returns that same gift of sharing. Intimacy is a prerequisite for falling in love and for forming a lasting bond with another person. To help you visualize the critical differences in male and female comfort with intimacy, we have employed a conceptual device we call the Intimacy Scale.

Imagine the need and wish for intimacy as falling along a continuum with Attachment at one end and Separateness at the other. Separateness represents the state of being alone, autonomous, independent. Attachment is the experience of feeling connected, intimate—at its extreme, fused with another person.

INTIMACY SCALE
Separateness --------------------------------------Attachment

Each of us has an optimal "bonding zone" which indicates at what level of intimacy we feel most comfortable.

Although men and women value love equally and place the same emphasis and importance on finding and sustaining a close union, their positions on the Intimacy Scale are often strikingly different. Such differences between men and women represent general patterns, and it should be remembered that exceptions always exist in specific cases. Some men relate to intimacy more as women generally do, and some women are more like men in the sense of having very strong needs for independence and autonomy.

**AFFINITY: HOW WOMEN BOND.** In our practices we have discovered that women are generally much more highly motivated by their need for closeness and attachment in a relationship than men are. A woman's bonding zone—the position along the Intimacy Scale where she is most likely to feel both comfortable and fulfilled—is very close to the Attachment end of the scale. This is where a woman seeks to position herself with a man.

WOMEN'S BONDING ZONE
Separateness----------------(Bonding) >>>Attachment

The origins of this powerful driving force, which we have called the Affinity Factor, can be found in a girl's earliest childhood experiences. An infant's world is completely centered on Mother, and the baby girl gains a feeling of strength by remaining bonded with her. Closeness becomes forever associated with security. Around the age of two—the process of developing her own identity begins, and the baby girl starts to imitate her magically powerful mother. Here, too, she learns that strength comes from being affiliated, bonded, close.

As the girl grows up she retains a firm and lasting memory of this idealized bond or depth of intimacy. As young girls become women, even as they become masterful or career-oriented, the feelings of security so strongly associated with the bond to the mother remain in the unconscious and exert a powerful influence. These early experiences are the origins of the Affinity Factor, the force that makes closeness and bonding so very important for women.

This does not mean, however, that the desire for closeness is always the primary motivator in a woman's life. As she enters adolescence and adulthood, independence and achievement become increasingly important to her; they can be as important to women as they are to men. But while the need for attachment may lie dormant during periods of high achievement, it is never lost nor does it lose its compelling power.

Because a woman associates safety with bonding, separation and aloneness are signals to her of loss of security, and thus represent situations to be avoided. Being unattached is, for many women, a negative and frightening state, for it evokes worries of never again feeling the warmth and security they value so highly.

**POLARITY: HOW MEN BOND.** Many women today feel that men are fearful of commitment. They see men as hesitant to take on the emotional demands of a relationship. They feel that men's ambivalence is a negative, that it connotes weakness, indecisiveness, even an inability to love fully or consistently. No matter whether a woman is single or has been married to the same man for years, she is likely to have experienced a man's approach/avoidance behavior: by turns he is strongly drawn to her and is romantic and loving, then he pulls away when emotional intensity builds. This causes the woman a great deal of confusion, resentment, and unhappiness.

Why do men act this way? It is our belief that there is a powerful underlying process or force that explains this often maddening behavior in men. It is not weakness or indecision or inability to love. Rather, this oscillation between closeness and separation is a basic law of male psychology. We have chosen to call this axiom of male behavior the Polarity Factor, and it too originates in childhood experiences.

In the same fashion as girls, boys form an incredibly dependent bond with their mothers. But while girls remain in close affiliation with the mother, something very different begins to happen with boys around their second birthday—they slowly become aware they are unlike their mothers and more like their fathers. Boys are then compelled to separate from the mother and model themselves after the father. Boys learn early on that autonomy is at the core of masculinity. This drive toward independence pulls boys, and later men, in one direction, while their less obvious but nevertheless powerful hunger to be taken care of pulls them in the other. These opposing forces create a pattern of oscillation in men— they tend to move back and forth between the two poles of Separateness and Attachment. Hence the term Polarity.

Visualize men's intimacy-seeking behavior as follows:


MEN'S BONDING ZONE
Separateness<<<<<(Bonding)>>>>>Attachment


Men alternate between a wish for Attachment and intense intimacy at the right end of the continuum and a wish for Separateness and autonomy on the left. They are uncomfortable remaining at either of these extremes for any length of time. When men reach a state of Attachment they experience anxieties about engulfment and weakness. Conversely, when they move too far in the direction of Separateness, they begin to feel subtle but nagging fears about abandonment, isolation, and aloneness.

Men feel most comfortable and are most willing to bond when they feel themselves roughly in the middle of this Intimacy Scale. When you compare this with women's ideal zone for bonding, it becomes clear that there is a built-in clash between what women want and what men want.

**CONFLICT: THE DARK SIDE OF LOVE.**
Women don't understand the bipolar tug that men feel from opposite ends of the Intimacy Scale because it is so foreign to them, so different from their own experience. Women don't oscillate in this fashion; as a rule, they prefer a bonding zone that is fairly stable and is closer to Attachment. Unfortunately, the bonding zone that is most comfortable for women is one that makes men feel engulfed and trapped! This discrepancy is at the core of many male/female conflicts and dilemmas.

Affinity and Polarity clearly suggest the inevitability of conflict. But not only is tension natural and predictable, it indeed forms the very basis of interest and attraction between men and women. We believe it is essential to understand that these differences never disappear; they are ongoing throughout our shared experience with a mate. We may mistakenly believe that differences exist only during the early stages of love and that with sufficient caring, trust, and time we eventually will become one with our lover and will experience no more conflict. We naively expect that love will magically alter fundamental psychological laws. It won't. The intriguing clash between men and women is always present. Men continue to dance between the desire for autonomy and the desire for intimacy. Women continue to seek affirmations of intimacy. But it is possible to understand these differences and learn to deal with them.

Our intent in this book is to unravel what seems to be mysterious about men's patterns of attraction and commitment and tell you exactly what goes on inside their hearts and minds as they relate to women. The first step on this road to discovery is understanding that love doesn't simply happen, it is learned, and its path can be altered.

## How Love Is Learned

Being a good partner or mate is not innate and not intuitive. Our behavior and expectations in relationships are, in large measure, shaped by all of our experiences, both as children and as adults. We watch our parents and, most often, imitate them, no matter how strongly we want to be different from them. Our parents' treatment of each other teaches us what to expect in our own lives and what attitude to take toward caring, affection, respect, and closeness.

As adolescents, we bring some of these early notions of what love is all about into the first relationships that go beyond simple friendship. We are often in for a shock as we find that others may deal with infatuation and attraction very differently than we do. One of the most critical things we learn at this time is how we feel about ourselves—our value and our attractiveness. For many of us, this is also a period in which shame, embarrassment, and disappointment result in our armoring ourselves against hurt. Many of us feel traumatized by teenage humiliations that left an indelible stamp. Many of us find our attitudes about dating and love arise from these adolescent experiences.

Our self-esteem is formed by these learning experiences. Most of the dilemmas we encounter as adults are the result of wounds to our self-confidence that occurred in our younger years.

The important point here is not that our lives are determined at an early age. In fact, it is the opposite. Most of our self-defeating patterns of loving can be modified, altered, even dramatically changed in positive directions.

## Influencing the Path of Love

We create our own dramas in life. Aside from early childhood experiences, we are responsible for the shape, direction, and quality of our relationships. We do not have to be the victims of our experiences; we are the writers, producers, and directors of them. People who have successful relationships learn from the past, but do not allow the past to tyrannize them.

No one escapes the excruciating pain and disappointment of relationship traumas. The content and story line of human scenarios differ, but one fact remains: everyone is hurt by someone, sometime. You can't keep from getting hurt, but you can reduce the probability of getting hurt in the same way again, and that requires learning.

What paralyzes a relationship and ultimately heads it in a destructive direction is one simple factor: both people involved continue to do exactly the same thing over and over. They hope things will change, but they go on behaving in the same old ways, often because they feel they have to change the mate's behavior, not just their own. This is not true—the power resides within each person, for when one person in a relationship changes, the other person must also—the mate is compelled to respond in a new way.

Having an impact on a relationship—creating attraction and influencing the path of love—starts with the first encounter between a man and a woman. The seeds for both positive and negative patterns are planted in the very beginning. Our fears, needs, and hopes are present as a kind of hidden agenda from the first "Hello."

When a man and a woman meet, what happens in

their first encounters that creates the "chemistry" that goes deeper than physical attraction—that goes beyond a surface feeling that he is "interesting, but . . ." or that she is "fun to be with, but . . ."? What behavior, clues, or signals trigger the much deeper hope or certainty that this is a person with whom we may be able to form a strong, enduring, nourishing emotional bond?

Without question, many of us make these important judgments about the limits of a relationship early on. Why, after only one date with someone, do we feel hopeful and exhilarated, or put off and wary? What a woman communicates in those initial moments or hours in many cases determines the direction, nature, and strength of a man's response.

Single people often fear that relationships pose insurmountable demands—that love is difficult to find, commitment even harder to secure. Married people often harbor the secret belief that the patterns they have established are so ingrained that they cannot realistically hope to change them. Most people believe the work that is required to get a relationship moving or get it back on the right track is monumental, requiring superhuman effort. The truth is, the insights and actions necessary to change a relationship can be learned and may not be as difficult as you think.

Change can be frightening to all of us. We fail to remember that it can also be an adventure—a growth-enhancing and empowering adventure—to experiment with new ways of being. We are too often pessimistic about our ability to break self-defeating patterns. Either we secretly believe we can't change, feeling "that's not me," or we insist on not changing, declaring that "this is me, this is who I am—take me or leave me." Whenever we act with such rigidity or fear, we inevitably lose out.

\* \* \*

In the following chapters in this section you will be reading about different kinds of women whose behavior contributed to negative patterns between themselves and the men they loved. As you read this material, look for these behaviors within yourself, not out of fear or apprehension but as a positive task, as a path toward new recognitions and discovery. Our purpose is enlightenment and personal growth, and for that reason we emphasize the various things you can do to break these self-defeating patterns, not for the man, but for yourself. Change within and for oneself is ultimately the most powerful way to enhance and enliven love relationships. Remember, taking chances, experimenting with new kinds of actions, is liberating, not only because it can lead to more fulfilling relationships with others, but because in the process of taking risks we become more confident and self-loving.

# CHAPTER TWO

# Woman Who Unknowingly Fear Intimacy

Helene, 38, a stunning and charming movie executive, is trying to climb her way out of a depression triggered by the breakup of her longest relationship yet—only one year. This woman, who seems to have everything going for her, asks, "Why do men always leave me?"

After four years of marriage, Agnes and Bill feel as though they're polite strangers with each other. Yet at parties, she sees Bill being funny, charming, even flirtatious at times, with other women. She's terrified he's going to break their painful silence one evening to ask for a divorce.

Greta brought her husband of seventeen years, Alex, into marital counseling after she discovered he was having an affair with his secretary. Certain that they had always had a terrific marriage, she thought he was just going through a midlife crisis. What she found out in the counseling sessions, however, was very different: he felt he had no emotional contact with her at all.

All of these women are attractive, intelligent, and well-intentioned. All deeply want their relationships to continue. Yet they're all at crisis points. With the exception of Helene, whose lover has already left her, the men in their lives are in the process of pulling away from them. Each for the same reason: these are women who unintentionally block a process that is absolutely necessary for a healthy relationship to endure, the development of intimacy.

## What Is Intimacy?

Intimacy is the essence of both love and friendship. To be intimate with another person is to feel a close emotional bond characterized by mutual sharing and understanding. There is a wish to know the other person's innermost dreams, wishes, and concerns while at the same time allowing ourselves to be known. Intimacy leads to feelings of warmth and security reminiscent of the trust and acceptance we felt as infants. Conversely, in its absence, we feel the acute pain of being strangers to each other, a sense of isolation or separation.

The capacity for intimacy is key in relationships, for it defines the ultimate limits or heights of someone's ability to love. Intimacy requires a good deal of trust. We must be confident enough to expose the most private and vulnerable aspects of ourselves, and we must believe that we can accept the other person's private and vulnerable aspects and not be overwhelmed by them.

Intimacy is not the same as neediness or dependency. Two people can be totally dependent upon each other's physical presence even though no honest, deep communication of feelings takes place. Other couples exhibit another tendency often mistaken for intimacy—excessive communication that is not received. The man and the woman can both share

their innermost thoughts, dreams, and feelings openly
and vulnerably, but if either of them fails to genuinely empathize, to "receive" or acknowledge what
the other is sharing, the couple is not intimate. This
is pseudo-intimacy—intimacy in which each person
ultimately remains isolated. This phenomenon commonly occurs in the early romance phase of a relationship, during which projected feelings and fantasies
are often mistaken for empathy and love, and it isn't
until much later that the individuals involved gradually sense they aren't being heard.

## Fear of Rejection, Abandonment, and Loss

Why would anyone be apprehensive about being
emotionally close to another person? After all, true,
real love—having a partner who knows us and accepts us, who loves us for who we really are—is a
matchless life experience. But the strange truth is
that intimacy is, in practice, avoided by many men
and women and may even be terrifying to them.
Many of us are not as open to intimacy as we would
like to believe we are, because love, as wonderful as
it feels, can trigger intense fears of rejection, abandonment, and loss.

First and foremost, in order to feel comfortable
being known and loved by another person, you have
to accept and love yourself. If you have doubts about
your sense of worth, if you feel the hidden facets of
your personality or character are bad or unaccept-
able, you may fear your lover will judge you in the
same harshly critical light you turn on yourself. Revealing yourself means offering yourself up for judgments, both positive and negative. As therapists, we
hear on a daily basis such anxious statements as "If

he really gets to know me, I'm afraid he won't like me." When you learn, however, to accept both your good and your not-so-great qualities, and to feel generally self-confident—"I'm not perfect, I'm flawed and human, but, on balance, I'm a lovable person"— you begin to feel more comfortable being known by another person. Intimacy then becomes not simply tolerable but valuable, comforting, and pleasurable.

Fear of abandonment—"Why reveal myself, why get that close, care that much, when he's going to leave me sooner or later?"—is another epidemic killer of intimacy. Ever since the increase in divorce rates over the last few decades, fear of abandonment has moved from a predominantly neurotic or unrealistic concern to one that is grounded in very real statistical probability. "Till death do us part" has been replaced by a conditional brand of love tempered by the awareness that love may not last, that many couples do break up. Anxiety about freely investing oneself in a relationship often evolves out of the awareness that "nothing is forever." But what is also clear to us is the ironic reality that men or women who choose to insulate themselves from the normal risks involved in loving openly often bring about the very abandonment they fear. People who are too guarded, who fear intimacy, often set in motion a process of estrangement and ultimate rejection—the very calamities they want so desperately to avoid.

Some people avoid or limit intimacy because they remember the excruciating pain they felt when a loved one died. A secret warning bell goes off when they begin to feel loving toward someone: "Don't get too close—you'll lose this person and endure that pain again!" When a loved one, especially a lover or a parent, dies, we typically respond in one of two ways. Some of us deeply grieve the painful loss and then slowly move on to fill the vacuum with new loving relationships. For others, the loss is so devastating that we forget that the love was nourishing; we remember only the pain of the loss, the danger inherent in loving someone. In this case, new love is clouded by the apprehension of loss. Such past hurts must be resolved before we can fully love someone new.

The truth is that a deeply caring closeness does mean the risk of rejection, abandonment, and loss. Self-acceptance and self-esteem are what give us the courage to run these risks and, by doing so, to reap the wonderful, nourishing rewards of intimacy.

## Fear of Losing One's Identity

Women are typically more comfortable than men with closeness and the sharing of feelings and are more likely to encourage intimacy in a relationship. But there are some women who are afraid that if they become too close to a man, they risk losing their sense of autonomy and independence. They fear that their separate identity will be lost or compromised, that their personality will be merged with the man's.

You may have had moments tinged by this type of anxiety. Perhaps after several weeks of intense togetherness, you have experienced an almost desperate need to spend time apart, alone, or with your own old friends. What's happening is that you want to feel the familiarity of your own, separate personality. This is natural and positive.

Sometimes, on a more conscious level, a woman may fear that intense closeness will somehow become a silken web that constricts her. She fears she will not be able to handle the man's emotional needs and requirements—that he will demand too much of her time and energy. She therefore limits the level of intimacy to protect her independence and hard-won accomplishments. Without a doubt, there are men who, despite their conscious wishes, still have difficulty emotionally accepting the career woman. Such a man secretly wishes for more involvement and care-taking on her part than is reasonable. The solution, as we shall explore in later chapters, is not to prevent intimacy, but to let it evolve slowly and, with growing trust and love, to negotiate its terms, making sure it is never one-sided.

## Fear of Being Overwhelmed by a Man's Needs

Another reason why some women block intimacy is that a man's vulnerability threatens them or diminishes their respect for him. They fear being overwhelmed by the man's worries, anxieties, and self-doubts, which inevitably surface as the relationship deepens. Honesty is an integral part of an intimate bond. Yet for some women, a man's honest disclosures may trigger the fear that he is weak and unable to care for her. During the romantic phase of an involvement, there is invariably some idealization—she sees him as strong and confident. But with the passage of time there is inevitably some disillusionment: he is not the gallant prince, not always strong and self-assured. By blocking intimacy, a woman can prevent this new and perhaps not very appealing image of him from emerging.

Women who fear being overwhelmed by a man's needs and emotional demands are often justified in their reluctance to listen endlessly and to give of themselves. The fact is that there are men who expect too much from women. In order to determine whether a man wants too much, a woman must understand men's need for, and fear of, emotional connectedness.

## Men's Fear of Dependency

One of the most important concerns of this book is the conflict that a man's emotional dependency on a woman causes him. Because of the Polarity Factor, nothing creates as much conflict in a man as being dependent on a woman. From the cold isolation of Separateness, men are drawn toward the warmth of Attachment as to a glowing hearth. But men are concerned about their wish for closeness and worry that Attachment will weaken and engulf them. It is crucial for women to understand the conflict men experience, because it is the primary determinant in how they bond with women, in whether they love or leave. If a man's deep wish for warmth and caring is neglected—all too easy to do, because this need is usually below the surface of his awareness, and he never talks about it—the neglect can inhibit his potential for closeness, create anxiety, and force him to build impenetrable emotional walls.

As we have noted, boys develop their sense of masculinity through a gradual process of detachment from the mother and imitation of the father. While girls feel empowered by affiliation and connectedness, boys feel empowered through separation and autonomy. They feel good about themselves when they are being independent, when they ride their bikes, spend the night with a friend, or drive a car for the first time. But in a related aspect of this process of autonomy, boys also learn to hide their feelings. Emotions sadly become admissions of weakness. We have all seen a young boy squirm away when his mother tries to embrace him. Why? Because to be taken in his mother's arms and accept the embrace, a boy must relax, lose control. This feeling evokes memories of infancy—of helplessness and weakness, the exact opposite of the self-reliance and strength that characterize the masculinity he is increasingly striving to achieve. We may call what he experiences when he becomes too aware of his need for closeness a fear of "engulfment" or "smothering," but it is basically a fear of loss of masculinity.

When boys depart forever the safety and comfort of connectedness with their mothers, they retain both a desire for intimacy and a fear of it—a conflict they will be engaged in all their lives, the Polarity Factor. The seductive lure of being nurtured is always there, tempting them, but they learn to give in to it only in certain situations, and never for long. For example, men frequently regress to a childlike state when they are physically ill. But this lapse into dependency feels acceptable—most men can let themselves be taken care of and fussed over without fear of losing their "manliness" when they are sick, because they know it's only temporary.

## When Men Feel Alone

There are few men who do not desire the rewards of intimacy, even though they may be reluctant to do half the work to create it. Women who prevent intimacy stimulate men's basic fears. In the absence of closeness, a man feels alone and negected. If he tries to communicate these feelings, he risks feeling humiliated, because he exposes his neediness and dependency. And he *is* humiliated if his attempts to make known his wish for a closer and richer experience with a woman fall on deaf ears.

As we described earlier, the Polarity Factor suggests that men feel actively bonded at some rough midpoint between Separateness and Attachment. It is within this middle range that they feel and express the greatest degree of passion, interest, and involvement. But when men feel themselves drifting toward Separateness, they experience both discomfort and anxiety. The woman who prevents intimacy is inadvertently allowing the man to drift away.

When a woman denies a man the love and intimacy he needs, his response may take one of several forms. First, he may feel frustration and resentment, which he probably will be ashamed to acknowledge to her, and even to himself. Then, as a way of protecting himself from feeling isolated and disconnected, he may pull away from her emotionally. He may also begin to numb himself to his growing pain and sense of estrangement. The final stage may be an obvious and pointed neglect of her, which often is an unconscious retaliation for her neglect. Rather than retaliating, however, many men simply withdraw. He may stop communicating, recede into his work, sports, or hobbies, become uninterested sexually or have an affair. Or he may simply leave the relationship altogether. And he may do this without even being aware of the specific reasons why he's taking flight.

## The Rock

Barbara, 34, has been divorced twice. She shares custody of her two children with their fathers. A free-lance book editor, she has been seeing Frederick for nearly two years. He's a former actor who currently works as a real estate salesman while he awaits a "big score" in one of his many speculative invest-

ment ventures. The years they have been going together were characterized by Barbara as they began
couples therapy as "chaotic and draining," though
she said this with a smile. Frederick agreed with her
description, but was not so entertained by the drama
of their involvement. It soon became clear that he
was in much more pain than she. He admitted he
instigated most of their battles, but revealed he was
now despairing of continuing the relationship, a crisis which had prompted them to enter therapy.

Barbara saw him as excessively needy, demanding, and even infantile in the extent of his need to be
close to her. "I need time alone," Barbara explained,
"probably a lot more than Fred does, but what really
gets to me is not just his need to spend more time
with me, but his need to talk endlessly about his
problems. It's not particularly interesting, and it's
certainly not very romantic." She longed for the
early days in the relationship when he had seemed
more carefree, dashing, and adventuresome—qualities
which her two rigidly conservative husbands had
lacked totally. She sincerely believed Frederick was
asking too much and that he had to work out his
own neediness—it was his problem. In Frederick's
mind, this was not so. He saw himself as a reasonably mature and self-sufficient man who, as a result
of his tumultuous career history, needed a confidante, a caring listener with whom he could share
the good things as well as some of his apprehensions and occasional bouts of self-doubt. He accused
her of being tough and ungiving, wanting only excitement and not love. "Look," he said to her, "I'm
not asking for anything I'm not willing to give. You're
so secretive about the things that worry you—I know
they are there but you never talk about them. Well,
I'm not going to play the same game. I don't think
that's what love is about."

Barbara gradually came to see that her anger at Frederick stemmed from a fear not only of his vulnerability, but of her own. Openness and the expression of feelings had always been difficult for her. She could be a very perceptive listener, a fact which her many friends attested to, but not as a steady diet, and certainly not in the context of a close male/female relationship. Barbara was trying to protect herself from having to give too much and deplete her emotional reserves. Initially, with Frederick, she thought she had finally found a man who would be her counterpart. She felt that he, too, wanted passion, intensity, and stimulation and did not want to drain his partner with "childish" needs or be drained by her.

What Barbara failed to see was that Frederick was, in fact, the man she thought he was. However, like most of us, as the bond deepened, a broader set of needs became part of the union. Being vulnerable at times and needing some caretaking is inevitable. In the right proportions, it is natural and healthy. By rejecting this normal component of intimacy, Barbara was foreclosing the possibility of her involvement going beyond a stormy and passionate romance.

*Overcoming the Fear of a Man's Vulnerability.* Barbara turned herself into stone for fear of being emotionally exploited or drained by a man. If you identify with Barbara's dilemma, there are positive steps you can take that will help you overcome this fear. But first it is important to understand what a man wants when he talks about his worries to a woman.

While you may feel he somehow expects you to solve whatever problems he is having, the truth is that most men simply want an interested and receptive sounding board. They want someone they can voice their concerns to openly and honestly without

holding back. They want to be heard and understood, not necessarily helped. For many men, it is
far easier to talk frankly with a woman than with a
man about aspects of their lives that are worrisome.
When he reveals his soft underside to a woman, a
man doesn't have to concern himself with the inevitable comparison and competition that accompany
all his interactions with other men. You can see,
then, why it is so important for a man to be able to
talk about his concerns to the woman he loves.

The first step in dealing with any fear is understanding more clearly what it is about—in this case,
understanding what makes you want to pull away
from a man when he is vulnerable. This type of
clarity is necessary to get a grip on what creates your
discomfort, for only by understanding its source can
you begin to deal more effectively with it. For example, ask yourself how you really feel about a man
with whom you are involved when he tells you his
deepest and most private worries and concerns. What
are you afraid might happen? How might you feel?

For some women, the concern goes something like
this: "I only have enough strength to handle my
own problems. If I have to give energy to someone
else's, I won't have enough left over to take care of
myself." This fear is based upon the assumption that
when a man expresses his worries he expects you to
do something about them—to solve them. Understanding that you aren't expected to do anything in
particular can be enormously freeing, for listening is
not draining—ultimately it only feels that way when
we believe it is our responsibility to do something
with what we hear.

Another common concern women have is typically expressed like this: "When a man talks about
his problems it makes me think of him as weak, and
I hate thinking that the man in my life can't take care

of himself." Obviously, having problems doesn't make anyone weak, for problems are ubiquitous. The test of strength and character is never the presence of worry or adversity, but how we handle it. When a man expresses inner concerns it doesn't automatically mean he is weak or can't really take care of himself. The fact is that many men will admit such feelings only to a woman they love. To the rest of the world they show the armor they've been taught to wear. In a very real way, it is a compliment to a woman when a man expresses his insecurity and self-doubt, for that expression reflects loving trust, not weakness.

Women who become rocklike in their response to men's emotional needs often fear the recurrence of old painful feelings from the past. This anticipated dread serves as a warning sign. For example, perhaps a woman saw her mother giving lovingly but endlessly to her father and receiving too little in return. That memory gives rise to a secret fear that if she starts giving to a man she will have to keep on giving—and eventually become mother as well as wife.

The task is basically to trust your ability to maintain an equitable balance in the relationship. Withholding so as to avoid depletion or exploitation by a man leads only to continued fear on your part and resentment on his. Giving to a man with the firm expectation of his giving back to you creates a better atmosphere, one in which mutual respect and caring are possible. In fact, giving without the fear of depletion can actually leave you with even more to give, for it is strengthening to love freely. Love is weakening only when it comes with strings attached and is haunted by the specter of resentment.

But what about when a man actually does want too much? The solution is for the woman to simply expect reciprocity, insist on it! It is no one's job to give unilaterally; certainly it is not the woman's role. Be open and clear with him about your concerns and be very definite with him that you're not his mother and you expect as much generous caring from him as you are willing to give. Women who give too much, who allow themselves to be exploited, are typically those who never raise the issue with the man in their life. Such women are hesitant to be clear and direct about mutuality and reciprocity. It is when this directness is missing that a woman can eventually feel overwhelmed by a man's demands.

## The Sphinx

Occasionally a man encounters a woman who appears to have everything going for her, and yet she has an odd history of never being able to sustain a close relationship. It is as puzzling to her friends as it is to herself, since she typically is everyone's ideal woman to fix up with a terrific man.

Helene is one such woman. She is 38 years old and has never married, although she has gone with a veritable pantheon of the most desirable men. Her work as a motion-picture producer brings her a high level of acclaim in her business, even recognition by the public. She is beautiful, intelligent, successful, and at ease in a tough profession. She is a tenacious negotiator as well as a very charming woman.

When Helene took inventory of her past relationships, there seemed to be a consistent theme to the men's leavetaking, a sameness to the comments she had heard from men over the years. Some men saw her as too perfect; her perfection made them uneasy. Others felt she had no real sense of humor, which she knew was true, even though she tried hard to be light and easy. There were other men who after a time became combative and competitive with her. She had always viewed those men as too weak to handle her success. One man she had dated never clashed with her, but he did joke about never really knowing her. His nickname for her was Mona Lisa, and for a time he was enticed by the enigmatic quality she projected.

The men in her life did, indeed, sense a very real barrier. As Helene describes, "I've never believed I could get involved in an intimate relationship and maintain the standards I have for myself. I know I can't always be understanding, witty, smart, strong, or even pretty all of the time. I think by holding back, I feel more in control, feel I'm not going to risk disappointing someone."

Helene was afraid that if a man got too close to her, her deepest feelings would be exposed, and he would be repelled by what he saw. Her secrets? Nothing really terrible—her father's terminal illness many years ago, and her mother's depression after her father's death. But as a girl, she had felt embarrassed and ashamed of these tragedies in her family, and so fearful of looking less than perfect to others that anything that might possibly trigger her own sadness and insecurity was systematically removed from her persona . . . or so she thought.

In an ironic way, Helene is one of those people who are cursed by the exquisite delicacy and efficiency of their psychological defenses. She learned early on how to appear attractive and appealing. She was so good at this that she forgot that she originally had developed these skills to protect herself from vulnerability and hurt. Her mask, her facade, no matter how lovely, proved to be a barrier preventing men from getting too close. Men eventually tired of the almost ineffable sense of loneliness they felt with her in private moments.

Now, Helene is learning to take risks. "I realize now that by always jumping in to smooth things over in an awkward moment or cutting off a man with some light remark when he was attempting to share something painful with me, I was making everything very bland and distant. I thought I was making men want to be close to me by making things as perfect and smooth as possible, but what I'm finding out is just the opposite—it's in those awkward or sad or hurt moments that we experience intense closeness, and those wonderful feelings flowing back and forth between us. I've had some very tender moments with the man I'm seeing now." As Helene continues to shed her layers of protective defenses, she is confident that instead of ultimately leaving her, a man will be drawn even closer to her.

*Learning to Risk Exposure.* Women who are superficially quite desirable and engaging can blind themselves for years to the ways they may actually prevent intimacy. If you see a bit of yourself in Helene, if men never seem to stay in a relationship with you even though you have a wealth of positive traits, it may be that you have built a protective facade which acts to block real male/female chemistry. Why we adopt such strategies typically has to do with old wounds and fears that may be more dominant than we would like to believe. We erect these barriers presumably to shield people we care about from our imperfections. In reality, this shield serves only to block what we need the most—the acceptance and trust that accompany intimacy. When we worry about showing our flaws it is because we are unsure of how they will be received—whether we will be loved along with them or judged because of them. While we all know that no one is perfect, we are also most acutely aware of our own imperfections. The trouble is that hiding them from others prevents us from ever finding out if we are lovable despite them. This only perpetuates our worries that they might pop out unannounced and sabotage us. It also tends to make us rather bland and colorless. Men connect most intensely to women who are vivid. The "rough edges" created by being yourself are the real adhesive in a close relationship.

The task is to find the courage to risk a fuller expression of yourself. The risk invariably pays off, for it heightens the possibility of greater intimacy. The first step is to isolate the specific fears you have about being close and therefore "known." Ask yourself: What exactly is it that someone will find out if he really gets to know me? What facts or feelings about myself are so distasteful or alienating? Typically, our fears are greatly exaggerated, even irrational in the sense that others would not view them as truly shameful or embarrassing.

From childhood, it is not uncommon to fear being disliked, or being different. We all tend to struggle with false pride, embarrassment, and the wish that somehow our flaws didn't show. A problem arises, however, when we feel compelled to be perfect to avoid being seen as defective, diminished, not enough.

You can free yourself from these fears as you find the courage to risk. Take a chance in showing more of yourself to others. You will be surprised to find that people easily accept you as you really are. The mere act of personal exposure makes us look and feel more alive and engaging, and more likely to encourage intimacy.

## *The Cheerleader*

Greta, 39, had been married to Alex for seventeen years. A highly energetic, intelligent, and well-organized woman, she's active in a variety of political and social causes. Her wide circle of friends think of her as extraordinarily vivacious, determined, and charming. But her husband knows the truth about Greta. She is not the warm friendly woman she believes herself to be. In fact, she is afraid to let anyone really know her.

Greta brought Alex with her into counseling after she discovered that he had an affair. Greta wanted to believe that it was primarily a sexual fling, but the fact was that the woman was the same age as Greta, and, objectively, not as physically attractive. She was hoping the affair would blow over and might only be a "midlife crisis" for Alex. She felt their marriage was basically okay; they had a terrific sex life and wonderful children, and they were out every other night at parties and benefits.

Greta genuinely tried to search her soul for reasons. Her friends, all of whom adored her, were no help, as they concurred with her that Alex had, indeed, "flipped out." Alex, tellingly, refused to discuss their marital crisis except in therapy sessions, insisting that his attempts to communicate with her in private usually failed because Greta turned them into pep talks, attempting to sell him on the great marriage they had.

For years Alex had felt totally alone in their marriage, without knowing why. It was only after he began the affair that he realized how emotionally malnourished he had been. Whenever he wanted to confide in Greta she lovingly but firmly changed the subject or responded with safe bromides. The net effect was that Alex was in great pain and felt completely estranged from the woman he had lived with so long.

Greta's way of dealing with her fears was to keep them bottled up inside and present a false air of well-being to the world. What were her fears? There were many, not just one. In many ways she typifies many women and men today who attempt to appear upbeat and positive as a way of disguising obvious and long-standing inner doubts about themselves. In effect, Greta long ago made a decision to construct a life-style and a marital relationship in which she would never see a shadow—never deal with the raw, gritty underside of life. Her parents had divorced when she was just entering adolescence. Her father had always been loving to her, but quiet, passive, and oddly aloof from the daily fray of the household. Her mother was more vocal but colder, and constantly criticized the father. When he finally left the family, Greta secretly blamed her mother and vowed to be as unlike her as she could possibly be. Because her mother was bitterly negative, she would be positive. Because her mother was a chronic complainer, she would ignore those things that hurt, upset, or angered her. She would not make the mistakes her mother had. She would not be left. She was going to be different.

The problem was that when Greta muted all the negative feelings she saw as dangerous, she limited the range and richness of her relationship with Alex. Greta was by no means a superficial woman, but the rigid constraints she placed upon her emotions made her appear that way.

*Getting Beneath the Surface.* Being upbeat and positive all the time creates not only a lot of unnecessary internal pressure but an impossible standard for one's partner to meet. Being around someone like this tends to make a person feel more bad-tempered, irrational, and maddeningly demanding by comparison. He begins to feel guilty about having normal moods.

How does one become free of this eternally sunny prison of false cheerfulness? It's not easy, but it can be done, and there are some very positive rewards. First, you must realize that there is a secret, slightly sanctimonious, satisfaction one derives from consistently being nicer than one's mate. And while you may feel that being so nice is good for the relationship, actually it is not because you are depriving both you and your partner of your real feelings.

Relationships are composed of a balance of both positive and negative feelings. People who have become overly invested in being positive tend to have two common fears, both of which are essentially unfounded. The first is that they have censored angry, sad, or hurt feelings for so long that if they ever gave vent to them they would be overwhelmed by the torrent and they would then overwhelm their partner. The second fear is that they have so accustomed their partner to their behavior that to suddenly change would not be acceptable. Wrong on both counts! Change such as this requires always takes time, and there is rarely any torrent of negativity. In fact, being a bit cranky, showing your sadness or hurt more openly, and making more honest demands can give the other person some real relief.

The reward for doing this is twofold. You will find that you have a lot more energy and are a lot less prone to feeling depressed inside, for hiding what you feel consumes much more energy than letting it show. And your partner will have a real three-dimensional human being to relate to—one who is far more complex and interesting than the cotton-candy person who always tried to be nice.

No marriage can survive without mutual sharing and disclosure. Without that, there is only a cold, quiet coexistence that someday will erupt when one party takes action. Greta, like Helene, must take the chance of revealing more of herself. A woman who reveals herself need not fear that the man will become disillusioned; the very act of allowing herself to be known will nourish the bond with the man.

If you struggle with these hidden concerns, understand that we all have them. None of us grows up unscathed, free of self-doubts regarding our value and attractiveness to others. But to succumb to those fears is to put roadblocks in the way of closeness and intimacy.

## The Loner

After dating for a year, Mickey, 35, and Irene, 30, got engaged on New Year's Eve and set a June wedding date. They moved into a spacious new apartment and threw a big party to celebrate. But by mid-March, Mickey was seriously considering calling off their wedding plans.

"I had never been with a woman so alive and funny as Irene. In the beginning, we laughed ourselves silly—even our fights ended in laughter and then lovemaking. We spent probably three or four evenings and nights a week together and talked on the phone every day. I thought we'd spend even more time with each other after we got engaged and moved in together, but we're drifting apart.

"She took on a big project at work and goes right into the study after a quick dinner a couple of nights a week, spends another evening at a women's therapy group, and works out or meets her friends for drinks a couple more evenings a week. We go out to dinner and a play or a movie on weekend nights, and that's about it. And about half the time I want to make love these days she puts me off. I thought we'd get closer as a couple—instead, I'm here trying to round up a friend to go to a game or a movie and getting pushed away in bed."

Irene experienced a similar slide into disillusionment. "I thought I'd finally met the right man. He has a great sense of humor, and he was a real romantic on top of that. I don't know why it had to deteriorate. From my point of view, he's becoming too clutchy, always in need of reassurance . . . and that has turned me off. And I guess part of why I've gotten so busy since we moved in together is that I don't want to lose my independence. I don't want to be one of those couples that do everything together. I want to spend time with friends and do things by myself, like going to the health club or spending a couple of hours browsing art galleries on Saturday."

Irene is experiencing some anxiety about their pending marriage. She's afraid of losing her identity and becoming one of those couples whose names are always said in one breath: "Mickey-and-Irene." But she's not only more of a loner and more independent than Mickey, she's also afraid of letting him get too close.

*Trusting Your Sense of Self.* When two people choose to become intimate, there are understandable accommodations and compromises that occur. This is true of any partnership. But does that mean we therefore are diminished in some way by that choice? Of course not. When we have a sense of our own boundaries, of our own sense of identity, our notion of who we are and what we are entitled to, then we are not fearful of bonding or intimacy.

You must trust that you will retain your sense of identity, your unique feeling of autonomy and specialness. Allowing a man to become intimate with you does not mean losing your identity—in fact, it strengthens you when you take the chance. It is a wonderful validation and acceptance of who you are.

Having an important, loving relationship with a man does require an investment of time and shared experiences. Try to stay clear in your interpretations of a man's behavior: don't equate his wish to spend time with you with a wish to be dependent on you. And don't confuse his wish to feel important to you with a wish to ensnare you by some subtle manipulation and make you dependent upon him.

It is true, however, that women with a more recently acquired sense of autonomy and independence can become apprehensive about getting close to a man. This is not an irrational fear, for there are men who secretly or unconsciously want a woman to feel responsibility to the relationship first and to herself second. Concerns over autonomy need to be discussed in the relationship, aired openly rather than suppressed. That's the easy part. Some women, however, feel an anxiety based on their ambivalence about independence in general. Many women today aren't sure just how autonomous they wish to be, and this uncertainty creates a fertile soil for anxiety over loss of identity. Women who secretly doubt their sense of self are most vulnerable to anxieties regarding closeness. But when you are sure of your commitment to independence and to yourself, you will be more confident of your capacity for intimacy.

If you feel that your sense of identity is not well defined, begin to keep a daily journal. Write down thoughts about yourself, your goals and values. Becoming conscious of them on a daily basis serves to affirm them as part of your identity. As you gain greater confidence in those uniquely personal aspects of yourself, as you define them with greater and greater clarity, bring them into your relationship.

## What Is the Man's Responsibility?

None of the women whose relationships we have explored in this chapter are to be seen as the "villains." While we have focused on their behavior and their impact on men, this is not to imply that they are solely responsible for the ways in which tensions are played out in their relationships. Unfortunate or negative patterns of relating always require two participants. In each of the cases we've explored, the man could have been more active and direct in his response to the woman. He did not have to passively allow her behavior to set the tone for the communication or lack of it. Too often, men will complain, get angry, or just become silent and incommunicative when they fail to get what they need from a woman. In the instances we've described, all of the negative patterns could have been held in check if the man had been more direct—if he had told the woman what he was feeling rather than what she was doing wrong.

As in any negative connection between a man and a woman, one also has to ask why the man chose this type of woman. Maybe he was unconsciously more comfortable with someone who did not encourage intimacy. Perhaps he was seeking a relationship in which he could continue to keep his own doubts and fears hidden, while at the same time proclaiming his desire for closeness. But while these certainly are important considerations, our goal in this book is to explore what women do that draws men to them or pushes them away—and, most important, what they can do about it.

## Recognizing a Lack of Closeness

There are a number of indicators that tell us when intimacy is diminished in a relationship or, worse, nonexistent. Does the man come to you with a wish or need to talk about his concerns—does he exhibit a need for you in this fashion? If you open up to him about the state of your relationship, does he genuinely listen and share his feelings as well? If there is no give and take, something is wrong—there is some reason why he doesn't feel safe sharing his thoughts and feelings.

Often men convey their wishes in rather oblique ways. For example, does he complain about a lack of time spent together? Does he talk wistfully about vacations together? Whenever complaints are aired between two people, it is wise, of course, to take them at face value. It is also wise to look beneath the surface and ask yourself whether he is communicating something else. Men who criticize and complain frequently do so as an indirect way of expressing their real underlying feelings: "I don't feel cared for," "I feel alone." This does not mean you are supposed to jump up and start trying to fix things. That's not our point here. But often if you read between the lines of a man's vague, cranky complaints, you will find another, deeper, more poignant message.

Intimate partners are also friends. The stereotype of the man as the staunch provider and the woman as the dependent homemaker with no identity or importance of her own is long gone. Deep friendships are always a product of shared, intimate experiences. Contrary to what many women think, men want to get closer to and be friendlier with the women in their lives, and when they cannot they tend to feel cheated, alone, and ultimately disappointed. This is true despite many a man's unwillingness or inability to put such wishes into words.

Another area that is guaranteed to reveal the level of closeness between a man and a woman is sex. We don't mean the mechanical quality of it, or the frequency, but rather the tenderness and expressions of love present when intimacy exists. Do you look at each other when you make love? Can you look into each other's eyes without that subtle hint of embarrassment that is a sign of underdeveloped intimacy?

A common expression that indicates a lack of intimacy is "I really feel I don't know you." When this is uttered, it usually means exactly that. Regardless of how certain you are of your attempts to be known, if the other person still says, "We seem like strangers," you are! While it may be unclear which person contributes more to the block, intimates don't make this accusation. Listen to it, and begin to look for ways to dissolve the barriers.

## Encouraging Intimacy

As a beginning, try to remember the most intimate moments you had with men. Often they are not obvious ones filled with intense love or passion. It could just have been a walk in the park, sitting under a tree in silence, walking together holding hands. What created that moment? How did those intimate feelings evolve? What triggered them? Searching your memory in this way can provide important clues.

What about moments of shared warmth and pleasure? What allowed those to emerge? For some couples with children, being together as a family, exchanging proud and warm acknowledgments, is a time of great intimacy. Shared pleasures and dreams are important. Have you experienced them recently, or discussed them with the man in your life?

As you remember back to those times when you felt closest, understand that it was no accident. The experience of closeness comes when we are most vulnerable and open. Make sure there are no walls between you and him—either those you have placed there or those you both have allowed to remain through a conspiracy of silence. Take a chance and open yourself up to him. Talk about those personal self-revealing things that may have quietly slipped out of your dialogue, and encourage him to do likewise.

Renewing and enhancing intimacy always requires action—some sort of real behavior, not simply hoping and wishing it were there. The most effective way to foster the growth of openness and sharing with a man is to present yourself as a model of these behaviors. Again, remember we are not implying it is your task alone to do so, but if you want to be an agent for change, there is no better way than to be open and self-revealing without automatically expecting it in return. This latter point is critical. People who feel vulnerability is being demanded of them rarely reveal themselves. Instead, they feel resentment and close themselves up even tighter.

As a first step, realize that breaking patterns requires action and communication that are different from your usual exchanges with him. For example, try something different in your physical expressions of affection. Express your love in a nonverbal fashion, again without the expectation that the gesture will be returned or even acknowledged at first. Holding hands in the movies, a back rub—these simple expressions can create new opportunities for closeness. Share previously secret or embarrassing thoughts, something you always wanted to say or do, but didn't. Share fantasies, let yourself be playful—act it out, risk revealing some new facet of yourself.

Create some new experience together—take a class of mutual interest, start a project together, get away for a quiet weekend, anything that creates a new and shared time together.

Remember, intimacy is always associated with vulnerability. Make personal statements about what closeness means to you, making sure they are not disguised complaints, demands, or judgments. And don't assume automatically you understand him. It's good every now and then for us all to start from scratch and assume we know little about each other.

Being direct about getting closer is often a delicate task. With some men, it is best to inquire gently whether they feel good about the relationship and whether there is anything they would like to change. Even discuss this as a game. Do it at a light moment. Never explore these topics in a heavy face-to-face encounter unless you want a real uphill struggle.

Be honest with yourself about how many of his inner thoughts you really want to hear. Are you afraid of his vulnerability? Do you have a vested emotional interest in seeing him in the same way you always have? Can you risk seeing him in a new light?

Don't permit the dangerous ruts of boredom and habit to set in. Boredom is not the natural accompaniment of day-to-day living, but it is the enemy of closeness. Do something to intervene, do something out of character, realizing that in truth, you are only revealing an aspect of you that has been kept under wraps. Self-revelation is always a catalyst for intimate exchanges.

Don't go overboard. Remember, becoming close is a gradual process. Don't try to accomplish this in one evening—it doesn't work that way. As we have noted, men can become satiated with too much closeness and even with too much dialogue about closeness.

Intimacy is not easy for any of us. Both men and women struggle to find someone with whom they can feel close, loving, and tender. And yet, it is that very vulnerability required to become intimate partners that can arouse so much anxiety. It requires revealing the most secret facets of our being. But taking the chance, finding the courage to risk this exposure, will lead you to new and more fulfilling levels of caring and companionship.

# CHAPTER THREE

# How Innocent Expectations Become Dangerous

Gloria asks only for what she is so willing to give—romance, and those "simple little things" that would make her feel more loved and special.

Cara protests with chiding annoyance, "I don't feel very secure with Chuck. He wouldn't have the foggiest idea of how to protect me if we found ourselves in a dangerous situation, and he's an absolute klutz around the house."

Belinda, describing her relatively new but promising relationship with Ray, says, "It seems that if he loved me as much as he says he does, he would want to get married. I don't have time to wait for years for him to make up his mind."

When we enter a love relationship, most of us harbor unspoken expectations that our partner will change in certain ways. We secretly believe that little flaws, irritating habits, and assorted quirks will somehow magically disappear. An important part of our desire to be with another person is based on wishes and expectations, so when our lover doesn't change, we feel puzzled, then disappointed and disillusioned. As we gradually become aware our mate will not or cannot change to suit our needs, we often begin making subtle but insistent demands that inadvertently can push our mate away.

When is expecting something from a man expecting too much? Should you have to worry that you're being overly demanding every time you tell a man what you want? Isn't feedback about likes and dislikes what communication is all about in a relationship? What is reasonable, and what is too much?

First, no one sets out to have such exaggerated needs and expectations that they ultimately suffocate the love needed and wanted from a partner. Both men and women make demands in a relationship normally and naturally. But there are certain pressures women may exert on men that may damage love and lead to resentment and, ultimately, to the loss of trust and comfort.

Let's go back to the beginning. If we look at the earliest stage of romance, we find it is based on acceptance. Initially, we all tend to think our partner is terrific. We either overlook his or her flaws or consider them virtues—part of the total picture of charm and attraction. In the first weeks and months, love is not necessarily blind, but it is certainly shortsighted! Acceptance, the wonderful feeling of lovability, is perhaps the most important ingredient in the bonding process between women and men. We feel our lover likes what he or she sees, and our insecurities slowly melt in the warmth of feeling valued for what we are. We can't keep our hands off each other, our friends see a lot less of us, and in our love we feel gloriously complete.

As infatuation deepens into love, acceptance becomes more discriminating and conditional. As we grow more comfortable and committed, we also can become more critical and more easily disappointed. We begin to see our lover's feet of clay.

When hopes and expectations dissolve into disillusionments, we often do an odd thing. Instead of concluding that our wishes may be unrealistic, we start to generate more expectations or complain more vocally about the ones we had. Expectations, even when ignored by our mate, begin to pile up; they take on a cumulative quality as we insist on having our wishes met. The result of this buildup is a kind of toxicity that may infect the relationship in negative and even destructive ways. We all know people who complain endlessly about some flaw in their partner we know hasn't the slightest chance of being altered. Yet they go on relentlessly, not realizing their lack of acceptance may sow the seeds for later resentment by their mate.

## What Are Reasonable Expectations?

What are your rights when you wish to make demands on your mate? How do you know when a healthy sense of personal entitlement crosses the line and becomes excessive or unrealistic expectations? The answer is not as simple as you might hope, for certain demands are appropriate, others are not, and some of the least appropriate demands may be the hardest to give up.

In our day-to-day lives, we all make demands on our mates. For the most part, they live with these demands, and within their capacity they change to meet them. There is a whole variety of realistic demands that are not only reasonable but also necessary —when we don't impose them, we run the risk of being taken for granted and discounted as individuals. Let's look at some of them.

First, we all have the right to expect tolerance of differences. We are not fused-at-the-hip Siamese twins; we will not think, act, and feel the same. We can all justly expect support of our basic needs for security, partnership, and affection. It is healthy for all of us to expect support of, or, at the very least, noninterference with, our individual growth and self-expression. It is appropriate to want a relationship fundamentally based on equality. And while all relationships are constantly evolving, we can expect honesty, clarity, and integrity with regard to issues of mutual concern. And that's about it—all the other demands we make of our mates are a bit questionable.

We cannot expect a mate to think and feel exactly as we do, particularly when it comes to emotional expressiveness and comfort with closeness. Nor can we expect to have the same sense of timing when it comes to commitment. And above all, we cannot expect a partner to take responsibility for solving our personal problems, particularly struggles with insecurity and poor self-esteem.

When we feel secure within ourselves and good about the way we are, the demands we place upon our partners are never too out of line. It is when we are trying to quiet our own inner doubts or fears that our demands can become unjust and we put unrealistic and unfair pressure on a partner to change.

Excessive expectations are self-defeating because they seek external solutions to very personal and internal problems. How many times have you heard someone say, "If he really loved me he would want to marry me as much as I want to marry him"? Men are every bit as capable as women of deep love and attachment, but their timing is often very different from a woman's. In fact, the basis of a man's resistance to marriage may even be his discomfort with the depth of his need of and love for the woman. The woman who pushes for commitment too soon and too unrelentingly does so out of a need to reduce her anxious feelings of uncertainty—not out of love or any real mutual sensitivity. Such poorly timed demands typically backfire, for the overriding focus is the woman's needs rather than what is truly comfortable for both parties.

Another aspect of unrealistic expectations grows out of our desire for personal completion or validation. We all want to feel cherished and valued. Such feelings add to our self-confidence and lovability. The woman who feels incomplete without a man, less than whole without the added status gained through affiliating with a man, may end up seeing men as solutions rather than partners.

## When a Man Feels He Is Not Enough

Men have an instinctive response to a woman's demands—they know what expectations feel right, even though they may have a hard time acknowledging them, and also know what feels excessive. That doesn't mean the man is always right, but it does indicate how sensitive men are to being told they have to perform. During most of their adult life, men feel an obligation to live up to certain standards, whether in their jobs or with the women in their lives. For men, having to perform well is both a goal and a burden. Men have to "get it up" in the workplace as well as in the bedroom.

From childhood on, men struggle with the challenge of measuring up, being strong and able to compete, not being a sissy. Men have always been on the receiving end of expectations. This is not to say that women haven't; they experience similar pressures from childhood onward as society tells them in no uncertain terms what they must do to be a "real" woman.

When a woman, whether directly or by implication, suggests to a man that he change to meet her expectations, he feels the bitter sting of her disappointment; he feels he has fallen short and is overwhelmed and resentful. More often than not, the man may not be able to put that resentment into words. Such accentuated demands launch a downwardly spiraling sequence of events in a relationship. First, they make a man feel he is becoming increasingly responsible for a woman's sense of well-being. And men shy away from that, just as a woman may shy away from the responsibility for a man's well-being. Demands also expose a man to possible feelings of inadequacy and shame for somehow not being "better," for not being more like what the woman wants him to be.

At a primitive emotional level, demands by women can even trigger unconscious but powerful memories of being scolded by one's mother and feeling helpless under her scorn. This is especially true when demands take on a relentlessly critical tone. They create conflict in a man, since he instinctively wants to please the woman he loves. He wants and needs her acceptance and approval. When a man constantly feels he has fallen short in a woman's eyes, it sets in motion a conflict between trusting the acceptability of his own conduct and wishing he could be her idealized version of himself and thus gain her approval.

Men's reactions to excessive expectations are unfortunately often disguised and hidden. Rarely does a man openly acknowledge he feels inadequate or is ashamed of not living up to certain standards. Instead, his only indication of this discomfort may be anger and overt resentment. Men don't feel at all comfortable with the prolonged embarrassment of being a disappointment, but they are also uncom-

fortable telling a woman how they feel. For most
men, there is an almost predictable sequence of responses. The conflicts these demands trigger lead
first to feelings of guilt, then to a stubborn resentment, and ultimately, if the demands are unrelenting, to angry rejection and the withdrawal of love.

## The Romantic

As far as Gloria was concerned, Tim had managed to
spoil everything. It wasn't just the energy she had
put into it, although it had been considerable. It was
what it all meant. She had planned her special surprise for Tim's birthday for weeks. When the day
arrived, Gloria picked Tim up at his office at lunch-
time and put her plan into action. She had Tim close
his eyes while she drove to the historic country inn
where, that morning, she had rented the most romantic room: four-poster bed, antique lace curtains,
and, in the bathroom, a claw-leg bathtub big enough
for two. As she led him into the room and told him
to open his eyes, she was filled with anticipation
and excitement.

Everything was perfect—the lunch, the chilled
champagne, even the spring flowers she had so carefully arranged. Everything was perfect except for
one critical element—Tim's reaction. "Oh, he thanked
me and said what a surprise it was, but I could tell
he really didn't love it the way I did. We had lunch
and toasted his birthday and all that, but when he
looked at his watch the second time, I knew he was
worried about getting back to work. I felt hurt, disappointed, and embarrassed."

More than anything, Gloria wanted to feel special,
to experience the "thrill" of love. She felt hurt, for it
seemed to her she had to beg Tim for the few ro-

mantic gestures she got from him. Her pointed need for romance was beginning to take a toll on him. Even when Gloria was doing something special for him, it felt to Tim more like an implicit demand than a gift. Gloria failed to recognize that while Tim loved her, men and women often love each other in very different ways. Gloria felt starved for romance in her marriage. She wanted Tim to love her the way she loved him, and he didn't. Her heightened expectations became unrelenting demands for closeness which actually had the opposite effect on Tim.

Gloria's wishes for more aliveness and romance created a vague and discomforting feeling of inadequacy in Tim. As he described it, "I really enjoy our candlelight dinners on the weekend and an occasional evening spent in front of the fireplace with a bottle of wine, but she thrives on a steady diet of that, and I don't. As far as our sex life goes, she's always talking about making our lovemaking an 'event.' I hate being made to feel guilty when I'm exhausted or uptight and I'm just not interested." Her insistence on romance stirred up anxiety in Tim instead of the passion and tenderness she so desired.

Tim felt a slowly growing resentment, for he knew that in his wife's eyes, he was failing her, was not making her happy, was not enough. And, the more she pushed, the worse he felt, and, sadly, the less he was inclined to give her what she wanted.

*Letting Go of Romantic Fantasies.* Women are often more openly romantic than men. Because of their greater ease with closeness, women tend to delight in the gestures that symbolize the importance of the relationship: a sweet note, a touching gift, a surprise evening out. Men, on the other hand, tend to feel vaguely uncomfortable about so directly expressing their love. It's not that a man doesn't care. It's just that for a man, romantic gestures are experienced as graphic measures of the extent of his intense attachment to and need for the woman. Clearly, women tend to be more relaxed about such acknowledgments. Gloria believed that if Tim's love equaled her own, he would necessarily be as interested as she in romance. Tim didn't love Gloria any less, but for him, romantic behavior and caring were not synonymous. Gloria didn't understand that unrelenting romantic demands can be tiresome; occasional demands are not.

Women such as Gloria need to relax, back off a bit, even create a little distance. That doesn't mean being less loving—a man's trust in the warmth and consistency of a woman's love enables him to feel less guarded, more comfortable, and more capable of intimacy. But a man also needs some degree of occasional distance between himself and a woman to feel most actively engaged with her. He needs to feel that she is not excessively dependent on him.

Heightened expectations created by romantic fantasies may be dangerous not only because they can push men away, but because they often disguise a more basic issue the woman needs to address—self-esteem. Women, and men too for that matter, will sometimes seek external solutions to internal problems of self-worth and well-being. Romance can be one such attempted solution. It not only makes us feel more interesting and worthy, it provides a kind of lift or excitement to our lives.

Boredom is a problem, for most of us experience it at one time or another. We may feel that if we're not doing something wonderful, our lives are bland, even worthless. The quest for excitement, for "highs," is often intended as an antidote to this boredom or sadness. In the course of therapy, Gloria discovered she really had been mildly depressed most of her adult life. Her hunger for romance was an attempt to feel more alive, to infuse more meaning into her daily existence.

If you see a bit of yourself in Gloria and her concerns, there are some things you can do. First you can ask yourself some questions. What will I feel about myself or my relationships if they go on the way they are, if they are not "boosted up" on a regular basis with intense moments of romance? Who am I without these moments, or without these validations of my worth? Am I enough? Am I a person of value?

This is not to imply that we should live without romance. But we do need to consider whether we can feel good about ourselves just because of who we are, without depending on how others respond to us.

The task here is ultimately to discover the difference between reasonable and unreasonable expectations. Unreasonable ones are really expressions of unresolved personal dilemmas.

## The Perennial Bridesmaid

Belinda, 34, a pediatrician, wants to get married and have a baby, and she feels Ray is the right man. The problem is that after being a steady couple for eight months, the issue of commitment and marriage is coming up not as a joyful discussion but as a source of ongoing frustration and pressure. Belinda is feeling insecure and disappointed that Ray is not ready. Ray feels pushed to make a decision which, from his point of view, seems too hurried because he feels he is still getting to know her. "I keep wanting to tell her, 'Don't push, don't ruin it,' " Ray complains. "But whenever I say anything like that, she gets her feelings hurt and I feel awful. I do know that I love her, but I need more time—I don't want to make a mistake.''

Belinda explains, "All of a sudden it hit me. I'm 34 and I really would like to have children. I'm around kids all day, but I want at least two of my own, and—let's face it—I don't have a lot of time left to have two or three children." Belinda is experiencing a different sort of pressure, one that many women today feel—that of time catching up with them after they have put off marriage and family for education and career.

The mistake Belinda is making with Ray is a serious one. Her wish and readiness for marriage and her eroding trust in the future of his love are making their time together strained and tense. The intensity of her need for a decisive plan places Ray in an emotionally difficult position. He feels forced to declare his commitment to her when it is only partially formed, not yet fully developed. She is exquisitely sensitive to her own sense of timing and comfortable with the thought of marriage but at the same time is being insensitive to Ray's need to take things a little slower. While some men certainly do need a bit of a nudge to take that final step, the seriousness of the marriage commitment necessitates that she recognize and be sensitive to Ray's sense of comfort and timing.

Ray does enjoy being with Belinda, and given some time and acceptance of his uncertainties, he would move toward a deeper union with her. But her hunger and growing need for permanence threaten to push him away.

*Understanding Differences in Timing.* One of the questions that plagues Belinda is whether or not she is wasting her time waiting for Ray to make up his mind. In the absence of guidelines regarding commitment and its timing, women of childbearing age are feeling a great deal of anxiety today. How *do* you know when the timing is right?

In our experience, men seem ready to begin dealing with commitment after they have been involved with a woman between one and two years. Women often feel the issue must be addressed seriously between six months and one year. Note the discrepancy. For most women, the momentum toward marriage is about twice as fast as it is for men! The discrepancy sets up the possibility of a great deal of misunderstanding and tension. It is interesting to note, however, that as men approach age 40, they are sometimes more receptive to making a commitment, even a surprisingly early one, than 30-year-old men, who still feel they have lots of time to decide about marriage and family.

## *The Eager Beaver*

A woman's anxiety about a man's feelings regarding marriage can surface in her first few dates with him. And that anxiety is only self-defeating.

Glenn, 42, an industrial designer, had dated a number of women in the year since his divorce became final. He was very excited about Sandra, 36, a personnel manager for a department store, during their first month together. She was bright and was involved in several of the same community and political causes Glenn was. But after only six weeks, Glenn began to cool toward her, and soon he told her he didn't think it was going to work out.

He describes what went wrong, in his opinion. "Looking back, the warning signs were there from the first. The first time we went out to dinner, San-

dra let me know right away that she was interested
in me and wanted to see me again soon, so we made
a plan to get together two days later. Then, every
time we saw each other, she would mention within
the first couple of hours some movie she wanted to
see or some plan for the following weekend, and
wouldn't let up.

"Maybe two weeks after we started sleeping together she asked me over dinner whether I wanted
to get married again, and how soon. I told her that I
did, within a couple of years, probably, and that I
liked living with somebody and didn't see myself as
staying single the rest of my life. She said she was
looking for an exclusive relationship and let me know
she wasn't sleeping with anybody else.

"It was as if she felt that I'd made some kind of
commitment to having a relationship, and that she
could expect a lot from me—a lot of time, a lot of
phone calls, and becoming a tight couple right then.
It was as though she had decided in her mind that I
was it. For me, we had about two great weeks, then
I started feeling pushed, and pretty soon it was over
for me."

*Containing Your Anxiety.* It is important and wise to
discuss your goals and your life plans early on in a
new relationship and also to find out what the man
is looking for. The question is, how early? And are
you simply seeking information or trying to allay
your anxiety? To wish deeply for an involvement is
normal and natural. To be frightened that it might
not happen for you is also understandable. But it is
important not to be overwhelmed by pessimism, or
to allow yourself to be sabotaged by self-doubt. Emotional hungers are never experienced as gifts by another person. Waning optimism about finding love
all too easily transforms itself into desperation, which

will somehow be communicated to a man regardless of how you may hide it.

When anyone transmits signals of excessive emotional hunger it has the all too predictable effect of pushing the other person away. Why? First, because desperation is perceived as being fueled by compelling needs that go beyond the relationship and are much more matters of self-esteem than of love. Second, because desperation feels overwhelming—the other person senses that the intense need cannot easily be satisfied. And third, because desperation leaves no room for the other person to love actively. The real feeling of love is experienced only when we are in the active "lover," not "lovee," role.

We are repelled by desperation and drawn to confidence and strength. How do you develop in that direction? Try taking a clearer look at what you bring to the arena of love. It's probably a whole lot more interesting and valuable than you think. Remind yourself of the value of your love, for that reminder can fill the void and gradually crowd out self-doubt. Desperation feeds on only one thing—despair. Self-encouragement and belief in one's lovability leave little room for despair. Channel anxious energy into social activities that reaffirm and expand your self-worth and provide you with new ways to meet men.

If you are with a man whose expressed goals are the same as yours, understand that although he may say he wants to get married and have children, it doesn't necessarily mean you're the one. And in the most ideal and promising situation, in which you both feel you're right for each other, take care to keep the desire to grow closer active and mutual on both your parts.

When your anxiety about marriage becomes dominant, it sets up a dynamic that results in making a man feel pushed, controlled, uncomfortably responsible for your sense of well-being. It prevents him from being an active lover, and it erodes any real hope for mutuality. He is likely to become passive, resistant, and even resentful, and ultimately inclined to move away from you rather than make a permanent commitment to marriage.

## The Status Seeker

"I think I've just about had it. No matter what I do or how much I give her, it's never quite enough." These were Al's words as he entered counseling with Frances, his wife of five years. She shouted back at him, "I don't think I'm asking too much of you—we both wanted the house, the vacations, the clothes. At least that's what you always led me to believe." Frances, 29, was right. Al, 43, had promised a lot, had tried to provide a luxurious life, but now he was getting tired.

As a couple, Al and Frances had developed a life-style that took every penny of Al's $70,000 yearly salary as an executive for an importing corporation. Frances was disappointed that Al hadn't been able to found his own company and had recently been passed over for the chief executive officer job he had campaigned so hard for. "Other men do it," she said. "They manage not to get stuck in a job where they can't make real money and be their own boss."

Although Al had a well-paying job with considerable responsibility, he felt he was a failure in Frances's eyes. "She gives me the feeling that I'm not good enough, that I'm not smart enough, rich enough, or tough enough to make her happy. But what really makes me nuts is that I've accomplished a hell of a lot more than she has or probably ever will." Frances had worked as a free-lance makeup artist in local department stores before she met Al but now worked only sporadically, considering her income as "mad" money.

Beneath Frances's elegant veneer, she felt sadly incomplete and inadequate. As a result, her connection to her husband was focused largely on getting a sense of validation and importance through affiliation with him. What Frances had not developed or accomplished on her own she attempted to secure vicariously through her marriage.

As we have noted, men feel saddled with the need to perform throughout their lives. Frances did not realize how much inner hostility was being stirred up in Al as a result of her demands. Most men place enough pressure on themselves to achieve, and they certainly do not welcome more from their mates. Just as women are burdened with a host of pressures of their own, men are chained to the idea that they are supposed to work hard, be successful, and, at the same time, master all the accompanying stress engendered by going after the American dream. Women who understand how men respond to these cultural expectations are typically cherished by the men they're with; women who ignore these unique male vulnerabilities are in danger of being left.

*Gaining Confidence from Within.* Whenever a man or woman feels inadequate, there is the fantasy that the partner can provide some of the solution. Both men and women are culturally conditioned to believe that a mate may enhance their sense of worth. Of course, this is never true in the long run, even though there may be a fleeting sense of pride for a man who has a stunningly beautiful woman on his arm, or a woman who is with a man of great power or wealth.

We all struggle at one time or another with the

question of whether or not we are "enough." But women have some important and unique problems in this regard. Traditionally, a woman's only path toward power and importance was through her affiliation with a man. What the culture implied was that if she wasn't with a man, she was nothing. Unfortunately, old conditioning, however inappropriate or anachronistic, dies hard. And for many women, that old conditioning can have a profound effect on their self-esteem.

The truth is that we all feel better about ourselves when we can provide for our own security, rather than trying to acquire it by affiliation with another person.

The task for most of us is to work at being "enough" just being who we are rather than who we are with. As a first step, ask yourself: If my mate never accomplishes more than he has now, can I love him? Will I feel okay? Or do I really need to solve my problems of insecurity by being with a man who, by virtue of his station in life, will make me feel I'm a worthy person?

Explore within yourself possible negative attitudes or feelings of self-loathing that may block confidence and self-esteem. We all grow up with inner doubts, shynesses, fears. There is a wonderful saying: "The more of life you master, the less of life you fear." The point is, if you take on the challenge of inner growth, you will be rewarded with a sense of self-respect that is quite impossible to achieve merely through association.

If you seek men as external solutions to internal problems, you need to work harder on building your own self-esteem. Get in touch with and trust what you like about yourself. Rather than feeling inadequate, make an effort to get out, and begin to work on those qualities you find lacking. Confidence is something we all can achieve, but it is always built from within.

## *The Hero Worshiper*

Cara, 30, wanted a "real man," one who was strong, mature, and protective. What's wrong with that? The problem was that Cara had a somewhat unrealistic view of men. Initially drawn to warm, sensitive men, she later came to resent their lack of aggressiveness and strength.

One night after she and Chuck, 35, had been living together for about a year, Cara thought she heard a prowler outside the kitchen. She ran upstairs and told Chuck, expecting he'd know what to do and would investigate the noise. "I was scared and I wanted him to do something. He listened and heard the noise too, and real nervously said he'd turn on the alarm and phone the police. I lost respect for him—he just seemed weak and fearful. I want a real man, someone who can take charge and protect me."

That was the last straw for Chuck. "I'm getting really tired of having to defend my manhood," Chuck revealed. "I'm comfortable with who I am, and, frankly, I'm not inclined to try to be someone else."

The acceptance Chuck felt from Cara early on in their relationship was rapidly fading. Cara wanted to find the mythic masculine man in Chuck. Fearful of the more dominant and aggressive man, she unconsciously sought to be in control by choosing a more sensitive and gentle man like Chuck.

*Regarding Men As Equals.* Men want acceptance just as women do. They do not want to be viewed as or needed as supermen or heroes. It's too much work to keep up false pretenses. Women who want a man to be larger than life will eventually find that the man resents them and is angry at them, even though this resentment and anger may be well hidden.

A woman's wish that a man could be more dynamic and protective is certainly understandable. It is the rough counterpart of a man's wish that a woman could be an all-knowing and all-giving earth mother. But at its core, this kind of unrealistic expectation about men is not just a simple wish but a reflection of a woman's feelings of helplessness or her lack of assertiveness. If a woman is to give up unrealistic hopes about men and what they can do for a woman, she must develop her own sense of strength, her own inner capacities. Women sometimes are afraid to seem self-reliant; they fear they will not be taken care of in the way they want to be if they appear to be strong. Studies of women's fear of success reveal this secret concern. Many women believe that if they are too strong, too self-reliant, and too successful, they will end up alone. Often they fear that men won't like them—that men will be threatened by their strength. Naturally, that isn't true, for most men respect and are drawn to strong, self-reliant women. But what is saddest about these women is that they fail to experience the joys of feeling strong and capable, when in fact strength and capability are the cornerstones for constructing relationships with men based upon a real sense of equality.

## When Are Demands Excessive?

How do you know when your expectations are dangerously in the red zone? The single most important indication is that your demands are fueled more by intense need than merely by wishes or preferences.

"Need" implies a certain level of imperative—that you will be lost or devastated if your expectations aren't met. This level of emotional intensity frequently gives rise to excessive demands. Expectations that primarily serve to reduce self-doubts and insecurities are likely to be excessive.

Demands in the context of a relationship have to do with wanting a mate to be different, to change, to meet our needs. Unquestionably, men are flawed—they are not the brave and gallant knights of old that women might hope for. But their imperfection is not the point. The point is that when a woman begins to tug a man in one direction, he recoils almost reflexively in the opposite. Repeated criticisms will make him feel he's "not enough," and will erode his feelings of being valued and accepted. Regardless of how much you tell him you love him, if you are also communicating that he must change, the net impact is not the warmth of love but the sting of disapproval.

A man's first instinct is to please the woman he loves. When a man believes a demand is reasonable, he will either make a sincere attempt to meet it or be fairly direct in telling you he cannot. The trouble comes when a man isn't sure whether what you're asking is reasonable and fair—when his own insecurities and need for approval make it difficult for him to decide what is reasonable and fair.

The first warning may be that he is relatively uncommunicative and vague when you attempt to discuss such issues; he doesn't give you any sort of straight answer. If you turn up the pressure, his feelings may shift slowly to resentment and then emotional withdrawal. Essentially, he is in conflict. He wants to stay connected to you, and while he is aware that your approval is an important ingredient in the connection, he doesn't feel able to satisfy you. This state of emotional limbo can be agonizing—he

can't seem to reduce the pressure he feels, and neither can he disconnect and get away from it. The
result is gradual emotional withdrawal.

In order to assess whether or not the demands
you make may be excessive, try asking yourself the
following:

1. Do I Want Significantly More from Him in a
   Particular Area? Excessive demands usually involve wanting more, not less—more time, more
   status, more romance, more manliness.
2. Am I Expecting Him to Be Different from Most
   Other Men? Excessive demands usually require
   the man to be not only "more than" and "better than" but different from other men.
3. Does He Seem Uncomfortable with My Demands? Excessive demands require a man to go
   beyond his level of comfort.
4. Why the Discrepancy Between What I See and
   What I Want? Does it have to do with something missing within myself—with feelings of
   incompleteness, questions of lovability, value,
   or security? Excessive demands often are efforts
   to force someone else to make up for what we
   feel is lacking within ourselves.

If you know the demands you're making are excessive, it's critical that you step back, even let him
know your expectations were unrealistic. That will
be the beginning of a real dialogue. Keep in mind
that genuine change always takes the form of small
but significant steps. Be realistic about the speed
with which change occurs.

When you want a man to make some sort of
change, choose the area carefully and be very specific about what you expect. When you are certain
your demands are fair, reasonable, and not exces-

sive, here is an approach you might take: "This is something that really bothers me. So we don't get into fights and because I love you, I want to know what I can reasonably expect to change in this area." If he is vehement about not changing, there's probably little chance for any significant alteration in his behavior no matter how right and justified you may feel or how wrong you think he is for refusing to change.

## Love Implies Acceptance

When we try to change the one we love, we make three primary mistakes. The first has to do with unrealistic expectations about love in general. It is a myth that we have a right, even a responsibility, to improve our mates. It is a myth that all aspects of interaction—personal needs as well as individual differences—are negotiable. They are not.

The second error has to do with a natural tendency to become self-righteous, believing that if we are willing to change for our partner, our partner should be equally willing to do the same for us. While that sounds reasonable, and in certain areas may be valid, the truth is that we are able to change relatively little. Remember, love implies acceptance. This wonderful feeling of lovability, comfort, and safety is the most important ingredient in the formula that holds couples together.

A third error women frequently make is not recognizing the basic nature of men. The women we have described want their men to be "much more" than they actually are. You can't have a relationship with "potential"—you have to accept and love a man for what he is right now. It is much safer and a lot less frustrating to be with a man the way he is, rather than the way you either wish he were or the way you hope he might become.

Many of you may feel sobered or even disappointed by how men respond to demands for change. But the truth is that women succeed well in encouraging change when they influence through loving acceptance and appreciation—it's a positive solution instead of a negative one. Your experience of love expands in direct proportion to the degree of caring and deserved acceptance you feel toward him. What he will give back to you will also be richer.

# CHAPTER FOUR

# Women Who Secretly Feel Contempt for Men

The word *misogynist* is centuries-old, with its roots in the language of ancient Greece. It means "woman hater" and has been used variously to describe a man who in one way or another disdains women or has contempt for them. Curiously, there is no analogous word for "man hater." We have a word for a person who hates everybody—*misanthrope*—but no word describing a woman who scorns men. Why? Until recent centuries, men were the primary carriers and refiners of language, for it was only men who were allowed to read and write. And it seems no accident that a word acknowledging women's contempt for men was somehow left out of the ancient vernacular. Might this be because men wanted to deny that women could have such hostile feelings? That they felt threatened by them?

Obviously, there are, and always have been, women who have strong negative feelings toward men. What is this about? What causes women and men to develop a sad and unfortunate enmity toward one another? Passions, both positive and negative, occur when strong interdependencies exist. The more we want, need, and rely on one another, the greater the potential for hurt and disappointment, and bitterness. This is especially so when, because of our dependency, we cannot just dismiss or avoid those of the opposite sex when they anger us. We have to continue to deal with them.

Certain of these basic angers toward men have been fueled in recent years by the women's movement, which exposed and decried the historical suppression of women by men. Feminism didn't create anger and distrust of men, but it did sharply focus and legitimatize such feelings. It provided a forum in which women could better understand and come to grips with some of the darker aspects and emotions of the male/female relationship. But even though the women's movement supplied a rationale for women's anger toward men, the true source of these feelings is rooted in much more primitive emotions.

## The Seeds of Contempt

The most basic sources of contempt are born in childhood. The building blocks of contempt/hatred/scorn are strong need on the one hand and hurt, bitterness, and fear on the other. The combined product of these forces is an intense and powerful conflict—needing and being drawn toward a person and simultaneously fearing that person. Typically, when something causes us pain we avoid it; we simply walk away. Few of us get burned repeatedly by a hot stove. But when we want and need that which can also hurt us, we are in conflict.

FAMILY INFLUENCES. Most often, ambivalence toward men arises when a girl grows up with a rather distant, disapproving, and unresponsive mother and a weak and unpredictable father, often one who had poor impulse control.

Darby, 38, recalls her alcoholic father—a powerful and respected attorney by day and an all too frequent drunk at night who would surreptitiously crawl into her bed to "sleep it off." While Darby has no specific recall of being abused sexually, she does have the disturbing feeling that it might have happened. "I think my mother basically just ignored what was going on because she didn't want to put up with him when he had been drinking." Her father became the only real source of "feeling needed or important I got as a kid." But the legacy of her father's behavior was far greater, for it also included feelings of terror, guilt, and revulsion. This combination of love and hate, need and fear, built an emotional framework within which Darby came to view and react to men as she became an adult.

Rene, 26, describes her father with painfully mixed emotions. "I did get love from him, and affection. He was always a whole lot warmer and more interested in what was going on in my life than my mother. But he also had these awful moods when he would get mad and yell at me. I know part of it was my mother—she would be mad at me about one thing or another and incite him when he came home. I guess deep inside I love him, but even to this day, I also feel a lot of resentment. I know he can't make me feel bad anymore, but I still can feel myself sort of cringe inside when he raises his voice."

Both Darby and Rene were hurt terribly by their fathers, and both have been left with emotional scars that have deeply affected their relationships with men. Both wish to have loving and positive experiences with the men in their lives, but neither does, for a thin but impenetrable veil of fear and contempt prevents the openness and trust which love requires.

Having a father who was "bigger than life" can also create problems with dependency, respect, and anger later in one's life. Catherine, a 32-year-old homemaker and mother of three young children, complains of her marriage to Jack, a gentle, rather average man. "He's nothing like my father, nothing at all. Dad was big, robust, and he had a deep, authoritative voice. He could be overly boisterous and even rude at times, but I loved the confidence he exuded, the raw energy he had. My mother sort of faded into the woodwork in comparison. I couldn't stand the thought of losing my identity in a marriage the way my mother did, and Jack seemed like the perfect answer because he seemed more gentle and understanding. The trouble is that I need him the way he is, but I also hate him for not being stronger." Afraid of becoming too dependent on or overshadowed by a man, Catherine chose someone she could dominate. But she dislikes herself for that choice and feels compelled to disparage Jack for being what he is.

**SOCIAL INFLUENCES.** Psychologists have long known that women have stronger affiliative needs than men. In part, these needs come from early-childhood fears that their very survival depends upon being protected. Even today, parents tend to be more protective of a girl than a boy. The effect this has on some women is that they look for protection from a man and simultaneously hate themselves and the man for feeling a need for it.

The fact that boys tend to be bigger, stronger, rougher, and more aggressive also plays a role in a girl's basic orientation and comfort with boys and later men. In many ways, the experiences girls have teach them to be afraid of boys—from the earliest skirmishes with roughhousing boys to later encounters with sexually aggressive teenagers. Men's propensity toward aggression and violence as well as the statistical reality of rape increase such fears, particularly in women whose backgrounds have sensitized them to such anxieties.

The fact that men have more real power in the world—more prestigious and better-paying jobs—is yet another painful contributing factor in women's resentment of men. Despite the changes in recent years, women continue to lag far behind men when it comes to the basic measure of power and mastery—making money.

**THE INTERNAL CONFLICT.** Many women grow up with both general and also highly specific reasons to resent, fear, and yet continue to need men. The anger that so intensely binds them to this conflict is precisely their ongoing dependency upon men. These women don't simply dislike men and decide to excise them from their lives, they also want an affiliation with men. They hide their bitterness, hurt, and distrust of men, at least partially, so they can also be with men. Such women experience tremendous internal conflict.

These women, sadly, are most contemptuous of their own perceived weakness, the need for a man. These inner feelings of personal judgment have farreaching repercussions in a woman's choice of man and her personal conduct with him. Sometimes she will choose a weaker man to disguise her own conflict, her mixed feelings about neediness and insecurity. And, at times, the angry woman will attempt to provoke a man about his weaknesses in an attempt to make herself feel stronger and less dependent on him. Such women may take pleasure in their ability to make a man feel uncomfortable, for he is then seen as having to experience the same fear and inadequacy they feel. Secretly, however, these women also resent the man's giving in—for they also need him and want him to be strong for them.

## When a Man Is the Object of a Woman's Scorn

Women who are angry at and contemptuous of men usually express their underlying feelings and attitudes in one of two ways: through emotional withdrawal, which makes the man feel isolated and neglected, or in more direct and aggressively angry ways, which intimidates the man.

**WITHDRAWAL AND NEGLECT.** A man feels isolated and neglected when a woman denies or disparages, either consciously or unconsciously, his need for emotional closeness. As we have already seen, men often hide their neediness or express it in highly disguised ways. Most angry women fall into one of two extreme groups: those who see men as excessively needy—"Men are big babies"—and those who view men as being tough, hard, and utterly self-reliant—"Men shouldn't need much of anything from women." Both are obvious exaggerations. Most men fall somewhere in the middle. They typically don't experience intense emotional hungers, but when they do, they crave satisfaction.

As we have described, contempt is an unconscious protective strategy some women adopt to shield them from feelings of dependency upon men. Risking hurt and disappointment, needing someone who might inflict pain, is too dangerous. The solution to this thorny dilemma is erecting a barrier of disdain. Women who are scornful of men withdraw from them emotionally for two basic reasons.

For a woman to engage a man fully—allow herself to be involved with him intimately and trustingly—demands a high degree of comfort with basic dependency needs. Women who fear their own dependency needs create distance in a relationship in order to reduce the level of closeness and intensity and thus avoid stimulating their own feelings of vulnerability. This psychological distance produces a buffer between themselves and the man, and even more important, between themselves and their need for him.

Another reason angry women withdraw is that accepting emotional involvement with a man tends to give him permission to expose his vulnerabilities. A woman who hates and distrusts her own vulnerabilities has trouble dealing with the man's emotional needs, for they are a painful reminder of her own.

In many ways, a man's response to feeling emotionally isolated and neglected does not differ from a woman's. There is a feeling of not being heard by and not being visible to the lover. But there is an additional edge for men. To be needy and to complain about it arouses a great deal of shame in men, because they have been taught to suppress and deny such needs. The Polarity Factor partly explains this. When men feel too isolated, they wish to move toward closeness. Indeed, extreme isolation in men adds a special urgency to this wish. When that need is blocked, and totally denied or neglected by the woman, a man is filled with a mixture of rage and sadness, both of which are difficult to express. Men feel ashamed to be so emotionally hungry and out of control. Ultimately, the only recourse they feel they have is to leave the relationship.

**ANGER AND INTIMIDATION.** When a woman expresses angry contempt for a man, the effect on him is a sense of humiliation or intimidation. Men who love women basically want to please them. The hostility and obvious displeasure expressed by a woman's scornful words or actions causes men to feel a growing apprehension.

Intimidation is an issue for both men and women. None of us wants or likes to feel intimidated. We want to feel safe and accepted, to be with a partner who encourages us, makes us feel strong and supported.

Intimidation is similar to fear but more subtle and complex. Fear is that accelerated heartbeat and adrenaline pumping into your system when you are presented with a clear and immediate danger. Intimidation is more insidious. It is a feeling of helplessness, cowardice, and somehow being made to feel smaller. It is a particular kind of fear that occurs only in the presence of someone you care about and need. The origins of intimidation lie in a curious mixture of components—courage, pride, insecurity, even dependency and love.

Intimidation always involves the presence of a strong emotional conflict. Because the man cares about and needs the woman, he doesn't want to withdraw from her. Neither does he feel able to be tough and confident, for fear of possibly losing her. The rather humiliating solution to this painful conflict is his feeling of intimidation—neither standing up for himself directly nor feeling safe and trusted.

What makes intimidation difficult for men to deal with is the acute sense of shame and loss of self-respect it causes them. A man especially hates feeling intimidated by a woman because he knows women tend to lose respect for men who are intimidated by them. Men understand this all too clearly. When we speak of a man's fear of a woman, we aren't referring to the electrifying kind of fear that accompanies physical danger—it's far more subtle.

Because of its subtlety, the telltale traces of this fear go unnoticed by the woman and denied by the man. Men aren't supposed to be fearful creatures; everyone knows that.

How can so common a human reaction as fear be so clouded with misunderstanding? After all, we are more accepting of a wider variety of feelings in men today, right? Well, maybe with the first quarter inch of our cortex, but not when it comes to our emotions. From the time they were little boys, men were taught that danger was to be dealt with, fear to be ignored.

Things really haven't changed all that much. Boys still want to be fearless, and women continue to be drawn toward men who are strong and confident. So when men experience the unmistakably unnerving messages of fear in the context of an important relationship, both partners are in for trouble.

## The Ice Queen

Judy, 27, has lost interest in sex with Gary. Even though their marriage is only two years old, an early frost has set in. As Gary, 32, said, "We don't even kiss much anymore. She interprets every expression of affection on my part as an overture to sex. Sure, I'd like it, but I'd also just like to have a little more contact. We used to, and . . . I don't know what happened." Judy thinks she knows. "He's become too insecure and demanding of me. There's nothing romantic anymore between the two of us. It feels more like he's clinging rather than wanting to make love."

Both Judy and Gary feel resentment. Gary feels lonely enough that he has thought seriously of having an affair, although the prospect isn't really attractive, for he loves Judy. What's really going on is that Gary feels emotionally neglected not only because his sexual needs are unsatisfied, but, on a deeper level, because his wish to feel warm and affectionate is, in his mind, rejected by his wife.

Like so many couples today, Judy and Gary are confusing lack of sexual interest with a sexual problem. They had a rich, inventive, and highly satisfying sexual ralationship prior to marriage. But Judy found herself getting progressively turned off by Gary's emotional demands, which Gary eventually channeled into sexual demands.

Judy could not respond easily to what she considered an unreasonable amount of complaining. When Gary experienced difficulties in his work as a pressured sales executive with a fast-expanding computer firm, he tended to walk in the door every night rehashing what the latest management blunder had been, telling her how anxious and upset he was. She quickly came to hate these nightly "debriefings." Secretly becoming disillusioned with him, she finally told him she needed a man, not an insecure little boy, and that he should get a better grip on his problems. Gary wasn't asking Judy to solve his problems, but he did need her as a kind of sounding board, for he valued her quick mind and generally tough perceptiveness. But for Judy, any crack in Gary's image of strength and competence was personally threatening, for it aroused within her the painful specter of her own uncertainty and sense of vulnerability. She saw Gary's weaknesses and she hated any sign of such flaws, for they reminded her of her own.

Judy's way of coping with her own discomfort was to progressively pull away from Gary. Gary's response to her withdrawal was to heighten the urgency and frequency of his sexual demands.

Unfortunately, whenever relationship dilemmas become sexual problems there is a rapid deterioration of warmth and closeness in a relationship. Fairly quickly, any expression of affection or physical contact becomes a signal for sexual contact. What eventually happens is that couples don't kiss, hold hands, cuddle, or even lie close in bed while sleeping. In that kind of atmosphere, no feelings of love and intimacy can survive.

In the case of Judy and Gary, the real question was not whether Judy could satisfy Gary's dependency needs, but whether she could accept them. As they came to understand over the following months, their marriage could survive and even flourish without her becoming a receptacle for his verbal outpourings. Gary needed to work on containing some of his hungers. He came to acknowledge that they were excessive, that he could talk more with colleagues, that he shouldn't use sex as a "pacifier" for his worries, as Judy put it. Judy, however, in some ways had a more difficult task. Could she accept the fact that men can be strong in some ways and quite needy in others?

*Accepting Oneself First.* Within every man there lives a boy who occasionally needs warmth and encouragement. Women carry within themselves a girl who needs the same things. Judy felt weak and ashamed of certain inner fears and did everything she could to deny and keep them in check. When she recoiled from sexual contact with Gary and humiliated him with her sharp, cutting barbs about his manhood, she was not simply being mean or insensitive. Internally, she was at war with herself—she was being even harder on herself, more critical and personally judgmental, than she was on him. She had strong and compelling needs for closeness and deeply insistent wishes to be protected and cared for. Early experiences with her harsh and emotionally constricted father made such feelings seem wrong, embarrassing, and dangerous to hope for. Gary's openly expressed desire for greater physical closeness threatened her shaky defenses.

It is foolish to say that there is no danger in the dependency that grows with open and mutual love. But how Judy handled her fears made lost love a self-fulfilling prophecy.

We are all vulnerable; we all have hidden concerns, wounds from the past that stir up worries about our value and our worthiness to be loved. What Judy might have done was to try telling Gary about her fears concerning dependency and her worry about making a relationship mean too much. Opening that kind of dialogue would have served two purposes. She would have exposed her deepest fear and, in the process, begun a gradual healing process. And second, that disclosure would have made her reticence more understandable to Gary, helping to free him from endlessly trying to reduce the emotional distance between them.

## The Competitor

Beth is a 31-year-old manager for a sporting goods manufacturing company. She is extremely aggressive and successful at her work and brings a competitive zest and enthusiasm to her job that all around her admire and envy.

As a girl, Beth learned that the only way she could ever get anything in her large family was to fight for it. She still views life in terms of either winning or losing. Issues are not negotiated, they are fought for. Her aggressive style worked during her childhood, and it works very well in her career. But it was disastrous in the context of her love relationships with men.

When she started seeing Charlie and began to fall in love with him, she was determined to make it work. She knew that her strength and competitive style had alienated men in the past, but she saw Charlie, a swimming-pool contractor, as extremely strong himself. "I felt I didn't have to worry about his being intimidated by me. I knew I had a strong tendency to test men, but I felt Charlie wouldn't let me get away with it."

Charlie recalls, "After about three months of seeing her regularly, the warning lights went on. I wanted her to have a lot of room to be herself and speak up about things, but I was getting really irritated with the way she always tried to better me, to play one-upmanship. For example, one night we were playing a board game at a friend's house and, sure enough, once again Beth treated the game like life or death. She seemed to go out of her way to put me down in front of my friends. I don't mind competing with my men friends, but with her, it was humiliating when she not only had to win, but had to rub my face in it."

Charlie's growing sense of dissatisfaction came to a head one evening when, over dinner at a restaurant, Beth said, "What's wrong? You seem down tonight." He told her he was feeling bad about losing one of his most lucrative contracts that day, with a hotel, and explained what had happened. What he wanted from Beth was simply commiseration and understanding. What he got was a lengthy lecture on how he should have handled the client. "Everything Beth said was right—everybody's hindsight is

twenty-twenty—but I was feeling bad, and she made
me feel worse. And that for me was the last straw."
It was only when Charlie told her he wanted to stop
seeing her, and why, that Beth realized her hostile
and competitive posture was damaging within a loving union.

*Dealing with Strengths and Weaknesses.* All men feel
some apprehension in revealing their vulnerability
to a woman. Charlie felt put off by Beth's need to
compete fiercely in every area. For him, it wasn't
simply "a little friendly competition," as Beth called
it. It had become deadly serious, and eventually
killed his feelings for her. Men such as Charlie have
had a hard time acknowledging how embarrassed
and shamed they feel in an adversarial relationship
with the woman they love and need. Beth felt she
was being playful or even helpful, while Charlie felt
she was being critical and patronizing.

Unfortunately, all Charlie ever really saw was Beth's
outermost protective shield. Had she allowed him to
peek inside, he would have seen a woman longing for
love but so unsure of how to handle it she did
everything to prevent it happening. Beth was so
afraid of really needing a man that she was always
putting him down. As long as she could view the
man as less than she was, she felt safe. In her mind,
if she was smarter, better, superior in every way,
she needn't ever worry about becoming dependent
upon him.

Women, particularly today, feel tremendous pressures to be independent. The emphasis upon autonomy, mastery, and career development has produced
an unfortunate by-product—fear and distrust of the
natural interdependencies in close relationships. Some
women fear any growing reliance upon a man as a
subtle manipulation of his to trap them, endanger-

ing their individuality and independence. Other
women see their reliance or need for a man as a
terrible weakness to be denied and overcome at all
cost. The sad result of this denial is that women feel
inadequate or guilty if they are not constantly
demonstrating that they are strong and, above all,
self-contained. The fact is that none of us is all that
self-contained. We are social creatures with primitive
and urgent needs for affiliation.

A woman like Beth needs to trust that her strength
and selfhood will not be eclipsed if she allows herself to get close to a man. It is only when she stops
having to prove herself that she will begin to trust
herself. Remaining outside of a relationship is a reflection not of strength but rather of fear of closeness
and union, and it inevitably results in a chilling
loneliness.

## When Sex Is Overemphasized

Sexual interactions between men and women can
create the most complicated and confusing of human
dilemmas. The anxiety men feel about their sexual
performance has been widely explored elsewhere.
Also well documented are the common sexual problems men have as a result of this anxiety. Not so
well understood, however, are the ways women can
unknowingly intimidate men by their sexual behavior.

We are living in a post-sexual-revolution era. Both
men and women have become less promiscuous.
This new conservatism is, in part, a natural swing
back toward more traditional sexual values, attitudes,
and practices that lead to more substantial benefits
in relationships. Although the sexual revolution is
certainly over, its legacy remains. As women claimed
the right to enjoy sexual pleasures more freely, men

became increasingly worried about their ability to be good lovers. Male performance anxiety is epidemic.

Every man's fantasy and many a man's fear is the sexually uninhibited and assertive women. Men dream of the delights promised by the woman who is expressive and spontaneous physically, who is able to toss aside caution and inhibition, who is aware of and trusting of her sexual hungers, who doesn't wait passively for the man to make the sexual overtures but instead actively and directly goes after what she wants and needs. Men do want and enjoy this woman—but with some important and not at all obvious qualifications.

A critical element when it comes to men's feelings has to do with timing and sexual comfort. Traditionally, it was the woman's role to put the brakes on sexually, to modulate the speed and intensity of the sexual involvement. Since men could count on women to operate as a sort of governor, they could ignore their own misgivings and act aggressive, decisive, and supremely confident. Women's growing ease with sexuality has changed all that.

## The Hot Number

Sharon, 28, recounts, "I really liked Bob from the first time we met at a friend's dinner party. We met for lunch, then dinner and a movie a couple of times, over the course of three weeks. We held hands, and got into some pretty hot kissing on my couch. But although he didn't seem shy particularly, he never tried to make love to me. I found myself wondering out loud, 'Do you have a hangup about sex, are you impotent, or what? Or maybe you're not attracted to me.' He looked upset, but just laughed my questions off.

"Well, the other night, I think I blew it. He took me to a baseball game and we had a great time. He drove me back to my place and we were watching TV, cuddling on the couch. I ended up asking Bob to stay over. I came right out and told him I wanted him to make love to me—actually, I told him I wanted him to give me a nice long, hard fuck—and all of a sudden what felt warm and romantic turned weird. He pulled away, got really uncomfortable, said he had to get up early—he was out the door in a couple of minutes! I felt horrible! I don't know whether I'll ever hear from him again." And she didn't.

*Acknowledging Differences in Timing.* Bob most certainly was attracted to Sharon or he wouldn't have continued to see her. But he was probably much shyer or more reserved about sex than he appeared to be. Sharon was attentive to her own needs and timetable of readiness but was blind to Bob's. Timing is extremely important to all of us, men and women alike. Don't assume that a man's timing will necessarily match your own. Men have performance concerns which can be intense and inhibiting, particularly when they are just beginning to know and care for a woman.

When a woman is sexually aggressive in the very explicit way Sharon was, it can be very intimidating to a man. Instantly, Sharon was seen as more powerful and freer and as requesting a level of comfort and performance Bob was unsure he could provide. This is not to say that women shouldn't be direct, honest, and assertive sexually, or that men can't handle that in a woman. But timing and sensitivity are crucial, for women and for men.

## *The Ball Buster*

Darleen, 29, is an attractive woman who is extremely comfortable with herself. Her irreverent humor, bright smile, and biting repartee charm every man she meets—at least in the beginning.

She and Doug, a junior-college track coach, got off to a passionate, wonderful start, or so she thought. During the first few weeks, they spent nearly all their free time with each other, telling their friends, "This is it!" But after the third week, Doug began making excuses why he couldn't see Darleen so frequently, and sometimes at bedtime he acted moody or picked petty arguments.

As Doug recalled, "I should have picked up on that cutting side of her from the first time that I slept with her when I obviously came too soon and she said, 'What's the matter, you got a train to catch?' I kind of laughed because of the way she said it, but it was really blunt."

Over the next week, Doug saw Darleen twice without having any real sexual contact. That weekend, ending up in bed with her, Doug was so anxious that he couldn't get an erection. Impatient, Darleen suddenly turned the light on to face him, and with obvious frustration, said, "What's the matter now? Whoever taught you how to make love?" Feeling humiliated, Doug pulled away. He went out of town the next weekend, and when he returned, he phoned Darleen only to say that he would be too busy with the coming track season to continue to see her.

Upset and confused, Darleen phoned him a week later and insisted that he tell her why he had broken up with her. "Did you meet somebody else?" No, he replied, he hadn't met anybody else, he had just gotten very busy. It was only under her intense questioning that Doug finally told her what had pushed him away: "Too much emphasis on sex—I felt too pressured and I was starting to feel bad about myself." As she pushed for something more specific, he told her, "All that kept going through my head was, how do you try and talk to a woman like you without seeming like some kind of wimp? It made me feel pressured to be the great lover every night, to live up to what you expected. I couldn't keep it up."

*Letting Go of a Tough Facade.* Is Darleen simply an insensitive woman? Not at all. Darleen wanted someone in her life, wanted to find love, but in a basic, and largely misunderstood, way, she was afraid of men. Having grown up with an angry father who subtly terrorized her mother and never permitted any real affection or closeness, Darleen unconsciously viewed the men she was drawn toward as potentially dangerous.

If men could be kept on the defensive and a bit insecure of themselves, they would never be strong enough to hurt her the way her father had. Where she felt powerless as a child, she would now feel powerful, where she felt humiliated and weakened by her need for love, she would make sure it was the man who had those concerns so she would never again have to experience such pain. Her solution was sadly self-defeating: the price for dealing with her fear of a man was to end up pushing him away.

Women who have been hurt by a man and feel fearful of the need love exposes within them have other options than the one Darleen picked. But a prerequisite for choice is awareness and understanding of what drives our feelings, words, and actions. Darleen's problem was not how she treated Doug, it was how she treated herself. She had been wounded

by lack of love, and she was unfortunately perpetuating that same lack of love in her life.

We do have choices. And one of the most important of them is to choose to recognize past hurts,
understand how they affect current experiences, and
allow the future to be different. For Darleen, that
meant having the courage to allow Doug to be confident and strong, taking the chance that he would
love her in his strength and not abuse her.

There is perhaps nothing so crippling as fear and
nothing so maddening as being afraid when we are
not sure what we are afraid of. Fear is perpetuated
by old, repetitious experiences that reaffirm our dark-
est and gloomiest thoughts. The antidote to fear, the
only real and effective one, is change. And change
requires new experiences, not familiar old ones. Conquering fear requires facing it, opening the closet
and letting the light shine in; if you keep the closet
door sealed tight in hopes that somehow the dread
will creep away, you will never conquer it.

Women who have fears of men, fears of getting
close to and then needing a man, can overcome
them not by ignoring them but rather by talking
about them—and talking about them with the man
they care for. It takes choosing a man wisely but
giving him a chance to be different. And it takes
paying close attention to those differences and trusting they will remain. Above all, don't close yourself
off to new experiences with a man by perpetuating
old and unfulfilling ones.

## The Scorned Woman

Wendy's unresolved bitterness from her early marriage is polluting her current relationship. Now 35,
Wendy married Ralph when she was 20. She loved

and trusted her husband, and it was her willingness to work that made it possible for him to complete medical school.

Although Wendy wanted children right away, she deferred her longing because motherhood would have interfered with her working to support Ralph's education. He promised they would start a family as soon as he finished medical school. After his internship, in the seventh year of their marriage, Ralph applied for a residency in internal medicine, which again postponed children.

She was patient and accepting of the situation until she found out that Ralph had had a number of casual affairs with nurses and woman doctors at the hospital. He confessed, moreover, that he had started having affairs during the first year of their marriage. She felt betrayed and bitter.

The divorce that followed, along with a number of unsatisfying subsequent relationships, led Wendy to create a hard, brittle armor around herself. It is this armor and her understandable anger and distrust of men that Wendy brought to her relationship with Steve.

As much as Steve enjoys Wendy's company, he is beginning to back off from her, have doubts; he senses that their relationship will be a limited one. He is perceiving subtle hints of her underlying bitterness toward and distrust of men.

"Wendy's told me pretty openly that she doesn't think much of men, but I'm getting this disturbing feeling that she really hates them. She talks a lot about the shabby things guys do to her girlfriends—this one stood a girl up; another friend found out her husband's chasing a woman at his office. She told me about her husband's cheating, and I understand her feeling betrayed by him, but I'm beginning to think she thinks most men can't be trusted. She tells me she thinks I'm special, but I know I'm not all that different from other men, and that one of these days, I'm going to screw up and do or say something insensitive and I'll just be another man she hates.''

While Steve finds much about Wendy that he likes, he is also beginning to resent her. Her deep anger is only thinly disguised and acts as an invisible barrier between them. She is afraid to trust Steve and open herself to being hurt again.

Were Wendy able to communicate to Steve her fear of getting hurt again and her need to go slowly, he might be able to respond in a way that would allow her to heal and trust again. Instead, her unresolved pain is preventing her and Steve from growing closer in the warm and safe connection they both want.

*Carrying Anger from the Past.* Unfortunately, the risk of hurt, disappointment, and pain exists in any love relationship. Realistically, we cannot hope to avoid ever getting our feelings hurt or causing hurt feelings. However, when old hurts become unresolved baggage we carry with us into a new relationship, they prevent us from loving openly.

Men are particularly uncomfortable with the suspicious and bitter anger of a woman who has been hurt before by a man. Even though a man may understand that he didn't cause the anger and is not responsible for it, it can make him uncomfortable and afraid.

When a man cares for a woman, the anger she brings from her past can have a profound impact upon him. It stirs up disquieting feelings of anxiety. Anger, particularly when a man knows he is not the original cause of it, makes a woman seem capricious and unpredictable. At the most primitive emotional level, such feelings are those of a boy who is terrified and helpless in his dealings with an inconsistent mother—a mother who at some moments loves him and at others takes her anger about other things out on him because he's conveniently there. No one wants to be the target of misdirected anger.

No matter how much interest, friendliness, and caring you project in your initial encounters with a new man, if he also picks up messages that you're bitter or angry at men in general, he is going to have a hard time trusting you or wanting to become intimate with you. Even though you may assure him that you feel he's different or special, he is nonetheless a man. He knows he will inevitably feel the force of your negative attitudes, and he therefore is likely to protect himself and shy away from you.

Looking at this in reverse, what would your emotional response be to a new man who let you know, whether directly or jokingly, that he "hates women," "can't trust women," or "always gets screwed one way or another by women"? You'd be likely to back off from him, wisely concluding that his attitudes spell trouble. Men have the same reaction: to move on to someone else who encourages their trust and love.

## Releasing Old Anger

Stored-up and unresolved old anger hurts us. If we don't let go of it we typically do one of two things: either we direct it back toward ourselves, eroding our self-worth and falling into depression, or we hurl it in a misdirected way at others, particularly those we care about. We hurt ourselves or someone we like—not a very good selection of options!

But there is a third option, a much better one:

getting rid of old anger and moving on with your life. Like any other kind of change, releasing old anger takes work and the courage to face yourself openly and honestly. For many of us, there is a temptation to cling jealously to old, archaic resentment, using it as a kind of righteous justification for feeling the way we do. But however justified our resentments may be, however hurtful our old wounds are, this tenacious attachment to them is self-defeating. It binds us to an unpleasant past, distorts and interferes with the present, and presents a better and more gratifying future.

There are five basic steps involved in the process of releasing old anger:

1. **RECOGNITION.** The first step involves recognition. Frequently, one of the most difficult things for us to do is to discriminate between old and misapplied anger and new and appropriate anger. The difference is that new anger feels roughly proportionate to the cause, while old anger feels excessive, somehow bigger than the crime warrants. New anger can be explained in terms of what has just happened to you, and it seems justified. Old anger can't be understood in terms of what just triggered it—the intensity and depth of your reaction seem to go beyond.

2. **GETTING BENEATH THE ANGER.** The second step is understanding that anger is a protective device we use to cover hurt. We are not simply angry, we are hurt. And old anger represents the deepest of hurts, hurts that continue to torment us. The reason anger is protective is that, unpleasant as it is, it is less devastating than the pain of being hurt. Getting beyond old anger, however, requires fac-

ing up to old hurts. It takes acknowledging how we were hurt, who hurt us, and how much we were hurt.

3. **EXPRESSING THE HURT.** Once you have identified the source of the hurt and what it is about, you must then express it. Let it out, put it into words, cry, scream, or write it down. Often, with old anger the people who hurt us aren't still around or, even if they are, couldn't understand or constructively deal with our anger. It's not necessary to confront them directly anyway. But the feelings must be translated into words and ventilated.

4. **FORGIVING THE HURT.** Release from old hurt and anger ultimately requires forgiving. Remember, though, forgiving is for *you*. It is your ticket to freedom from old pain; it is not to relieve the person who caused it. Forgiving is not necessarily excusing the people who hurt you; it doesn't imply that whatever they did was justified. But it is the process that breaks the link in the chain that binds you to old hurtful feelings and that begins to heal you. You might say to yourself, "But I could never forgive him"—but remember, the other side of that declaration is "I'll always be hurt." Try saying something like this: "You hurt me terribly, and I forgive you and release myself from that hurt."

5. **VIGILANCE.** Getting rid of old anger is a process that takes some time. Anger tends to recur occasionally even long after we think we've freed ourselves from it. When that happens, understand and acknowledge it, tell the person you're with about it clearly and openly, and then reaffirm to yourself your freedom from it.

Experimenting with these five steps may yield gratifying results. Whenever we free ourselves from any negative emotion, we create room for new, more positive, feelings and attitudes. Anger, secret contempt, resentment, are invariably debilitating regardless of how justified these emotions may have been at one time.

# CHAPTER FIVE

# How the Need to Control Backfires

*Controlling* is the word Vince uses to describe his wife, Sara. When he says it, there is more than a trace of resentment in his voice. The first few times Vince shouted this epithet at her, Sara thought he was just being dramatic. Even now, when her alleged control of Vince has already driven him to have an affair and think of divorcing her, she is mystified as to why he feels so enraged.

## What Is Control?

The word *control* has ominous connotations. It suggests totalitarian regimes—helplessness on the part of those who are being controlled, and malevolence on the part of those dictating the rules and restrictions. When we describe people as "very controlling" of their mates, we may see them as tyrants, essentially power-mad at the expense of their innocent partners.

But is this really true? Are people who wish to control their loved ones driven by harmful intent?

Or are they, instead, choosing an ultimately self-defeating means of bolstering their own security? We believe it is the latter. The wish to exert control over one's mate is understandable and quite common, for being in control makes us feel more comfortable. Feeling in control allows people to be less anxious and more certain that everything will go along in a predictable and satisfactory fashion.

The need to control typically begins as soon as we start to fall in love. There is a saying that love and hate are closely related, but it might be more accurate to say that love and control are tightly linked. Loving someone carries along with it a growing need for that person. Emotional need bestows great power on the one who is needed. When we give that power, we often feel fear as well as an unspoken resentment that we have put our sense of well-being in someone else's hands.

Allowing ourselves to love someone creates strong and frightening feelings of dependency on that person. The link between dependency and control begins in childhood. Children can be most clever in conjuring up ploys to control their parents' behavior. For example, in order to feel safe and maintain a connection with mother and father, a child may attempt to create enough guilt in the parents so they won't leave the child with a baby-sitter, fake illnesses to stay home, or painfully complain, "You don't really love me," to elicit a reassuring "But of course I do" from a parent.

If you have ever tried to control a loved one, you probably know that the urge comes not from strength but from a feeling of insecurity—you don't believe he truly loves you, you don't trust his love. If you did, you could allow him the freedom to be and do more as he chooses. In the absence of trust, there is often a growing need to make sure you know exactly where your partner is and whom he is with, to restrict his activities or even to make him increasingly dependent on you.

Most of us at one time or another have experienced trying to reach someone we care about on the telephone, not being able to, and then frantically calling every few minutes. When you cannot make contact, it feels as though you are losing the person, as though he cannot be counted on to return again. Another example is when you are meeting a new lover at a restaurant and he's late. You wait, and wait, and continue to look at your watch. For a brief moment, the thought crosses your mind that maybe he won't show up—maybe this is it! It's all over! We are all capable of these private and painful flashes of anxiety over the possibility of loss. One common solution to that anxiety is to exert more control.

There are numerous ways control is achieved in a relationship. The most obvious pattern of controlling involves the restriction of behavior—dictating how the other person is supposed to act and not act by encouraging or discouraging that behavior. For example, pushing a man to act more "mature" sometimes has very little to do with simply expecting him to behave in a responsible way. Rather it is often a veiled attempt to make him less free and uninhibited and therefore less unpredictable.

Control is frequently exerted by some direct monitoring of our partner's activities. Checking up on him, even when disguised by an innocently caring "Just wanted to see how you're doing," may be motivated by a worry that he doesn't care enough, that the union is fragile.

Perhaps the most disguised and yet most common way to control is by playing the role of generous and loving caretaker of one's mate. This form of control may masquerade as supportive behavior, but in fact it is an attempt to secure a position of power in the relationship by making the other person need us.

There are those who say marriage itself is a form of institutionalized control, bondage rather than bonding. In the narrowest sense, there is an element of truth to this, for marriage does, to some extent, involve issues of territory, possessiveness, and control. By definition, marriage forces us to take some position on sexual fidelity, on time spent with one another, and on major leisure-time activities. Areas of personal responsibility may be redefined, and intense friendships with the opposite sex may be considered threatening to the union and therefore off-limits. But, in a broader sense, all of us need agreed-upon boundaries in order to feel secure and confident within a relationship. When we feel most secure, we're also most free to love each other fully.

Control is an issue in every relationship. The ideal union both provides the continuity of a secure and predictable partnership and protects individual freedom. Positive, mutual accommodation and compromise result in intimacy and the preservation of uniqueness and individual expression. Excessive control far overshoots its mark: rather than enhancing one's life, as love can, it diminishes personal freedom, creates resentment, and ultimately makes one want to break free.

## How Women Learned to Control

When issues of power and dominance are explored between men and women, it is usually the man who is cast in the role of the controller. In truth, men have attempted to control women through the ages, most commonly by restricting or containing female sexuality, which men saw as threatening. Men have also been repressive in areas in which women could achieve power, such as literary and artistic accomplishments, as well as work. But while these various manifestations of men's anxieties and insecurities are well documented, the ways in which women wish to control and often succeed in controlling men are not so well known.

The wily, cunning, and devious woman is a common theme in mythology and literature. From Eve's seductive temptation of Adam to tales of sirens luring men to their destruction, there has always been the fantasy of the powerful, controlling woman. Undoubtedly, these mythologies are derived from men's intense and lifelong need for women and the anxiety that need arouses. Creating myths is one way we attempt to understand and put into perspective what we fear.

Because men have often exerted control over them, women were forced to develop more subtle techniques to get what they wanted from men. Women, in general, are more astute about and comfortable with the emotional give and take in relationships than are men. Because of this, a woman who wishes to control is likely to be fairly successful, for the man is generally not conscious of what she's doing.

As we have indicated, control is one way to feel secure. By making sure the man acts and feels in particular ways, a woman can predict his behavior and thus feel reasonably secure about him and his presence in her life. But most women, irrespective of the amount of control they have, remain somewhat ambivalent. Women don't really want ultimate control no matter how hard they may fight for it. Women who are controlling invariably insist that they want the man to fight back, not to yield totally, because if he does, he appears weak in their eyes. If a man gives in too easily, the woman comes to believe that he is with her only because of her power to control him, not because he values her. She knows that he is caving in out of fear—fear of losing her love—and this makes her anxious and afraid herself. She says to herself, "If he is so weak, so pliable, how can he be strong enough to take care of me, to love me and protect me?" So paradoxically, the very efforts she makes to feel secure may end up causing her even more insecurity. No woman wants to really control, for when a man ends up becoming too easily dominated, she feels anxious and alone.

## When a Man Feels Controlled

Men hate feeling controlled. On an unconscious level, it evokes primitive and scary memories of the powerlessness of infancy and childhood and the dominance of the mother. When men are conscious of being controlled by a woman, and the control persists, they feel even worse—they feel emasculated. The Polarity Factor helps explain a man's reaction to feeling controlled. Men want to be connected and intimate with the woman they love, but not at the expense of their ability to control their own destiny. When men feel constrained to remain in a position of being fused, forced to remain too close, they feel rage and resentment, even though they may not express it directly.

One reason for a man's feeling of helplessness over being controlled is that he is to some degree dependent on the woman and therefore reluctant to take certain steps that might threaten the bond with her. What happens then for some men is that they are angry about being restricted and controlled yet at the same time feel that it is dangerous to express such feelings. They then silently grow even more resentful. Men in this predicament feel as though they're stuck—they feel they can't leave or retaliate directly, so their only recourse is to stay put and see them with negative emotions.

More specifically, if a man has attempted to make his dissatisfaction about feeling controlled known, and the woman does not acknowledge that his anger may be justified, he may slip into a posture of quiet resentment. Women sometimes miss the signs of a man's irritation over being controlled because men hide it well. Men often feel ashamed of their resentment; they don't want to seem plaintive, and don't like admitting that they are uncertain of how to change the situation. As a result, a woman may have few hints of the inner turmoil and subsequent rage a man is experiencing until it is too late and the man abruptly leaves the relationship.

To be on the receiving end of control is to feel fundamentally untrusted and unloved except within the narrow confines of another person's perceptions. As a result, a controlled man eventually feels alone and estranged while at the same time suffocated by his need to maintain the relationship. That kind of negative connection with a woman is akin to bondage, not love.

When a man is with an excessively controlling woman, he often feels caught in a bind: if he yields to her control because of his wish to please the woman, he worries that she will view him as weak, a "pushover." Men know that women don't really like to control a man. So on the one hand a man's first instinct is to try to please a woman, and on the other he is afraid he'll come across as a "wimp" if he is too yielding.

Women who control men are typically well-intentioned and caring. They usually do so unknowingly and without conscious intent. Regardless, this behavior is primarily self-involved and self-defeating, and rarely leads to a woman's securing the love she wants.

## *The Princess*

Laurence, 29, describes why he decided to stop seeing Rita, 31, after only three dates. When they met at a friend's Sunday barbecue, "I liked her a lot. She was pretty and friendly and seemed easy to talk to. I called her a couple of days later and asked her if she wanted to go to a certain movie.

"First she said she wanted to see it, then she mentioned a couple of others she wanted to see more. I didn't care that much which movie we went to, and told her to choose. She did, then asked me, 'Well, is it okay with you, or would you rather see the one you suggested first?' I finally had to choose the movie, by this time feeling I didn't know what she wanted to see.

"It was the same thing when we got to the theater and started walking down the aisle. I asked her where she wanted to sit and she said, 'Where do you like to sit?' I found a couple of seats toward the middle and she said, 'Wouldn't you rather sit closer?' I came right out and said no, I like to sit in the middle, and I remember exactly what she said, because it irritated me: 'No reason to fight about it.'

"Overall," Laurence recalls, "I liked Rita. We went to a disco a few days after that, and the following weekend she took me to a party. She was sweet and affectionate, but there seemed to be no easy flow to being with her. Whether it was making a simple plan to go somewhere or even just having a discussion, there was always all this back-and-forth. She would agree to do what I wanted to do, then bring up all these little points about what was wrong with it.

"For example, she would ask me what I thought, then pick holes in what I said, then say, 'But you're right.' She would express her opinions or take a stand, then take it back. It was enough to drive me crazy. The result was that it was just easier and smoother to ask her right out what she wanted, first, and go with that. I ended up feeling she was trying to control and manipulate me, in an indirect way. The small things began to add up and irritate me to the point where I wasn't having fun or feeling positive toward her. At best, I found her much too set in her ways; at worst, I thought she acted like a spoiled princess."

*Loosening Up.* Whenever we meet someone for the first time, or go on a first date, most of us are a bit nervous—we want to make a good impression. That's normal and understandable, but how we handle that nervousness is something else. Some people may act very irritable or uptight because they resent the pressure they feel. Others are so anxious for approval they act overly sweet and compliant. And then there are people like Rita, who have an unconscious need to control in order to feel comfortable.

Rita's rigidity was her way of feeling secure, but it gave her trouble with men right from the beginning. Flexibility and accommodation left her feeling dangerously vulnerable to possible hurt, even rejection. Yet her manner of coping led to the very outcome she most dreaded.

The solution for someone like Rita is to become more aware of her social anxieties and, more specifically, just how she deals with them. Often it may even be appropriate to tell the other person that you're a little nervous and excited about the encounter, for that can help both people to relax a bit. Chances are he is nervous too.

## The Spoilsport

"Vince is childish and irresponsible," complains Sara, 40. "I'm a sports widow. Depending on the season, he spends his free time either playing softball or watching football on TV with a gang of his buddies." Sound familiar? The reality is that Vince is a deputy district attorney, highly committed to his work and diligent to a fault. But on the weekend, Vince likes to unwind and play, which in the spring takes the form of playing on an amateur softball team, and in the fall screaming and yelling his head off in the den with his friends as their home team wins or loses on TV.

Sara has been disappointed with Vince in one significant area during the course of their marriage. She thought he would be more attentive and generous with his time both with her and with their children. Lately, she has complained relentlessly about his "immaturity." The more she tries to close off his recreational hours, the more resentful he becomes.

Vince sought counseling after, unbeknownst to Sara, he had an affair that was meaningful enough to make him consider leaving his wife. He viewed the battles over weekend sports not as an innocuous marital clash, but as only the tip of the iceberg in the problems with their marriage. Beneath those complaints was his belief that Sara disapproved of pleasure either for herself or for him. Vince felt his wife regarded life as a series of obligations to be fulfilled, with parenthood primary.

In the course of their sessions, Sara revealed what was underlying some of her need to control Vince.

She has always felt uncertain of his love for her and afraid that one day he might just suddenly leave her. And after the children were born, she felt he wasn't as loving and caring toward her. Rather than dealing directly with these insecurities and talking them over with Vince, she gradually adopted a posture of becoming the more "mature" one in the relationship as a means of control.

*Understanding a Man's Need to Play.* Men are often described as just being boys at heart, obsessed with toys, games, and the wish to play. Sometimes this is said in a disparaging tone as though "mature" men were the exception. The fact is, however, that men not only want to play, but need to play as a balance to their intense drive to achieve at work. Play allows a man to recapture carefree childhood states of being. Tension is released, enabling him to put life in a more balanced and realistic perspective.

It is interesting that so many women love the boyish part of a man when they first get involved with him, but are disturbed by this very quality later on. There are women who have difficulty accepting the fact that men can be strong and dependable even though they may sometimes wish to be silly and boyish, especially with male buddies.

Sara didn't understand Vince's need for play and relaxation. He did not love her or his children less because he needed to take that time out. Her subtle disapproval of the playful parts of his personality ended up taking the fun out of his relationship both with her and with their children. Sara could not see how much resentment she had stirred up in Vince and how she was driving him away from her.

## *The Inquisitor*

Catherine, 30, felt as if she was going crazy. She found herself going through Gil's wallet after he fell asleep, checking their phone bill for unfamiliar numbers called on the evenings when she was in night classes, and calling him two or three times when he was working nights or weekends at the office. Even as she was indulging her suspicions, Catherine was embarrassed by her conduct, but she couldn't stop.

A few weeks into their relationship, one year earlier, Catherine had discovered that he'd spent the night with his old girlfriend, but that was well before Gil and Catherine developed an exclusive relationship. Other than that incident, Gil had never given her cause for suspicion. And yet, jealousy and possessiveness became central issues between the two of them as time went on.

As for Gil, he felt smothered by her jealousy and constantly on the defensive. He felt as if he had to account for his whereabouts every second, as if he was constantly on the defensive. No matter how much Gil reassured Catherine of his love for her, her jealousy and suspicion continued, and increasingly poisoned his feelings for her.

Gil was deeply hurt and disappointed by the deterioration of their relationship. He had felt sure they would get married and have children together.

"At first, it was wonderful being together. It was intense, but I thought that was because we were getting used to living together. But instead of getting easier, more relaxed, it got more and more tense. She became obsessed about this one-night stand that happened before we really were a couple. I tried to love her and make her feel secure, but I couldn't turn it around."

His resentment mounted until he hated every question she asked, even innocent ones about how his day had been. He began working long hours at his office, and before they'd lived together for even a year, he asked her to move out.

Catherine was so obsessed with discovering possible signs of Gil's infidelity that she had little idea of the impact of her behavior on him. He wanted to feel close to her—but not if closeness was an open invitation to interrogations. His spending more and more time at the office should have been a warning to her that she was pushing him away. Instead, she viewed his absences as additional proof that he might be having an affair, and so her fearful suspicions intensified.

*Conquering the Torment of Jealousy.* Jealousy is one of the most painful emotions we can experience. It can be obsessive and relentless and can lead to a feeling of being totally out of control. The fear of losing someone upon whom we depend can be terrifying. People who are jealous are in effect at war with an imagined enemy who may steal love from them. At its extreme, jealousy is similar to paranoia. Clues pop up everywhere. Each word or gesture takes on special and frightening meanings. When it's not resolved, jealousy can surely and swiftly doom a relationship. Even if the man doesn't physically leave, he withdraws emotionally and spiritually. Love and trust cannot blossom in an atmosphere of suspicion and resentment.

Jealousy often has a basis in fact: past infidelities. Catherine used Gil's one-night stand as a justification for her distrust, despite the fact that they had not yet discussed an exclusive commitment to each other when it happened. Regardless, her behavior destroyed what might have become a good and lasting marriage.

How we respond to jealousy is a highly personal issue. It involves our own level of confidence about how lovable and valued we feel. When we feel whole and worthy, we are not prey to ravaging bouts of jealous fantasies and suspicions. To be jealous is to be feeling insecure, inadequate, unworthy. While some degree of jealousy is normal in a relationship, it can get out of hand and become destructive when fed by self-doubt. Jealousy can hurt not only the object of our jealousy, but also ourselves, because it corrodes our sense of self.

If you find yourself struggling with jealousy as Catherine did, try to use these torturous feelings to begin helping yourself. Know first of all that you are no doubt exaggerating negative feelings about yourself and undervaluing positive ones. By allowing yourself to be enveloped by jealous feelings, by giving in to them, you are making yourself feel worse than you have to. You can begin to stop the downward spiral by addressing the real problem: self-esteem. The first step is to contain the jealousy. Talking about it, worrying about it, or acting upon it will only serve to breathe more life into fearful fantasies about your lover. Acting it out through suspicions and accusations not only increases its hold on you, but also drives your lover away from you.

Begin to channel the energy expended in worry and self-doubt into feeling better about yourself. Try writing down all of the qualities you like in yourself. Trust these affirmative statements, think about them, and remind yourself of them. Think also about what you need to improve in yourself. It is useful to even try thinking about what you fantasize your lover would like in another woman, for they are probably qualities in which you feel deficient. Don't then try to be like that other person, but perhaps there might be some aspects of your personality you might like to work on and change. Explore these not out of fear, not for the man in your life, but for yourself.

## The Lifesaver

Anita, 36, had been seeing Matthew exclusively since they met two years before. They had talked about getting married a year before, but he kept putting off setting a date, for a host of vague reasons. She was becoming increasingly upset, discouraged, and angry, because she thought she was so good for Matthew. Their friends thought he was crazy not to marry her. "Look what she's done for him," they said. Matthew, however, was not so sure. He did acknowledge that she had helped him turn his life around, but he had nagging doubts about his love for her. As the months passed, his doubts increased, and even Matthew wasn't sure why.

When they met, Matthew was coming off a major business fiasco in which he broke off with a somewhat unethical partner in a failing auto parts business. While he fancied himself an entrepreneur, and certainly had some good business ideas, Matthew had never quite succeeded at anything he tackled.

When he met Anita, a highly directed and successful interior decorator, the combination seemed perfect. Anita helped him get his new venture off the ground, and also became a kind of teacher to help Matthew with some of the "people skills" he lacked. She loved doing this for him, and he was deeply grateful.

But as the months went by, Matthew found himself beginning to resent the help and encouragement he initially found so welcome and special. While he knew she had his best interests at heart, he also felt controlled, even manipulated by her. Even though he became much more competent, she continued to be a kind of "overseer" making sure he did everything correctly. Even when her way of doing things was better, he started to push back, to try to do things his way. Eventually there were more power struggles in their relationship than moments of comfort and harmony. He knew that part of the problem stemmed from his lingering doubts, but nevertheless he felt a growing resentment.

Anita was only vaguely aware of Matthew's resistance to her help and didn't take it seriously. Unconsciously, she was afraid to let go of the control, as though Matthew might not love her if he didn't need her. Anita had never recognized the fact that she coped with her insecurities with men by becoming invaluable to them. Not that she was doing any of this in a calculated fashion, for she loved being a helpmate and a partner. But Matthew began to focus more on the negative controlling aspects of her behavior than the positive helpful qualities.

Anita believed he should have been able to handle her competence with less ambivalence. She was correct. If Matthew had been a more self-assured man, he could have spoken out more directly and stopped the negative drift to their relationship. But he was not. Does that mean the burden was on Anita to save the relationship? No. The purpose of this case is merely to illustrate how being a lifesaver can backfire. If you have chosen this manner of winning a man's love, be aware of the unspoken resentment that may surface if you do not allow him to develop on his own.

As it turned out, Anita and Matthew were unable to change their relationship, and they parted. Anita continued therapy and gradually resolved some of her personal insecurities. As her sense of self and self-worth increased, she began to believe in her worthiness to be loved by a man for herself, not for what she could do to "fix" a man who had problems. As she became healthier, she began to choose healthier men.

*Feeling Important for the Right Reasons.* If your drive to mold, shape, rescue, or guide your loved one is powerful, it might be helpful to take a look at whether your good intentions are producing the effects you desire. Women who become lifesavers are very attractive to men who have problems, and yet these same women also tread a delicate balance between being generous helpmates and being controllers. If you take an objective look at your impact, you may find that the man is slowly becoming less receptive or responsive to your guidance and help. This is a clear warning sign that he is feeling controlled.

There is nothing necessarily wrong with control as long as we remember that it has certain consequences. Controllers need dependent people to control, and dependent people look for more dominant partners to control them. It all fits together rather neatly, except for one hazard: hidden anger! Hidden because there is always ambivalence attached to being controlled—in effect, this weaker man doesn't want to lose the woman's help, but at the same time he is angry about being in a one-down position with a woman.

How then does one go about altering the power base of the relationship? Perhaps you know that you need to be needed, and that type of connection with a man has backfired. Two actions are required: you must be willing to give up some of the power that goes along with this sort of control, and you must start talking more openly with your mate. Does he genuinely want your help? Keep in mind that a person's resistance often occurs on an unconscious level. Therefore, even positive verbal response such as "You're the best thing that ever happened to me" must still be measured against a man's real behavior toward you. For example, does he agree with your ideas, plans, or goals, then invariably fail to implement them? Is he becoming more passive? Does he appear defensive or react as though he is being criticized? These are signals that you may be dealing with a man who is gradually assuming a passive-aggressive posture in the relationship.

Men cherish a partner and helpmate just as women do. But there are men who position themselves for lifesaving and then resent it because they end up feeling controlled. It is essentially their problem, but it can become yours! Finally, search your own patterns of relationship. Do you find yourself seeking men who are weaker than you are so you'll feel more in control of the relationship? If you do, take heed, for that kind of security may be short-lived. Ultimately, trusting and developing your own self-worth is a better goal.

## When Is Control Reasonable?

Attempts to control, in moderation, are part of all relationships. The giving up of some freedoms is more than offset by the wonderful sense of mutual caring and giving. But when control becomes excessive, the result is conflict and resentment. The first signal that controlling behavior is getting out of hand is when the man being controlled shows signals of protest—either verbally or in his actions. By "signal," we mean just that. A warning sign. That doesn't mean you should back off. What it does mean is that it's time for you to talk about what's going on. Find out how he feels and negotiate a new way of relating to each other that's comfortable for both of you. In the cases we have presented, no such communication occurred. The women felt they were justified—which in some cases they were—and the men felt constricted. Communication could have averted the crises that came about.

As to what is legitimate to expect of each other and the relationship, that's up to the man and woman to decide. Each of you has to decide how much of your autonomy and independence must be given up in order to make your mate feel secure. In any partnership or relationship there must be accommodations and compromises in order for there to be harmony and mutual satisfaction. The important question is, how much and by whom? There is no easy answer. We do know that in most good marriages, each person is 50 percent responsible for what is good and what is troublesome. The responsibility does not reside with the woman just because she is the one who is typically more sensitive to emotional concerns. However, you should also keep in mind that waiting for your mate to initiate changes may also be frustrating if he is not likely to make that step. As therapists, when we are asked that question, our response is that the one who most desires change or communication should be the one who takes the first step. But again, remember that flexibility and compromise are always necessary to achieve harmony. The purpose of any union is to achieve the unique fulfillment that togetherness can bring.

## Some Control Is Natural

When we love someone, we come to need him or her—loving and needing go hand in hand. It follows that in spite of the purity or unselfish nature of our love, we still wish at times to exert influence over our loved one. These attempts to influence are primarily in the service of strengthening the ties and usually are not meant to weaken our loved one's sense of individuality. Unfortunately, this does happen when influence becomes extreme or excessive.

In marriage and other committed relationships, there are built-in codes of conduct that are controlling, if we wish to see them in that light. For example, behavior that is prohibited includes excessive absence—we expect our mate to spend a certain amount of time with us and the family. Close friendships with the opposite sex are often seen as possible preludes to violations of sexual fidelity and are therefore seen as threatening. To say that these conventions are too narrow or petty is to miss the point. Codes of conduct have evolved as a means of increasing security in a relationship.

Both men and women need to have some influence and control over their mates in order to feel secure. None of us is so secure that he or she can do without any rules in a relationship. Rules also exist because we assume that, given a sense of security in a relationship, we are then free to love even more fully. In our experience, this proves true—couples who feel certain of their love for each other tend to be more expressive, trusting, and demonstrative of their affection.

## Letting Go of Control

If you found yourself identifying with the controlling behavior of some of the women in this chapter, here are some steps you can take to change this self-defeating way of finding security in a relationship.

First, look honestly at yourself and try to determine the degree to which you might feel insecure in a relationship. By this we mean how nervous or apprehensive you might be regarding your lovability. Do you truly believe that you are loved and that your lover is loyal? Some concern or doubt is normal. However, insecure people go beyond moments of doubting or concern; they begin to feel genuine anxiety.

We all have a need to make the unknown known, to strive for certainty in the face of uncertainty. One way we do this is by using control. When we are very dependent upon someone, we try to make their whereabouts predictable, we want them to be accountable. Whether we consciously recognize it or not, we all need to know where our mate is at any given time. Some of us are comfortable with some general idea—"He's at work"—but others of us need to know for sure, need to call several times a day just to relieve the anxiety of not knowing and ensure that we are on our mate's mind. This can become obsessive and self-defeating behavior. Attempts at control are actually ways of assessing our importance to our mate. Even when these attempts result in irritation and evoke a negative response, we may still feel relieved! Negative attention is still attention.

Control undermines love. The better, healthier way to feel secure in a relationship is to trust. Trusting your mate is not only having a belief about him, it is an act of faith—meaning that trust is not something you manipulate, it is something you feel only after you stop controlling or attempting to influence.

Insecure people who are inclined to control their mates will learn to trust only by letting go of their controlling strategies. If you let him be, if you give him space, if you grant him his independence, does he come to you? Does he still act in a loving way?

Does he still show signs of his affection for you? You can discover all of this if you tolerate the anxiety of letting go of control. Remember, you initially employed control to reduce your fears and insecurities, so if you let go of it, you will definitely go through a brief period of feeling more anxious and nervous. Tolerate it—you won't die, you won't be consumed by uncertainty. Give your lover a chance to demonstrate his love for you. But first you have to take the risk.

People feel much better when they trust their mates. People who use excessive control always have the secret belief that the love they receive isn't really deserved. If you risk letting go, if you learn to tolerate uncertainty, you will discover a much more genuine love. And, perhaps more important, you will discover a new inner strength.

# CHAPTER SIX

# Women Who Give
# Too Freely

In recent years, women have been taken to task for a quality that used to be admired—giving or loving in abundance. In the past, a woman was said to be fulfilled when she received love back as a reward for her bountiful capacity to love. Now, women are being told they "love too much." It is really almost impossible to love too much when love is healthy and genuine. It is our belief that love is the cure for many relationship dilemmas rather than the problem. But it is possible to give too freely. Women who appear too loving are really giving too much of themselves out of fear.

Women who become too self-sacrificing, who give too much, have often been characterized as sick, as masochists—women who are inexorably drawn toward painful relationships. We feel this is a harsh and distorted portrayal. In our experience, neither women nor men seek pain or suffering in love. But for many women, anguish does become an unwanted by-product of their attempt to find security in a relationship. There are women who have learned a pattern of giving and self-sacrifice that invariably serves to deplete their emotional resources and, ironically, re-sults in pushing men away—the very outcome they so deeply fear.

You undoubtedly know of women who find them-selves in such painful dilemmas. Perhaps you're one of them yourself. Does this sound familiar? "A num-ber of men have told me I come across as too desper-ate, but I don't know why." Or "I would do anything for him, but he doesn't appreciate it." Or "I find myself getting involved with men sexually a lot sooner than I really want to—I guess I'm afraid to say no." Each of these women feels she's trying her best to create positive feelings with a man. Sadly, each of them is unknowingly sowing the seeds for rejection. They try to be loving, but instead of fostering inti-macy, their efforts actually prevent a man from get-ting closer! The reason for this well-meaning but self-defeating behavior is that all these women give too freely.

Can a person give too freely? Isn't giving what love is all about? Isn't the real problem that the other person can't handle intimacy and being loved? Is it possible to love too much? Certainly giving and love are intimately linked. We all value and appreciate partners who are generous with themselves, who accept the notion that love must be attended to and nurtured. But love is more than simply giving, and healthy love has built-in constraints; it is conditional rather than limitless and unconditional.

For adults, a positive and enriching love relation-ship is ultimately based upon mutuality and balance. The needs and desires of each partner must be equally important. Love and balanced giving lead to mutual feelings of well-being, comfort, and trust. And yet, for centuries, women have been conditioned to be-lieve that more is expected of them than the man.

# Why Women Give More

In the past, women were always told they were the caretakers of the relationship, they were the ones responsible for making love last. Women were taught that their identity and their worth were in large measure dependent upon their ability to keep a man happy. Little girls grew up trying to please Daddy, and young women came to believe their self-esteem was tied to their attractiveness and their ability to get a man. Regardless of the particular strategy employed, whether it was through culinary skills or sexual allure, a woman's ability to captivate or enchant a man was of the highest priority for her. Even today in this time of women's liberation and concern with mastery, independence, and self-realization, women are still exhorted by advertisers and the media to dress, act, and look a certain way in order to attract men and keep them happy.

As the Affinity Factor demonstrates, women are inclined toward relationships as a crucial issue in their development, and because of that, they are more prone to engage in self-defeating behavior in order to ensure closeness and connectedness with a man. Keep in mind that men too suffer from a similar kind of excess in their quest for self-esteem. Where women may give too much, men try too hard in their work. Just as women may be driven by the fear of being alone, of not being loved, men are driven by the fear of failure, of not being "enough."

One would assume that in recent years the women's movement has influenced women to give more appropriately, to avoid falling prey to outmoded conventional views of what it means to be a woman, to demand that love be equal and reciprocal between themselves and a man. In our view, that has not

happened as much as one would hope. There are
two reasons why women continue to love too much
and give too freely, even today.

First, for single women, the so-called "marriage
crunch," the compelling wish to find a man and
establish a family, has forced women into a number
of excesses in order to find love. Giving too freely
has been one of these excesses. The anxiety over
being alone is sufficient to cause some women to
revert to old ways of relating to men. Such women
naively believe that men still want the old-fashioned
woman whose primary offering to the partnership is
willingness to be the nurturer. Second, for married
women, there is anxiety connected to the awareness
that marriage is not necessarily forever. There are
wives today who secretly fear their husbands will
suddenly, in the midst of a male midlife crisis, pick
up and take off in quest of a younger woman. While
these concerns are based on some fact and are therefore not entirely irrational, giving too freely is not
the solution, because such giving is rarely interpreted by the man as love.

## Loving Is More Than Giving

Why would a woman give too freely? We have relationships because we enjoy the person we are with
and because that person enriches our lives and makes
us happy. Doesn't that come about because we give
lovingly and freely, without any concern as to whether
it is returned? Not quite. In fact, the woman or man
who gives too freely may not even be loving at all.
As wonderful as acts of loving and giving may seem,
they may also be disguised ways of satisfying deeper
needs. Love is frequently an arena in which we try
to work out our own problems. Obviously, solutions

to these problems have nothing to do with love, but all too often, we try to gain relief from them in the context of the love relationship.

The one common difficulty that characterizes women who give too freely is insecurity. They have hidden fears that what and who they are may not be enough. The solution is to make up for what they fear is lacking by excessively doing for and providing for the man.

For many such women, this insecurity stems from unresolved childhood conflicts. When they were children, love was absent or so inconsistent that a hunger or yearning was generated that could last for a lifetime. When we have been unloved, there is a continuing attempt to undo the pain we have suffered. Women who felt neglected or unappreciated as children often shower love on a man in the hope that he will return it fully enough to erase their deep lingering sadness.

Women who set forth on a lifelong mission to gain love from a man as a way of filling a void naturally come to believe that self-sacrificing is what is required of them. Such women believe it is the woman's job to be an endless source of nurture and emotional support. They don't feel worthy of being loved for themselves. Deep down, they fear abandonment, and it is that fear that makes them so vulnerable to giving excessively to a man. As Rosemary, a married woman in her forties, explained, "I hate to admit this, but I think I extend myself a whole lot more out of fear than love. Even though I've been married for fourteen years and I have certainly done more than my fair share, I still feel as if I should be grateful. I'm afraid I might lose Paul if I give less or stand up for myself and ask for more."

What Rosemary is really doing is rushing headlong into the very situations that are so frightening

to her. Loving a man is so scary that she copes with
the fear not by loving less, but by loving more. She
naively believes that clinging ever more tightly will
protect her from what she really fears—aloneness.
Unfortunately, her clinging will lead exactly to what
she most dreads. When women give too much, men
don't simply feel grateful, they feel suffocated.

For other women, one-sided or excessive giving
helps them to feel more in control. They find needing a man uncomfortable and threatening. They hate
being on the receiving end of love, strange as that
may seem. "I can't stand needing a man," Carol
exclaimed. "It makes me feel nervous." It is much
easier for Carol to give than to receive. She prefers
that the man need her. "I give from a position of
power and control, but when a man gives back to
me, it makes me feel weak. I start worrying about
how important the relationship is becoming and that
I might lose it. I don't feel any of those things as
long as I'm the one doing the initiating."

There is a third type of giving that really has very
little to do with love, and that is giving for the
sensation of giving. The term "love addiction" refers
to this kind of love. There are women, and men too,
who rarely feel alive or invigorated unless they are
caught up in the drama of romance and the pursuit
of love. These women become addicted to the search
for completion or validation by a man. The feeling of
longing becomes an exhilarating end in itself. Romantic entanglements, even when they are anguished,
become the intense signals of aliveness. When these
women give, they feel fulfilled for the moment, "almost" loved. What they fail to discern, however, is
the terribly negative and alienating effect this "false"
love has on the man they are with.

Women like Rosemary and Carol both give out of
a basic insecurity. While they may express their inse-

curity in very different ways, it remains the common element that fuels their continuing need to give, accommodate, and defer. Such women set up self-defeating forces within the relationship. Acts of love are not gifts when they are fueled by fear of loss or abandonment or when they are secretly designed to manipulate. The woman who gives excessively risks triggering feelings of resentment and emotional engulfment in a man.

## How Love Can Become Overwhelming

You have probably been in a relationship in which you felt the man cared more for you than you cared for him. He did all the phoning. He was always the first to express his affections. He brought you small gifts and sent you flowers. He expressed real concern if he couldn't reach you, even for a few hours. He wanted all your free time. He wanted to look deeply and lovingly into your eyes and have long, meaningful conversations. And you wanted none of it! The more he pushed and the more he gave, the more turned off you became. You know that feeling. It's awful, isn't it? Well, that feeling is what men often experience when women give too freely.

Love always feels more alive and important when we are in the position of active loving. The role of "lover" is always more invigorating and vital. When we are in the active mode we feel no obligation, no guilt, no encroachment of territory, no suffocation. Ideally, a relationship is constantly dynamic: each partner takes turns being the ardent lover. Each partner continues to feel renewed by the special magic that accompanies the role of "lover" and never has to languish for too long a time in the role of "loved one."

Remember the Polarity Factor. Men feel most actively loving and involved with a woman at some relative midpoint between Attachment and Separateness. It is in this middle range that men are in touch with the greatest degree of passion, involvement, and interest. Women who give too freely inadvertently press all the wrong buttons in men. Wishing only to please and attract, these women push men away, stimulating in them a determination to give less and less as the woman gives more and more. Why?

First of all, a man needs to give love to retain his interest in a woman. Women who give too freely tend to overwhelm men by quickly satiating their needs for closeness. If the woman does it all and gives it all, there is little motivation for the man to do anything. It triggers a man's fear of emotional engulfment, which causes him to pull away from being lovingly close to her. As his discomfort and need to distance himself begin to worry her, she is likely to feel this estrangement is her fault. At the very time she should be giving less, she does just the opposite—her solution is to give more. And so it escalates. The more one-sided her giving, the farther away the man will move from her.

Men don't feel comfortable with, appreciate, or even respect women who give without expecting love in return. For a man to stay actively involved with a woman requires his giving, his respect, and his willingness to put energy and feeling into the relationship. If a man is not giving to the woman, loving her in an active and involved way, he is pulling away in a process of distancing. Relationships don't ever remain static. They are either in a state of growth and redefinition or they are in a state of gradual deterioration. Excessive giving has a very consistent and predictive outcome—it leads to lack of interest and of respect, and it discourages meaningful closeness. In its extreme, giving too freely can even create an atmosphere in which men become exploitive.

To exploit someone sounds terribly malevolent, but there are forms of exploitation that are not necessarily conscious in intent, though they still result in men's depreciating women. What predisposes a woman to potential exploitation invariably involves powerful feelings of insecurity, an excessive need to bond with a man, and denial of the possibility that a man's character and ethics are questionable.

Both men and women obviously are afraid of being taken advantage of, for it shatters self-esteem and fundamental trust in others. Yet it occurs. How often have you heard single women, for example, bitterly recount tales of dating men who seemed to have no other intent than "using" them for sex, or married women complain that they feel neglected and taken for granted by their husbands?

Exploitation on the man's part means taking advantage of a woman's strong need to bond with him. Because of her desperation, she misreads the man's true intent. What he is looking for, rather than mutual love, may be much more immediate and basically self-centered. She is blind to his self-involvement and unwittingly projects onto him wishful fantasies of bonding and love similar to her own. His dishonesty shows up in his evasiveness about the importance of the relationship. Usually, his crimes are ones of omission rather than commission—he allows her to bask in misguided speculations about the future.

Regardless of the level of the man's dishonesty, the woman's hunger may be so great that even if he wanted to love her, he would be overwhelmed. Sens-

ing his detachment makes her even more frantic. By
the end of all this struggle, the man remains focused
on what he can get from her, not on loving her.
Sadly, women who give too freely get left rather
than loved.

## The Rescuer

Brad, a 41-year-old electrical contractor, sees all
women as pretty similar and, unfortunately, all too
reminiscent of his mother. He feels he never got the
love he needed from his mother. A single parent,
she was gone a good deal of the time, either working two jobs to make ends meet or out on dates.
Brad felt he was always trying, unsuccessfully, to
get her attention, love, and approval.

Janet, a 36-year-old elementary school teacher, recalls feeling protective of her father, whom she saw
as a gentle victim of her mother's unrelenting demands and angry, abusive nature. He would passively withdraw into reading his Bible while Janet
fought his battles for him. "I always felt as though I
had to make up for my mother. She was pretty
awful to Dad. I'm sure I didn't understand the whole
picture of what he did to provoke her anger, but I've
always seen Dad as a kind of saint who somehow
got saddled with having to put up with my mother
the 'bully.' "

Janet's involvements with men are all determined
to a large degree by her attempt to show them that
women can be loving. As Janet says, "I have this
thing about feeling responsible for making up for
other women's failings. I can't stand for men to see
women as hurtful or not to be trusted."

As a result of these childhood influences, Janet
always finds a hurt and often embittered man to try

to work her healing magic on. When Brad came along, he was a perfect match, given his emotionally impoverished background.

Brad and Janet have been living together for two years. Janet would like to marry, but Brad keeps putting the decision off, using his previous hurtful relationships as an excuse. Instead of feeling resentment or giving him a deadline to make a decision, Janet is patient. She believes the power and sweetness of her love eventually will win his trust.

Essentially, Brad takes in Janet's caring and generous sensitivity to his needs without ever feeling the need to reciprocate. He is unmoved and unmotivated to allow the relationship to evolve to a deeper, more committed level. Janet trusts Brad, and basically he takes advantage of her. And he will go on doing so until she puts an end to it. As Brad candidly says, "I wish she wasn't so nice sometimes. She's never done anything to hurt me, and yet I disappoint her all the time. I feel as if I can get away with anything and she will still love me. It's crazy, but instead of endearing her to me, I end up losing respect for her even though I know she deserves better."

*Getting What You Deserve.* Janet's eagerness to do all the work is in some direct way responsible for Brad's increasing disrespect and distance. Obviously, Brad also needs to take responsibility for his inability to accept and give love in a mature fashion. But the problem is that Janet's willingness to give without getting back tends ultimately to condone Brad's behavior. If you find that you have been in a situation similar to Janet's, there are steps you can take to develop more of a sense of entitlement with a man.

Women such as Janet are essentially working out old childhood problems in current adult relationships. By assuming the role of the rescuer, Janet was attempting to find some meaning in her life, some way of feeling good about herself. As a child, she was not only protective of her father, she was also trying to win his love. A passive man like her father no doubt drove her mother crazy with his inability to do anything but live out life as a kind of self-righteous victim. Janet was unaware that not only did he deprive her mother, he also was negligent in expressing his love for Janet and allowing her to play the role of his defender.

Being a savior or rescuer can become a way of getting close to a man, encouraging his dependency, and having an illusory sense of security—at least for a while. Eventually a man loses respect because he senses that the woman never really expects to be treated fairly. If this type of woman had more self-esteem and an appropriate sense of entitlement, she would expect and even demand reciprocity. Giving too much and being a rescuer, an unconscious strategy for feeling more secure, never really works.

What a woman like Janet can do is to recognize that her giving is fueled by insecurity and not love. If you have these problems, you first need to acknowledge the presence of deeper fears and anxieties about being worthy and lovable. Then ask yourself whether you truly believe you have any value beyond your capacity to cater to a man. Whenever a woman or man asks that important question of themselves, there is often a quick and detailed response in the affirmative—we are interesting or bright or accomplished in a variety of ways. Sometimes we actually have a greater sense of self-esteem and confidence than we think we do. Ultimately, it is our actions that provide the true answer to this question. Women who feel deserving of mature and reciprocal love do not remain rescuers for long, no matter how intriguing a "rehabilitation" project the man is.

In order to break these old patterns, it is necessary to take the chance of expecting more, of making demands when love seems out of balance. But here's the catch. In order to feel good about taking that risk, you first have to feel better about yourself. It's really not critical which comes first, the expectation or the self-esteem; each feeds and builds upon the other. The important point is to act, to take the first step. If you stop giving so much, you will begin to discover what else about you a man may love or cherish. If at first it seems he only cares for your ability to rescue, defend, or problem-solve, then perhaps it is time for you to move on. Rest assured, the very act of feeling entitled to getting love back will make him take a fresh and very often positive look at you.

The payoff for breaking these patterns and taking these risks is enormous: more mutually satisfying relationships and being loved for who you are rather than merely being needed for what you do. And beyond that, expecting love in return has the effect of opening yourself to the opportunity of being with men who are healthier and more able to give.

## The Siamese Twin

Some women deal with feelings of emotional deprivation by attempting to establish an almost symbiotic or fused relationship with the man in their life.

Gail is 28 years old and recently married. She grew up in an emotional vacuum. Ignored by her busy mother and discounted by her father, who never had the boy he wanted, Gail recalls, "I can remember trying to do boy-type things—things I thought would please my dad. But I always got this awful feeling that instead of making me more interesting to him, it just made him even more disappointed that I was a girl."

Gail's eight-month marriage to Jack has been rocky from the start. From her point of view, she is doing everything to make Jack happy and feel loved. The truth is that she is slowly suffocating him and killing the genuine love he feels for her. "I thought she would feel more secure after we got married," Jack confides. "The fights we used to have all centered around her worrying that I didn't care as much about her as she did about me. It wasn't true. I did care, and even though I told her I loved her, it wasn't enough."

After they got married, her expressions of love accelerated. "She constantly sends me romantic cards, writes notes, even calls me at work, sometimes three or four times a day. She thinks she's being sweet and loving, but it's too much."

Jack goes on to say, "There are a lot of things that I enjoy doing with Gail, but she wants to do everything together. I remember on our honeymoon in Hawaii, she wanted to hold my hand when we went scuba diving. At the time, I thought it was touching, but lately this nonstop togetherness is making me a little nuts. What I wanted in this marriage was a partner, not a Siamese twin. I'm having serious doubts about whether we'll last. Regardless of what I do, it doesn't seem to be enough. I've always been pretty affectionate, but now when she asks me for a hug, I can feel myself cringe inside."

Gail's emotional isolation as a child left her with deep feelings of deprivation and insecurity. She doesn't trust that she's lovable as an adult mate, for she never received as a child the support and validation she so desperately needed. Gail would do anything to demonstrate her love for Jack. However, her hunger for its return makes it seem like an emotional demand. Gail makes the fatal mistake of trying too hard. Her efforts don't translate as freely given love but rather as an insatiable wish for completion and validation.

*Becoming More Separate*. Despite Jack's genuine caring for Gail, his inability to make her feel secure in his love leaves him feeling powerless and depleted. Unknowingly, Gail stimulates primitive feelings of discomfort and anxiety in Jack. Her intense need for closeness is suffocating him and going well beyond the bounds of healthy intimacy.

Women who feel as Gail does need to work on backing off and allowing a man some breathing room. Men are not put off by feelings of insecurity, only by how those feelings are expressed. But in suggesting that a woman back off, we are aware it is that very behavior she most fears, for she only feels safe and valued when she is "doing." Letting go is tantamount to feeling alone and abandoned. A woman who needs to be this close feels overwhelmed by anxiety if she backs off, for she loses contact with why she should be loved.

In order to break this pattern, the anxiety stirred up by aloneness must be experienced; it cannot be avoided. It is similar to breaking any habit. Time away from the man—with women friends or even alone—is critical. Find out what you feel inside when you are not with him. Typically, the first feelings stirred up are like those you may have felt as a child—loneliness and fear. But as you allow more time to pass without connecting with a man, you will find yourself quickly feeling better, stronger, more self-reliant.

As you learn to grow and feel better without the

constant reassurance of a man's love, you will begin to discover that, in the past, what seemed like a gift of love was, in many instances, merely a disguised expression of your own deep-seated doubts about your value and desirability.

## *The Easy Lover*

Over the years, Terry, 34, had slept with many different men. She felt comfortable with her life-style, but her friends cautioned her that she was far too "easy." Terry told herself that she was sexually liberated and perfectly comfortable with going to bed with a man on the first date provided the "chemistry" was right. However, Terry was not merely out there to have a good time, she was intent upon getting married—and was not aware of the negative impact her dating behavior had on her chances of finding a mate.

Terry believed that being sexually open or available might secure a man's continuing interest. But at an even deeper level, Terry had the unfortunate fear that she might not be "enough" without offering herself as an easy and accommodating sexual partner. The combination of her emotional hunger and low self-esteem acted to push her into relationships that were ultimately shallow and emotionally unsatisfying.

Moreover, the casual sex that Terry perceived as a gift was not valued the same way by the men she slept with. Men who initially were drawn to Terry for her wealth of positive attributes—she is attractive, interesting, and intelligent—and who conceivably would have been interested in building a mutual, caring relationship with her sadly ended up valuing Terry as little as she valued herself. Because she too quickly encouraged sexual relations, she thwarted the possibility of real intimacy.

Sex almost never becomes the hoped-for adhesive in a relationship. A woman who offers herself too casually will find that it merely invites a man to use her for fleeting gratification. Men rarely find themselves drawn to women who are "one-night stands." Men make quick judgments about easy lovers and rarely appreciate their other very real qualities or values.

*Respecting Your Real Worth.* In order to restore her self-esteem, Terry had to move against her instincts, to do something that seemed paradoxical. At the beginning of a relationship, when she wanted to move closer, she had to learn to tolerate a bit of distance and contain her insecurity. She had to face and master her most basic fear—fear of abandonment and feeling unattached. But this does *not* mean being cold or withdrawn, for that scares men away. Instead, as Terry discovered, a stance of positive self-containment creates mild uncertainty in a man and sparks his interest.

With her goal of a long-term relationship based on balance and respect firmly in mind, Terry, in her new relationships, is taking things very slowly. "Before, after sleeping with a man right away," Terry recalls, "I would feel very anxious about whether he would phone me again—it was as though I put the ball in his court as soon as I slept with him." After she entered therapy, she says, "For about eight months, I just dated casually and didn't meet anybody I wanted to get seriously involved with, so I didn't sleep with anyone at all."

By taking the chance of giving less, Terry gained more. She found that men appreciated facets of her personality that were previously hidden behind her *femme fatale* pose. But she had to take the risk. As we have already noted, the very act of trusting that you are worth more serves to indeed make you feel more worthy. It is a kind of courageous leap of faith, but, in truth, you actually have little to lose by trying this.

Because sex has been so overemphasized in our culture, there is a mistaken belief that it is a surefire way to attract a man. That is simply not true. In fact, sexual conservatism is enjoying a resurgence precisely because men and women really seem to prefer it! For example, take that old admonition not to go to bed with a man on the first date. Well, not only is it very good advice, but we would go one step further —we think it's wise not to become lovers with a new man until you have spent enough time with him to know his goals and his character, and to have established with him some level of trust and mutuality. This separates out men who are capable of caring from those who are merely exploitive. This advice is based on the fact that men, while seemingly more liberated, still function according to old unconscious programming. Men may push for early sexual involvement, but at a deeper level, most men believe sexual relations should really be an expression of caring and involvement. When this caring is absent, then it's just a "lay." Attraction can be present from the first moment, but caring cannot exist in the beginning of a relationship. Caring grows gradually as a function of experience and over a period of time. It does not come quickly no matter how much a woman may want it or how much a man may tell her he feels it.

While some of these comments are directed to single women, there is a corresponding suggestion for married women. Wives who always give in to their husbands' sexual overtures because of their fear of saying no will invariably encounter later difficulties. First and most important, to accommodate and cater to a man's demands in this fashion only leads to your feeling a growing resentment. Moreover, men eventually become aware of this resentment. They sense you are not "making love" but are acquiescing in order to hold their love. While you may think a man is grateful to you for being so accessible, he may secretly feel as estranged as you do. Even men who are so dense that they don't sense this absence of genuine desire in your sexual responses will end up not being appreciative but merely taking you for granted. Regardless of the outcome, giving too much even in the sexual realm will corrode a marriage.

## The Martyr

What causes a woman to become a martyr? By far the most basic and consistent ingredient is poor self-esteem. Martyrdom is never a gift regardless of how it is disguised. In fact, it is often a hidden aggressive act designed to control by inducing guilt in one's partner. When a woman chooses to relinquish her power, when she refuses to acknowledge and stand up for her own needs, she is vulnerable to becoming a martyr.

Jackie, 38, has always felt inferior to Sheldon, her husband of six years. She went to work straight out of high school; he has a master's degree in engineering. She is quiet; he is charming and outgoing with people. Secretly, she fears she "married up" and one day he will tire of her. Instead of developing herself personally and learning to feel more comfortable in her marriage, she became self-effacing and self-sacrificing and put her husband ahead of herself in virtually every area of her life. For example, Jackie would shop for Sheldon at the best men's stores, feeling that expensive clothes were important for his career. Yet when it came to herself, she shopped at discount stores.

Early in their marriage, Sheldon was touched by her seeming generosity, but soon felt vaguely guilt-ridden. He encouraged her to take classes, not in a patronizing way but because her self-deprecating comments saddened him. And when he gave her expensive presents, she invariably returned them. The day after he presented her with a lovely gold bracelet, an anniversary present, he came home to find a costly leather attaché case waiting for him. Jackie, once again, had returned his gift and put his wants above hers. He blew up, precipitating a crisis that led to their seeking professional help.

What happened here? Why did her apparently loving and caring husband erupt? From Jackie's point of view, it came out of the blue. "I've always done everything for him, put my life in the background." Sheldon had a very different point of view. As he looked back over their marriage, he became aware that he was choking with guilt.

Jackie was a martyr. She felt most secure when she was giving up her needs for his. Filled with self-doubt and insecurities, she foolishly attempted to control the relationship by making her husband feel sorry for her. Her secret belief was that he would never leave anyone so willing to sacrifice and give. Sheldon later commented that he was always made painfully aware of her sacrifices, which led to guilt and the slow buildup of resentment. "I never really felt good coming home. I used to wish that I had one of those wives who had her own friends and activities, not someone who would rush home from work to greet me at the door with a drink and a special dinner."

What were the warning signs Jackie missed? First, she never really believed Sheldon cared. In a strange way, her martyrdom was terribly self-centered. Her anxiety made her so myopic that she never believed he could love her. When Sheldon tried to change the balance in the marriage and make the two of them more mutual and equal, she thwarted him at every turn. There was no vessel to receive the love he wanted to give. She was threatened by his wish for equality—she was afraid that she wouldn't be up to it, that somehow she wasn't really lovable or intelligent enough to sustain his interest.

*Letting Go of Self-Sacrifice.* A martyred partner always creates serious inequalities. Men today don't want to be in an unequal relationship; they don't want self-sacrificing women. Such women breed a growing sense of guilt and its companion, resentment. Instead of making the man feel better and more secure, martyrdom does just the opposite. Men with martyred partners feel alone.

When a woman does not respect herself, it is difficult for the man to feel for her. But if she takes the chance of developing and trusting good feelings about herself, a woman will find that men will respond positively and lovingly.

If you found yourself identifying with Jackie's martyr-like behavior, it is important to understand that you are engaging in a strategy that will not endear a man to you but will actually stir up resentment in him. Self-sacrifice and other guilt-inducing behaviors will only cause conflict between you.

Women who become martyrs typically lack assertive skills; they are fearful of standing up and expressing legitimate needs and wishes to their mate.

Instead, they hope their suffering will make the man feel pity. There is even the fantasy that such sacrificing will lead to admiration, since others often admire the martyr as someone who staunchly gives her all in order to create harmony in the home.

As with other women who give too much, the way to break the pattern is by gradually doing less and at the same time beginning to expect more. See if his loving increases as you begin to act in a way that commands respect. Initially, doing less will stir up anxiety in you; it may even trigger the fear he will eventually leave you. The anxiety you will feel is an emotion that you have been running from all these years by being a martyr. Remember, even though you learned these patterns as a way of coping with a lack of love during childhood, you don't have to let your past control you. You don't have to be a victim, which is what the martyr so often secretly feels she is.

## The Caretaker

Women who take on the role of caretaker with a man have a number of traits in common. Most suffer nagging concerns about self-worth and feel distinctly more comfortable in the giving rather than the receiving role. These women fear that expecting love in return may precipitate their worst fear—"You're not worth it if I have to do something in return." Ellen, a 35-year-old legal secretary, is a woman who became a caretaker in her relationship with Jimmy. When they first met, Jimmy, 33, had a part-time job teaching word processing at corporations and was in his first year of graduate school. He seemed to be everything she was looking for—best of all, he also seemed to really like her.

Their first few months together were genuinely wonderful and led Ellen to ask Jimmy to move in with her. Their schedules allowed little in the way of free time, so the time they spent with each other was doubly precious. In order to squeeze out a few more hours, Ellen first offered to type a couple of Jimmy's papers. She did this joyfully and was pleased that it gave them more free evenings together. Ellen had always had an ease and facility with words. Before long she was not simply typing Jimmy's papers but writing them.

Jimmy was having a difficult time with his heavy academic load. He enjoyed the more and more frequent "boys' nights out" with his men friends, leaving Ellen at home struggling with one of his papers. While occasionally feeling a bit resentful, Ellen explained away Jimmy's lack of self-discipline as temporary and related simply to his needing a break from the unrelenting pressures of school.

Jimmy enjoyed talking with Ellen, for she was a warm and receptive listener. She was not only understanding and accepting, but also had a calming and immensely reassuring effect on him. Jimmy talked endlessly about the pressures he felt, and Ellen was always ready to take on yet another task or errand to help him out.

Ellen loved Jimmy and enjoyed his growing reliance upon her. She felt a sense of closeness and love reaffirmed by her active and intimate involvement in every aspect of his life. Without knowing it, Ellen had slowly and consistently set up a pattern with Jimmy that unfortunately encouraged a growing exploitation and discouraged a passionate attachment to her. Her willingness to do things for him and to make up for his failings and deficiencies had a predictable effect on Jimmy. An only child, he was accustomed to having things done for him by an

overly indulgent and sacrificing mother. The step
from mother to Ellen was all too easy for him to
make. Ellen had inadvertently become a kind of sub-
stitute mother—one who gave unquestioningly and
expected little in return.

*Becoming Less the Mother and More the Woman.*
Many women envelop themselves in a kind of moth-
ering role. Some feel comfortable doing this, for it
makes them feel like "earth mothers," women who
are larger than life. This is not to imply that the
warm maternal woman is consciously hiding something else with that behavior. Unconsciously, though,
she may be neglecting her own potential to be more,
to be viewed in a more complex and encompassing
way than she is now. Sadly, these women may go
through life being mother to their husbands as well
as mother to their children. Giving too much in this
way encourages a man to neglect a woman and take
her for granted, but more important, it may prevent
the caretaker from ever discovering who she can
become.

As we have noted, women who become caretakers
often assume that role because it enables them to
avoid dealing with other facets of their personality.
For example, there are women who feel sexually
inadequate, and being maternal is a way out of con-
fronting this self-doubt. Sometimes the man may
even be a co-conspirator in this regard. A man who
wants his wife to be a mother may not want her to
be too sexual, for this can become confusing. This is
a variation of the sacred/profane dichotomy—other
women can be sexy, but one's wife must be pure
and above such base pleasures.

In order to break the caretaking pattern, you have
to trust that the man does want a woman and not
just a mother. You must take the chance on express-

ing more facets of yourself. Reveal more and give less. Let him discover you. If a man seems to be taken aback by a sudden shift in your behavior, you can discuss this with him. Lovingly put him on notice that by giving so much, you've made yourself less than you could be.

## Knowing When Love Is One-Sided

The most direct way to determine if you're giving excessively is to take a good look at the way in which the giving is received. Is the man engaged by your generosity and your love? Does he respond with appropriate appreciation? Is your giving reciprocated over time? Women who give too freely typically do not look for signs of reciprocity—rather they are forever hoping it will come. When you ask yourself these questions, don't look for answers immediately. It takes time. Some men fail to respond right away. Sometimes it takes a few days, sometimes a week, to get an indication of a man's manner of receiving your caring.

Does he seem to pull away from you after you have been particularly loving? Does his appreciation and respect grow with time together, or does it diminish? After a few weeks or months, if you are really paying attention, you should be able to sense the impact of your warmth, giving, and caring and know whether you are being taken for granted.

Do you feel an anxiety over the passage of time? Women who give too freely tend to be impatient, and then quell their anxiety by giving even more. It's as though giving could secure the love they so desperately crave.

Do you find yourself making excuses for him? Are you being too understanding and forgiving? Women who give too freely invariably have some sneaking suspicions that they are going overboard. They are often aware they are making too many excuses to explain why the man behaves in the way he does, why he isn't more giving. If you find yourself explaining to friends and family why your relationship seems one-sided, that is a definite sign that the imbalance has gone too far.

And finally, do you find your giving coincides with your own doubts about lovability? Do you feel you are "enough," or, like so many women who give too much, do you find your insecurity is always channeled into some behavior with the man that is really a disguised way of getting approval? If so, you secretly know it's not working.

## Learning to Expect Love Back

Men must be required to give. They must be expected to behave in a mutual way with a woman, and we do not mean that simply for the sake of fairness and balance. Rather, in accordance with the Polarity Factor, this demand for reciprocity in a relationship is necessary for the formation of a man's bond to a woman. When a woman offers too much and expects too little, the bond, from the man's point of view, doesn't form properly. That isn't to say that with this type of pattern a man can't become dependent upon a woman for favors, creature comforts, and services. But this connection is not emotional, is not based on respect or passion, is not the love a woman wants.

One-sided relationships in which a man is allowed to give too little inhibit him from moving toward closeness. Women who do all the work dampen the man's desire to do any on his own account, and that is a serious and self-defeating mistake. On the other hand, the woman who knows she's worthy of active loving and lets a man know she fully expects this to happen in return will draw him continually to her.

To avoid the pitfalls of giving too freely, you must be clear about your own expectations. Take a long hard look at how easy or difficult it is for you to feel worthy of being given to and loved by a man. If you come to value yourself and act in accordance with that value, you will avoid exploitation, because your awareness of your own dignity will prevent it from happening. Women who experience exploitation are blinded by their own emotional hungers; judgment is set aside. Being in touch with your worth acts as a friendly beacon in your search for love.

The woman who gives too freely feels time is against her; she acts as though her chance for love is almost slipping away. If you are single, learn to take your time with a new relationship. Allow sexual experiences to flow out of the slow development of trust, knowledge of each other, and caring. Distrust both your impulse to hurry it and his impulse to hurry you. Understand that no matter what a man tells you, he will basically trust and respect you more if you value yourself.

Take a chance and talk about your feelings—tell him of your fears, and point out your responsibility for and participation in the whole process. From then on you must assume the attitude and posture of asking for more and setting limits on what you will give. When you believe you have the right to expect love back, he will move closer to you. If he does not, it's best to find out now and move on to what you truly deserve.

# PART TWO

# Women Men Love

# CHAPTER SEVEN

# The Path Toward Commitment

The desire for love is a fundamental human drive. No matter who we are or what we do, whether we are male or female, married or single, we all want the exact same thing when it comes to love: someone to enjoy life's experiences with, someone to make us laugh, someone who understands our fears and sorrows, and someone to make us feel good about ourselves.

In this section of the book we will explore how men are drawn to women and why they fall in love. But no worthwhile exploration can be complete without an understanding of the process of love itself, from its tumultuous onset through its various stages, from the heightened expectations of romance to the depth and security of mature commitment.

There is one basic underlying reason why most of us find love so difficult to achieve. We begin our search for love not only with sincere and realistic goals, but also with primitive deep-rooted fantasies. These unconscious forces, rather than the conscious ones, shape our need to love and be loved, and create many roadblocks as we move from aloneness along the path toward commitment. We believe that in order to break out of self-defeating patterns, to stop sabotaging one's attempts to find love or to make a marriage stronger, as a first step it is essential to understand the fantasies that accompany the search for love.

## Love's Three Secret Wishes

The quest for love is motivated by three powerful unconscious wishes: the desire for fusion, validation, and aliveness. No matter who we are, regardless of how sensible we believe we have become, no matter how reasonable our conscious expectations, embedded in our unconscious are these primitive desires. But here is the problem: not one of these wishes has anything to do with giving love to another person! They are instead needs, all of which involve a primary concern with oneself and one's own satisfactions. Because these wishes are fueled by the need to get rather than to give, they eventually bring a clash between us and the person we hope will gratify these wishes.

Where do these wishes come from? As we develop from infancy to adulthood, we move along a path of individuation, of becoming truly ourselves, constantly creating and expanding a more defined sense of who we are. Some of this change is positive, some negative. For many people, life is experienced as an ongoing struggle, as a coping with inner anxieties coupled with a fearful avoidance of outside pressures. More fortunate individuals develop a healthy and positive desire to greet the challenges and risks of life. Most of us tend to oscillate between fear and confidence, self-doubt and self-acceptance.

**YEARNING FOR FUSION**. Perhaps the most primitive drive related to love is our wish for completion, for fusion. This wish stems from the fear of aloneness and a sense of incompleteness. Initially, every child exists in a symbiotic or interdependent union with his or her mother before healthy separation and individuation occurs. From the moment we separate from our mothers until our last breath, aloneness or its possibility is our constant companion. Very early we develop what are called narcissistic needs, self-love, the need to care for ourselves. Narcissistic needs are natural and healthy, in moderation, and they come about in the following way.

When we have healthy, attentive parents who lovingly care for us, we develop a positive sense of ourselves. Gradually, we learn to incorporate, or internalize, our parents' love for us and their ability to soothe and comfort us. In perceiving ourselves through their eyes, so to speak, we learn to soothe ourselves and to administer self-love. Through this process, we learn to be less anxious, less in need of fusion, and we feel more complete within ourselves.

Unfortunately, this process is never perfect, for parents are flawed and inconsistent in their loving. In a healthy upbringing, children can easily handle minor parental inconsistencies as they learn to deal with frustrations and an imperfect world. The child's sense of self gradually becomes stronger, better-defined, more resilient. But if the parent is neglectful and unloving, the child's sense of self may remain fragmented and underdeveloped. Sadly, such a child is unable to comfort himself or herself and eventually resorts to seeking external sources of comfort—other people, drugs, even love; any intense outside stimuli that will block the pain of self-doubt and incompleteness.

Fusion becomes one fantasied solution to these feelings of a deficient self. For example, a woman with a background of incomplete parenting may unconsciously fantasize that if only she could merge with a man she could achieve that wonderful secure state she felt with Mother. Most people have this wish or fantasy in some degree; it is merely more pronounced in very needy people. In times of stress or emotional deprivation, especially, we may dream of fusing with someone who will give us the love we don't feel for ourselves, someone who will make us feel whole.

**THE SEARCH FOR VALIDATION.** Another powerful wish fueling our search for a loving connection is validation—the need to feel good about ourselves, to have self-esteem. Again, because of incomplete and less than perfect childhood experiences, we may feel unworthy and desperately seek outside validation.

Good parenting involves encouraging children to think for themselves and through their experiences to come to value themselves. But some parents don't encourage autonomy, they keep the child dependent on parental approval. This results in a lifelong quest for external proof of one's value or lovability. Some people look in the mirror and smile: "I like what I see!" Others look and wonder anxiously, "Will so-and-so like what he or she sees?" They look for someone else to tell them they are okay. Adults who haven't learned to validate themselves hold the strongest potential for becoming love-obsessed, forever in search of that person who will make them feel good enough.

Most men and women seek some validation in their choice of lovers. To some degree, all of us regard a potential mate as a measure of our own worth and status. For example, you may have had the experience of introducing a new man in your life to friends, secretly hoping they will think more highly of you because of the kind of person you attracted. The secret belief here is that if an attractive or accomplished person loves you, somehow it elevates your own worth.

The problem with validation as a dominant solution to feelings of deficiency is that we fail to love the other person genuinely; we love instead the illusion of our own boosted self. In addition, there are always those dark moments of aloneness when our insecurities clamor and remind us how we truly feel about ourselves. Personal validation through another person's love really does not work.

**THE WISH FOR ALIVENESS.** The third wish driving our search for love is aliveness. In this very stressful world, it's a true challenge to recharge our own batteries, to make ourselves feel alive and excited about life. This is a key reason why we place such a tremendous emphasis on sex; it is one of the easiest ways to feel stimulated, vibrant, glowing. A second way many people create aliveness today is in the pursuit of romance, a guaranteed source of intense emotions. Still others, perhaps more pessimistic about the rewards of relationship, seek aliveness through eating, drinking, drugs. Such people feel a momentary sense of inner well-being as long as the chemical high will last—which is never too long!

The origins of our intense hunger for feeling alive and stimulated again can be traced to childhood experiences stemming from a melancholy that results from the loss of the warm and safe mother. All children need contact and closeness in order to feel an alive sense of well-being. In fact, children who fail to receive such physical contact and warmth often develop serious physical and emotional illnesses. Sadly, people whose early childhoods were insecure and bereft of loving contact carry with them a lingering sadness. The antidote to this feeling of chronic emptiness is stimulation—any kind. Typically for men, substance abuse or sexual activity is used as a solution to this dilemma. Women more commonly become addicted to the emotional highs and lows of romance. But when such women capture the object of their obsession, they invariably experience an emotional letdown. As infatuation gives way to reality and routine, the intensity pales. The love addict thus compulsively moves through scores of lovers.

As we grow up and leave our less than ideal childhoods, we all may yearn in varying degrees for fusion, validation, and aliveness. And we seek in varying degrees for external solutions to these internal needs. We all grow up attempting to compensate for a variety of things that were missing in our childhood; none of us is the product of perfect parenting. But there are solutions that are healthy and go beyond unrealistic fantasies. Loving and being loved can be learned. But this learning necessitates an understanding of the evolution love takes. A clear view of the twists and turns in the love process helps one avoid the unrealistic expectations and disillusionments that happen so often in our relationships.

## The Stages of Love

All love relationships evolve along a discernible path. The first phase is romance, infatuation, or falling in love. The second stage is a period of adjustment where illusion and reality collide. The final phase is mature and enduring love.

**ROMANCE.** In our quest for love, the first thing we all look for is that exquisite feeling of excitement and infatuation with another person: romance. Romance involves a sense of fusion, oneness with another person, a feeling of exhilaration and passion, even flights of ecstasy. We experience a heightened sensitivity to beauty, not only in our lover but in the world at large: other people, sights, smells, the whole spectrum of the senses. In this phase we extend the boundaries of our sense of self to include the other person. We feel we have known our lover forever, yet delight in discovering him or her anew every day. The experience of romance embodies all of the three basic things we wish for—fusion, validation, and aliveness.

There is a dark counterpart to this experience. You may find yourself feeling anxious, secretly fearful: "I'm afraid if he really gets to know me, he won't like me!" Or "It feels as if it's too good to be true, too good to last!" This undercurrent of apprehensions, while painful, also heightens the emotional charge of the drama; uncertainty and fears add to the mystery and excitement.

This is a time of innocence when the lover's virtues are magnified and in the foreground. His flaws or annoying behaviors are in the background and may even seem incredibly charming. The cheapskate is seen as "a liberated man who lets me share costs equally." The self-obsessed man who talks incessantly about himself is "open and vulnerable." The withdrawn man is "strong and mysterious."

There is no question that romantic love is one of life's great experiences and adventures. But like everything in life, there is always the risk-reward ratio. Romance, with all of its intoxicating rewards, carries with it the inevitability of serious psychological hangovers.

**THE INTRUSION OF REALITY.** What happens when we bring these unconscious wishes, needs, and heightened expectations into relationships? What happens when reality intrudes on fantasy? In the second stage of a relationship, the period of adjustment, reality and fantasy either clash so violently that the connection is severed irreparably, or merge successfully to form healthy and realistic expectations.

As the initial romantic intoxication wears off, one of the first hints of change may be something as simple as boredom. In the beginning, being in the presence of the lover is stimulation enough; we are entirely at peace, content to gaze into the lover's eyes for hours, rapt and fascinated. As a result, many people feel that the first sign of boredom is a signal that "it's over." The relationship just wasn't what we thought it would be, not the "real thing." "Maybe I made a mistake" is the first secret doubt that may occur to us.

As lovers become familiar with each other, the unflattering light of reality throws imperfections into stark relief. Irritating habits and minor differences that previously were overlooked now march onto center stage. Suddenly, the partners are annoyed, irritated. "Constructive" criticisms, snide or disparaging remarks, even outbursts of anger and annoyance may now be directed toward the lover who previously could do no wrong. The period of faultfinding has begun. His clothes are wrong, his friends are tedious, his laugh is weird, his kiss is too wet. Lovers can sense, of course, when their partner's image of them is changing, and they become defensive and guarded. Wholesale, across-the-board disapproval may even set in: "What did I ever see in him?" Resentment builds: "What did I ever see in her?" What is really happening is that the lovers' initial idealized and romanticized images of each other are being replaced by more realistic images. As areas of conflict surface and are not resolved directly by accommodation or compromises, the fantasy erodes, and the boundaries of two separate identities now become painfully distinct. The initial wish for oneness is replaced by a desire for breathing room, space. Even if a woman recognizes the need for some normal and reasonable distance, and conveys this need to her lover in a supportive way, it's likely to create anxiety, fear of separation and abandonment. For example, if he wants to spend time apart, with his friends, it may be interpreted as an accusation: "You are not enough." If she breaks several dates in a row, saying she just doesn't feel like going out, he may fear her next request will be one for a separation: "I don't like you anymore."

Even if the tension subsides, vague feelings of sadness, despondency, and melancholy take over. As a result, the third of the romantic wishes, for aliveness, begins to diminish. The sense of isolation that was felt before the beginning of the relationship returns. "How can this be? Who destroyed what was so precious to both of us? This sense of loss I feel couldn't be my fault! I wanted this so much! It must be your fault!" Blame leads to anger, and either or both partners begin to withhold love, tenderness, and sexual delight.

Sex is the most sensitive barometer of these changes. Even in the most harmonious, most passionate relationships, normal cooling of sexual desire occurs eventually. However, the first time a partner indicates lack of sexual interest can be traumatic. Up to that point, sexual insatiability has been one of the indicators of the perfection of the relationship. But tension, conflict, and doubt invariably dampen sexual desire. Sexual needs mount. Refusals are interpreted as invalidations. The partner who's taking the sexual initiative and being rebuffed experiences growing resentment. So too does the one who feels pressure to give in. Over time, the one who says no hardens and slips into a pattern of withholding. It's not even conscious—she or he just feels "turned off." At this juncture, one or both partners may fantasize about having an affair and recapturing romantic feelings with a brand-new lover.

As feelings of fusion, validation, and aliveness diminish, disillusionment may trigger the thoughts "Maybe he is not good enough for me. Maybe we're not good for each other. Maybe I'd be happier with someone else!" Yearning for fulfillment of those old familiar romantic wishes returns. The decision may be made to end this relationship and begin anew.

While this sounds like an anguished scenario, take heart, for it is a magnification of the pitfalls that can occur when we unleash primitive unconscious wishes and expectations and let them dominate our behavior. Realistic expectations about the natural cycles of relationships can prevent sad and tormented melodramas.

It is essential to accept the notion of phases in almost every aspect of life, including love relationships. Clinging too tightly to romantic visions prevents us from dealing effectively with the inevitable period of adjustment and makes it impossible to move on to mature love. Realistically, we all must fulfill some of our needs outside the arena of love. We must accept our basic separateness even though we all want to love and be loved by a partner. We must also have a strong enough sense of self to be able to love another person successfully and genuinely. Self-worth emanates from our own estimation of ourselves, it is not something that can be acquired from someone else.

In a sense, the overall danger of romance is that we may get stuck at that initial phase of infatuation and fantasy, driven by selfish unconscious wishes and unrealistic goals. The more powerful our needs and illusions at the beginning of a relationship, the more tumultuous the period of adjustment is likely to be and, consequently, the less likely is it that we'll succeed in getting through this difficult stage and graduating to the final stage.

**MATURE LOVE.** Despite its inherent pitfalls, romance plays an indispensable role in setting the stage for enduring love. In fact, a passionate beginning to a relationship can be very beneficial in the long term. When lovers begin by experiencing the full range of intense positive and negative emotions, they are better able to weather the turmoil of the adjustment phase, because they have experienced how good, how passionate, love can be. That memory serves as a powerful motivation to stay through the rough times so those exquisite feelings can be experienced again. As therapists, we often hear people who have long and successful marriages say, "What we've learned is that it goes in cycles. We go through just hideous periods of really disliking each other, constant battling, and periods of boredom and restlessness, but even in the worst of times we know that sooner or later, we'll discover ourselves falling in love with each other all over again."

When we reach the end of the romantic phase of a relationship, we leave a certain delight behind. But letting go of romantic fantasies actually paves the way for a human experience that transcends romance. Granted, leaving romance is a kind of loss of innocence, but it allows room for something even more rewarding—adult, mature, and mutual love.

Mature love is not idealization, adoration, or infatuation. It is an appreciation of someone for who he or she really is rather than what we would like that person to be. Mature love is unselfish love; it goes beyond our own needs and concerns. As psychiatrist Harry Stack Sullivan has said: "Love exists when another person's security and satisfaction are as important to you as your own."

## What Love Requires

You have probably heard it said of someone that he or she lacks the "capacity for love." A capacity for love means being able to feel and exhibit caring and concern for another person. This is empathy, or the willingness to participate in the feelings or ideas of another person, the ability to put ourselves in another person's shoes, to be curious about what is going on inside someone else, and to understand how he or she feels.

The capacity for love exists when we give up our narcissistic posture with respect to ourselves and the rest of the world. What this means is that we move beyond self-absorption to a real desire to know and care for others. Narcissism is something we all grow up with and, in times of stress, occasionally revert to. Being narcissistic implies an excessive concern with ourselves and our need for attention, nurturing, and love. It represents normal development and normal needs, but sometimes can get out of hand, to the detriment of our ability to care in a more unselfish way. The three basic wishes we described at the beginning of this chapter all refer to narcissistic concerns.

Part One of this book was, in many ways, concerned with the ways in which we try to allay our insecurities in relationships. Mature love comes about when such needs no longer tyrannize us. We all have the tendency to occasionally revert back to self-involvement, such as in moments of extreme loneliness, but arriving at the capacity for mature love implies our energy is also freed up to love and care for others. One component in adult loving is the capacity to integrate tenderness and sexuality, the ability to "make love" to the person for whom you care. Love is not just one or the other, not simply caring without sexuality or sexuality without caring. Men and women who have not reached this level of caring find sexuality to be merely a validation of who they are. The female love addict feels worthy as long as attention is bestowed on her by the yearned-for man. The male Don Juan character feels whole and valued as long as he feels validated by the sexual conquest of yet another desirable woman. It is this kind of love, love as sensation, love as the vehicle for solving old childhood deprivations, that gets us into trouble.

When we speak of letting go of a narcissistic posture and being willing to embrace mature love, it should be clear that love requires the engagement of two reasonably mature and healthy egos. Only when we have a strong sense of self can we allow ourselves to love in a mature fashion. Real love requires a kind of yielding or surrendering to the other. In order to yield in this way, one must not fear the loss of one's identity in the love relationship. When we feel good about ourselves, we no longer need to invest energy in bolstering the ego—rather, we become free to invest that energy in loving another person. Expressed differently, mature love evolves

out of the realization that unselfish giving and caring
renews and replenishes us rather than depleting us.

Ultimately, it is not enough for us to have an
awareness of the specific dangers in the initial stage
of romantic infatuation or the second stage of adjustment during which illusion must deal with stark
reality. Nor is it sufficient for us to know how to
navigate these tricky waters well enough for us to
get along with a lover. We must be willing to make
the transition from romance, with its essentially selfish wishes and needs and its emotional intensity, to
the final stage of love: mature and enduring love
that is largely unconditional and unselfish, and renewed constantly through realistic accommodation,
acceptance, and compromise. This transition, when
we move from a love that is purely emotional to one
that is actually spiritual, is the moment of commitment.

## What Is Commitment?

Today, commitment is an issue with the deepest
meaning and importance to both men and women.
There are two ways of defining it: one definition of
commitment is the act of deciding to marry, and the
other refers to the unselfish feelings and acts of love
of those who enter into an exclusive relationship
with another person. Most people today think of
commitment as the former. While this definition is
obviously of importance to anyone who is waiting,
especially a woman who hears the biological clock
ticking ever more loudly, it is the broader definition
that has the deeper and more meaningful implications for a man or woman. Sadly, there are both
men and women who get married but who never
have really explored within themselves the more
far-reaching implications of the second meaning of

commitment. It is this latter definition of commitment as an intellectual or ethical concept that is, in our view, the more important one.

Let us first explore for a moment the notion of commitment as a decision, as a choice to marry. Sometimes commitment has very little to do with real love. A person who chooses to marry without any true desire to become close and intimate is making a decision, but not a commitment. He may not have given any real thought to issues of love, loyalty, and the making of a lifelong pact. Indeed, some people marry and then, later on, they evolve into a truly committed state.

When we move beyond the narrow definition of commitment—deciding to marry—we can then explore the broader one, commitment as an intellectual ideal. Commitment, in this sense, not only refers to a declaration of loyalty, but to a broader code of loving conduct, ethics, and honor. There are many men and women who truly believe they are committed to a relationship or marriage even though the content of their commitment may be vastly different. The person who secretly knows his or her love is tepid and perfunctory may be "committed" to another and may be faithful but has actually never believed in the possibility of passion and caring in marriage.

There are two facets of commitment, each of which poses challenges, each of which strengthens and enlarges our sense of ourselves and simultaneously frightens us and makes us reluctant to take on the responsibilities of marriage. First, commitment requires courage. In order to commit ourselves to another, we must have the courage to love, the willingness to struggle and risk engagement. This requires that we feel secure enough in our sense of self, that we can trust. No matter how much information we have accumulated, how certain we are that our love will be acknowledged and returned in equal measure, we still take a great chance that our belief will prove unfounded, that the person we love will perhaps one day not love us back. There are no guarantees in love, but nevertheless we choose to declare our intentions. That act is trust, pure, simple, and scary.

The second facet of commitment involves the ethical posture we assume when we say we are committed. As we suggested, commitment is ultimately an ethical declaration, a kind of code defining the conduct of love. It is a statement of intention that we will live out the terms of the agreement. Sometimes these terms refer to the traditional marriage vows: "to honor and cherish, to love for better or worse, in sickness and health, till death do us part." Powerful words! Certainly these vows, declarations, and intentions are not to be taken lightly.

## Commitment in the Eighties

Decades ago, men and women assumed marriage was forever. Today, we no longer can luxuriate in such naive projections; we know that marriage is dissolved relatively easily and that divorce is a common alternative to a troubled marriage. Because men and women today realize how shallow commitments can be, they are all the more resolved not to fall prey to such traps. Today, men and women want their commitments to have meaning, to be heartfelt rather than facile, and to endure rather than disintegrate.

Men today seem more afraid of commitment not because they don't want to marry or enter into lifelong bonds, but precisely because they do and they are taking it seriously. Because so many women are ready for a serious relationship today, and are outspoken about it, men in turn are outspoken about their reluctance, not about commitment, but to enter into what may feel to them to be a premature commitment. The facts are in: men are marrying at the same rate they always have. Men are not ignoring marriage as some believe. What they are doing is being very careful about expressing this wish and to whom they express it. Because women appear to be so eager to marry, often even desperate, men, in contrast, sound more cautious. Men are hesitant to discuss with a woman their views on marriage for fear that even an abstract discussion of what they would like in the future might serve to lead the woman on or be interpreted as an implicit promise. Even though men may seem to avoid the issue of future and commitment, they nevertheless do think about it, do want commitment, and do wishfully picture themselves in a bonded relationship with a woman.

Undoubtedly, commitment in the eighties is more difficult than in the past, but not because men and women are less caring. It is because they want it to work. And they know all the ways marriage and love doesn't work, all the ways that good intentions go awry.

## The Rhythms of Commitment

Many women have experienced wanting some form of commitment from a man they care for and being met with resistance. They may have waited and waited for him to make the first move to deepen the relationship, only to hear him say, "Don't rush things—I don't want to be pressured." Men may declare their romantic feelings early in a relationship, but this doesn't mean they are in love or ready to commit themselves to an exclusive, permanent bond. Feeling romantic and wanting to commit themselves are two entirely different experiences for men, and one doesn't automatically lead to the other. A man can feel he is falling in love and yet not be ready to even think about a permanent bond. Many women, on the other hand, allow romantic feelings to move them more quickly toward commitment. For women, strong romantic feelings often inspire a wish to bond; for men, they don't. It's not that the men have made up their minds against commitment. It may not even have yet occurred to them; they may simply not be ready. Most men do not feel the same sense of urgency that women do. This discrepancy is very common in relationships. Why?

Men's and women's different bonding zones, or tolerance of and comfort with closeness, clearly lead to different rhythms and a varying sense of timing in relationships. Women typically feel ready to make a commitment or to get married months before men. But there is something else that happens which may surprise women. Men are often willing to deepen the union yet totally disguise their willingness from women. They may even hide it from themselves. A woman may not recognize her lover's receptivity because he gives her little evidence of how attached he has become. Men are usually much more dependent and connected than they let women know. It is this fact about men's hidden dependencies that explains why well-timed ultimatums often work in getting a man to commit himself to a relationship. The man's oscillation between Attachment and Separateness does not mean that he doesn't care, for he may in fact feel very loving. So when he's given an ultimatum, he is forced to acknowledge to himself that he can't live without the woman he loves.

Commitment is fundamentally an attitude. When we give commitment we are affirming our love. It is an ongoing expression of how we value the other person, the position that person holds in our lives. Sustaining commitment is an alive and evolving process shaped daily by our encounters with one another. Commitment is intention, it is love in action. In a good relationship, each intentional act of love not only has meaning in the moment, but also serves to further solidify and reinforce the growing bond between the man and woman.

# CHAPTER EIGHT

# Giving Up the Prince and Finding the Man

In recent years, it has become fashionable to engage in "male bashing." Men were often described as being locked into a macho image, emotionally underdeveloped, and insensitive to women. Then when they did open up a bit, men were disparaged for being too soft or "wimpy." According to the latest round of faultfinding, men have become elusive and reluctant to commit to relationships. Needless to say, all of these castigations do nothing to create harmony and mutual understanding between the sexes. Our task in this chapter is to unravel some of the mythologies and present a picture of men that is free from the distortions arising from trendy rhetoric and facile characterizations.

One reason women do not understand men is because men make little effort to *be* known. Instead, men have allowed myths about who they are, how they feel, and what they think to persist. However, although it may sound contradictory, men do wish to be known, and they love women who understand and accept them.

Another reason men are not understood very well

is that women have been reluctant to look objectively at the male psyche. Such a clear and dispassionate look is even threatening to some women, because they are afraid of losing their fantasy of the prince. Men are not knights in shining armor; they do have flaws, often embarrassing ones. It is our contention that many women, even today, want a variation of the prince—a man who is strong yet sensitive, heroic yet tender, one who has the energy for romantic surprises yet is still masterful in the work world. Would that all that could be true. Such supermen do not exist. But if you give up the wish for the prince, we promise you that the man you will find ultimately offers substantially more.

Understanding a man creates power. A man gives his heart most completely to a woman when he feels the safety and trust that go along with being known and still valued. The most fundamental key to a man's passion and his desire to commit himself is a woman's capacity to understand and accept who he really is.

## Understanding Is Not Necessarily Acceptance

Understanding and acceptance are not synonymous. All men yearn for acceptance from the women they love. Understanding is only a part of that wish. Understanding is knowing who men really are beneath the posturing and bravado. It is knowing what drives and motivates them as well as what they avoid or fear. It is knowing how they respond to women and how they interact in intimate unions. It is being aware of the many ways they may be like you and also how they differ. While all that is wonderful, accepting goes far beyond.

Some women have a partial understanding of men, particularly their vulnerabilities, but don't truly accept or even particularly like men. Employing their exquisitely sensitive knowledge of men, they can sense a man's weak spots immediately and know how to play on them subtly. A man may be fascinated by being known by this kind of woman, but such fascination rarely evolves into trust or love by itself. Typically, this sort of male understanding is used for manipulation and exploitation, not befriending.

Other women have a deep understanding of men, but also fail to accept them. They are conscious of men's strengths as well as their weaknesses. Such women possess few illusions—they know what men can deliver and what they cannot. But while they value men's positive attributes, they harbor the sometimes hidden wish that men could be different—somehow better. They resent a man's human imperfection, for it prevents him from being the idealized rescuer, provider, or romantic prince they had hoped to find.

One form of acceptance we all are familiar with is the kind that is accompanied with a shrug of the shoulders and a fatalistic sigh: "Oh, you know what men are like!" Or "Men—that's just the way they are." This is not the kind of acceptance men are looking for. What a man hopes for is an appreciation of his whole self, and compassionate forgiveness for his annoying habits, deficiencies, and defects of character.

Full and loving acceptance demands a special kind of maturity. It means being able to care while at the same time perceiving both the good and the not so good. As one man described it gratefully, "I know living with me isn't easy. But I can't tell you how good it feels being with Sara. I never get the feeling that she expects me to walk on water. Even when I'm a total jerk—impatient, bad-tempered, or just

plain negligent in holding up my end of our marriage
—I know the bad somehow gets blended in with the
good and that she loves me. It's not that she doesn't
let me know when I screw up; it's that I know she
cares in spite of it. Her acceptance, forgiveness, and
love make me want to work harder to be the best
person I can be."

What this woman offers is love and acceptance
that is unfettered by "ifs" and strict boundaries. As
has often been said, it's no trick loving someone at
his or her best. The hard part is loving them at their
worst. This kind of love doesn't require looking the
other way or being unaware, and it certainly isn't
blind. A loving acceptance means simply that we
don't allow the less than heroic or the irritating
aspects of our mates to affect the core of our love.
When they come up, they are reacted to emotionally
and then dropped without either building resentment or undermining fundamental caring.

Acceptance requires that we let go of being per-
fectionistic and idealistic about either ourselves or
our mates. For if we are overly critical of ourselves,
we will also be that way with our mates.

Freeing oneself from the constricting confines of
idealism is accomplished by reversing what is foreground and what is background. For example, if we
allow a person's cough from the balcony to become
foreground, we'll miss out on the magnificent sym-
phony the orchestra is performing on the stage. If
you allow a man's absentmindedness or impatience
in traffic or habit of leaving his wet towel wadded on
the bathroom floor to become foreground, you may
miss out on his steadfastness in times of adversity,
his patience when the kids are cranky, or his loyalty
to and appreciation of you. Acceptance allows his
pleasing aspects to remain foreground, on the whole,

and those that annoy or disappoint you to reside, overall, in he background.

Loving and conscious acceptance are not easy. It requires letting go of unrealistic wishes. It's not liking or appreciating everything, but realizing that the flaws, however glaring, are nevertheless part of the whole person you love.

We are not cataloguing what should be acceptable to you and what should not. These are subjective determinations to be made by you. Unquestionably, acceptance is not license, and you should not put up with intentionally insensitive or mean-spirited behavior. What we are addressing is that broad range of typical behaviors which, although annoying, are very normal. Accepting minor flaws, particularly if they are outweighed by qualities we like and respect, will go a long way toward providing the comfort and freedom the other person cherishes.

## Who Men Really Are

To truly understand men, it is important to have an overview of their dramas, hopes, and dreams, particularly their ongoing quest for masculinity. This quest, which faces men from childhood onward, deeply affects the way they love a woman. For just as a woman loves and values the man who is supportive of her desire for achievement, a woman's understanding of a man's need for mastery and career success will draw him to her.

**THE DRIVE TOWARD AUTONOMY.** Autonomy is a prime component of the Polarity Factor: independence begins with a boy's separation from his mother. But a man's need for self-sufficiency soon grows beyond these early origins—it becomes a goal in itself. The quest for autonomy takes on value and meaning of its own.

A man's thoughts are dominated by his need to engage in activities that lead to feelings of strength and vitality and his related need to avoid situations that hold the dreaded potential of weakness or help-lessness. Most men are drawn toward action and abhor passivity. They constantly seek ways to make themselves feel strong and powerful, for such feel-ings are intimately tied to their sense of being manly. Although strength and manliness are defined by men in vastly different ways, the common thread is a feeling of power or "effectance"—the ability to have an effect or an impact on one's environment. Re-gardless of the specific paths they may take to attain this, most men have an important drive toward feel-ing more effective. When they achieve this, they feel more masculine.

For men, autonomy, the ability to flourish inde-pendently, is the foundation for achieving a sense of masculinity. This does not mean that men must be alone to feel manly. Nevertheless, the sense of mas-culinity sought by men is a feeling that usually oc-curs outside the realm of relationships, with the possible exception of the domain of sexuality. Men typically define masculinity in work- and action-oriented activities in which they ultimately experi-ence themselves as alone.

**THE NEED TO BE BRAVE.** In early child-hood, boys learn from their peers and their first model of manliness, their fathers, to be ashamed of fearful feelings, to ignore them. This is in sharp contrast to girls, who are taught more realistically that fear is appropriate to certain circumstances, that it is acceptable to both acknowledge and express it.

From boyhood onward, the issues of strength,

bravery, and measuring up become ever-present concerns for men. Most adult men still have vivid boyhood memories of not taking a dare hurled by another boy, "chickening out" in a fight, or secretly or openly comparing penis size in the locker room. While these experiences are sometimes remembered with amusement, other times they are still painfully tinged with anxiety and embarrassment. These events shape a boy's first images of his masculinity.

Competition and comparison are the primary barometers for measuring maleness. Boys who are willing to compete begin to see themselves in masculine images. The boy who is afraid to take the challenge, who is timid or who shies away from competition, is labeled a "sissy."

In primitive societies, a male spent his boyhood learning hunting skills in preparation for his initiation to manhood: the hunting and killing of a dangerous animal. Today's tests of courage and strength are less life-threatening, as a rule—drag racing and street-gang activity excepted—and are most often relegated to the athletic field. But even though opportunities for tests of physical and moral courage are more limited today in the lives of young men, the need and wish to be tough have little diminished. The enormous popularity of action-adventure films and television programs attests to this fact.

The film *Rocky* epitomizes the fantasy of the underdog who triumphs in the ring. Rambo shoots up an entire nation single-handed. Clint Eastwood and Charles Bronson have created film careers playing the lone avenger who triumphs over hordes of bad guys. The vast number of films that emphasize winning and revenge, whether in the context of sports, war, or the mean streets (cops against the criminals), all stem from the male need to transcend a sense of helplessness or powerlessness. Every man would like to feel that he can rise to the occasion, that he can meet the challenge and win.

In sum, boys don't "choose" to be strong, they "need" to be strong. This relentless drive toward self-reliance helps boys overcome feelings of weakness or helplessness. It toughens them up, helps them better define maleness, and prepares them for the rigors ahead.

**THE NEED TO WIN.** One of the finest and most poignant examples of the importance of winning and losing for men is the archetypal American drama *Death of a Salesman* by Arthur Miller. Its protagonist, Willy Loman, is a man who touches the hearts and stirs the fears of most men who view his painful struggle. No matter how much his wife insists to his sons that their father "deserves attention," no matter how hard Willy tries to convince them all that he is not just liked but "well liked," we know that because of his failure as a salesman, he is doomed. To be a loser in America is to suffer a terrible fate. In the course of therapy with men, we find that no matter how great their success, they are haunted by the specter of failure. Indeed, it is our impression that men are driven much more by the fear of failure than by the desire to succeed!

From early childhood, the emphasis on achievement is paramount in a young boy's life. Girls get conflicting messages about achievement and career ambition, but for boys, there is never any question about the absolute need to become economically self-sufficient and, beyond that, to become a provider for a family. A boy knows from childhood that he will spend his entire adult life working and to some degree being judged by the level of success he achieves.

Because America is known as the land of opportunity, men who fail in this country secretly feel it's their fault—they didn't have it or didn't try hard enough. The concept of "the right stuff," of being gutsy and courageous, is typically American and is the fuel for male achievement. As boys grow into men, their sense of worth is in large measure determined by their progress up the ladder of success.

Unfortunately, in America, a prime indicator of success is money. For some men, just making ends meet is a major achievement. For other, more affluent men, money becomes a measure not only of their ability to provide for a family, but also of their skill or cleverness at the game of power. Men tend to use the same terms to describe the pursuit of financial success as they would use to describe warfare or intense athletic competition. Managers fantasize themselves as field generals leading their troops into the fray. They "nuke the competition," "quarterback a squeeze play," "make an end run" on "the opposing team." If a man has the skills necessary to survive in the corporate world, he is a "winner."

Winners and losers, from the male perspective, are often also distinguished by the degree to which they are tough and "streetwise," which again likens the battle in the corporate world to the struggle of adolescents growing up in the streets.

Men think women do not understand their compulsion to succeed and be tough. Even though men have heard the message of feminism and the talk of the "new male," they continue to believe that women judge them as potential mates by traditional criteria— the more successful a man is, the more attractive he is to women. To a great extent, this is accurate. A man's career success, income, and accomplishments are high priorities in many women's choice of a lover or mate. The persistent message boys and, later, men get is: succeed at work and everything else will follow.

Given the tremendous social pressures men feel to be "winners," it is no wonder that they place such a high priority on work, often at the expense of personal relationships. As Larry, 32, a manufacturing executive, sadly expressed it, "I know my kids are first, although I have a sneaking suspicion that's more a heartfelt wish than actuality. But I do realize my marriage comes second to my career. I wish it were otherwise, but it always feels like the stakes are too high to take my eye off the ball."

We offer these observations not as a suggestion that women indulge the work-obsessed man in their life at the expense of their own needs, but rather as a clue to some of the underlying forces that motivate men. We are convinced that women who are successful with men are those who fully comprehend the power of the underlying forces that drive men in their careers.

**THE NEED TO PLAY.** Men are often described as being just boys at heart, obsessed with buying "toys" and overly involved with all kinds of games, from amateur baseball leagues to pro sports to elaborate practical jokes. Sometimes this is said in a disparaging tone, as though mature men were the exception. The fact is, however, that men not only want to play boyishly at times but, significantly, *need* to play as a balance to their intense drive at work.

As illustrated in the case study of "The Spoilsport" in chapter 5, many women misunderstand men's desire to play, to have fun, even to be silly. Men have told us that their wives feel threatened by their playful behavior, that they can't accept that men can be both strong, dependable, and mature and also boyish at times. But men do need to play, and not just with their lovers or mates—they also need the time and space to be boyish with their male friends. The reward for men is the release of tension and the ability to put life in a more balanced perspective. Women who truly understand men recognize their need to be serious as well as their need to be youthful and silly at times.

**THE NEED TO BE A HERO.** From time eternal, men have defined themselves in terms of their capacity for taking risks, being courageous and heroic. In modern times, these themes are often experienced vicariously in books or films, for it is difficult in our complex technological world to seek out tasks or journeys that are heroic. Nevertheless, acting with courage, taking that step that holds the potential for failure and even physical harm, is a fantasy most men secretly crave.

Today, it is a challenge for men to find a heroic context, a situation that demands risk, honor, and fearlessness. In a society where most endeavors are mundane, interdependent, and often anonymous, the heroic or courageous act is not within the grasp of most men. In this century, war and sexuality have often been the only arenas where this aspect of manliness could be expressed. Thankfully, the notion of a "good war" is long past us. And the sexual revolution rendered sexual conquest of women obsolete as a measure of masculinity.

In the past, men defined their manhood, in part, in terms of their ability to seduce women. But when the sexual revolution equalized the rules, men backed off. As soon as men realized that women have equal and at times even greater sexual appetites, and that men had to concern themselves with being good lovers, sexual conquest went the way of dragon slaying. The sense of mastery men gained from seduction gave place to an awareness that responsibility and performance were being expected of them.

Meanwhile, the women's movement ended male dominance in the workplace. Women proved they could take on just about any job that men were doing and do it as well or better. Women integrated clubs that before had been "men only," they were appointed to the Supreme Court, and they became vice-presidential candidates. Women became active participants in every work area from the space program to the boardroom. Women sports reporters even invaded the locker room! What testing ground remains that is man's alone? How can men define themselves within the concepts of traditional masculinity?

It is difficult for men today to find activities and endeavors which yield affirmations of courage and heroism. Maybe new ways of achieving such affirmations will never be found, but most men still secretly or unconsciously find their quest to be a compelling one.

## How Men Respond to Understanding and Acceptance

Most men are plagued at times by fears of inadequacy. Most men know precisely where their weaknesses are and could write out a list of their more glaring flaws. Confidence in the face of these limitations is often hard to maintain, for men can be more critical of themselves than they will ever let women know. The man who believes his mate basically accepts him is given a tremendous boost—he feels loved and good in her eyes. All men need to feel this, even if they are unable to express this need to women.

When men experience consistent and loving acceptance, they gradually become more open. They grow less cautious and guarded, less fearful of being judged harshly or being seen as deficient. All men absolutely dread being found lacking in some important quality or area. Acceptance allows men to feel "more" rather than focusing on the common male worry of being exposed as being "less."

As a result of these positive feelings, men feel more expansive and let more of themselves be revealed and known. The reward for the accepting woman is a man's stronger love for her. Both the man and the woman experience a richer union as a result of the intimacy and freedom of expression her acceptance encourages in him.

## The Confidante

Ken, 30, an administrator for a city arts center, describes his first encounter with Marisa, 27, an assistant to a prominent elderly art collector. They met when both volunteered to serve on a committee for a benefit art auction. They ended up sharing the responsibility for one aspect of the event, and met for coffee to discuss their plans.

"It only took us fifteen minutes to agree on our ideas—she was very open and encouraging to me, saying things like 'What a good idea,' and also suggesting things herself. Her warmth, her readiness to smile and laugh, made me feel charming and bright. She asked me about myself, where I'd gone to school, and we started talking about ourselves.

"Looking back, I can pinpoint the exact moment when it went beyond the sort of surface conversation between two people in the same business circle to the feeling that Marisa was somebody I wanted to go out with. We discovered we had a mutual ac-

quaintance, a man who has somewhat of a bad repu-
tation for being moody and difficult and never
showing up with the same woman twice. I had started
putting him down as a womanizer when she interrupted me and said, 'I've got a hunch he's really still
hurting from a couple of years back.' She told me he
had been engaged to a woman who had abruptly left
him for someone else. She described a couple of
instances when this fellow had gone out of his way
to help people out, and painted a much more sym-
pathetic picture of him. What she said was so understanding and compassionate, seeing the good in
someone most people criticize without knowing him.
And she began to talk about how tough relationships are on both women and men these days. I
found myself telling her about my last serious relationship and what I had learned from it. We talked
until almost midnight. When I walked her out to her
car, I asked her out for dinner the next night. Driving home, I realized that this was a woman I wanted
to spend time with. She was warm, open, and the
kind of person who really makes me want to open
up. I have a feeling we're going to be seeing a lot of
each other.''

*Triggering Chemistry.* So often, men and women fail
to realize how quickly they form impressions. The
case of Ken illustrates how early a man can sense the
possibility that a woman will become a confidante.
We erroneously believe that attraction is always the
initial catalyst for the beginning of chemistry. Yet,
sensing what we truly need and respond to may be
the spark that draws a man and a woman close to
each other. Ken sensed a capacity in Marisa for
acceptance that was obviously critical for him.

Molly is also a woman who became a Confidante. It was Molly and Ben's first wedding anniversary. After the last of many friends' toasts to their marriage, Molly stood with her arms around her best friends, Andrea and Brad, the three of them surveying the party, the house, and Ben. "I have you two to thank for all of this," Molly said, smiling.

"Hey, we gave the advice," replied Brad, "but you're the one who put it into action."

It had been just a year and a half before that Molly hit a near-suicidal bottom in her life. Three weeks into a passionate, intense affair with Stan, a restaurant owner, he had stopped phoning and hadn't returned any of her several calls to him.

Molly felt humiliated, rejected, angry, and, most of all, hopeless. Hopeless because, as she recalled all the disappointing three-week or two-month relationships she'd had over the years, this latest affair and abrupt rejection seemed just a dismal repeat of every other one she'd ever had—romance, excitement, passion, and then the disappearance of the man.

Stopping by her friends' house on her way home from work, Molly found herself sobbing, and, for the first time in her life, really asking for help. The feedback she got that night from both Andrea and Brad was honest, even brutal at times. Brad said, "Every time we introduce you to a nice honest guy who wants a family, you call us the next day saying, 'He's nice but boring,' or 'He wasn't sexy,' or 'He wasn't exciting enough.' "

Said Andrea, "When you tell us about your dates, all you talk about is how successful they are, what restaurant he took you to, how great he is in bed—nothing about just feeling comfortable together, being flesh-and-blood people."

"And when we double-date with you and one of these guys, you act differently than when you're just with us," Brad said. "You take on this stagy, flirtatious, baiting personality with men, really pushing your sexiness. That stuff might be attractive to a man for a short time, but in the long run he wants someone he can talk to honestly."

Molly didn't change overnight, just as her self-defeating attitudes and behavior patterns with men hadn't developed overnight. Even though Molly was an effective and aggressive professional in her career and a genuine person around her male and female friends, when it came to a lover, she played out the flirtatious, romantic behavior that she had deeply internalized from her mother during childhood. After her crisis, she realized that she had to learn to be a friend as well as a lover.

After a few one-date-only experiences with men who didn't truly interest her, she met Ben at a volleyball tournament. He was exactly the kind of man who had always excited her before: dynamic, sexy, and successful. She had an immediate powerful response to him, but in their first conversation, and on their first few casual dates, she forced herself, in line with her determination to behave differently with men, to talk to him straightforwardly and naturally rather than using the sexy body language she had employed in the past.

She felt very positive about her new behavior and taking it slow in her new relationship, but although she tried not to, she found herself thinking and fantasizing about him almost obsessively. And from the night they became lovers, Molly relapsed into her old behavior patterns: she became traditionally feminine, even childlike, Scarlet O'Hara to Rhett Butler.

Ben's response startled her. Shortly after they became lovers, he cut her short in the middle of a flirtatious, teasing joke as they lay in bed after making love. "Maybe we should go back to just being friends, Molly," he said, irritation in his voice. "We're getting into a whole other number that quite frankly doesn't appeal to me anymore."

Molly's immediate reaction was one of flushed humiliation and hurt—she felt he was rejecting her as all the others had before. She was ready to jump out of bed and go home, but Ben took her in his arms and held her close. "Let's talk."

In the long discussion that followed, he told her he had had a lot of romantic infatuations and intense sexual affairs with women, and that he was tired of them. He said he felt constant pressure in his career to be "on," to be a dynamic and self-assured powerhouse, and that at this point the last thing he wanted in a relationship was to feel pressured to be romantic and exciting. "What attracted me to you right from our first conversation at the volleyball tournament," he said, "was that I felt I could relax and be myself with you."

It required a major psychological adjustment for Molly to let go of the deep-seated emotional yearnings that had always equated the role of lover with that of a rescuer, prince, and romantic ideal. But she eventually did, with Ben's encouragement and support. Ben has found in Molly a woman he can confide in, a woman who draws him ever closer to her. In Ben and the radically different way she relates to him, as his confidante, supporter, and friend, she has found a deep and lasting love.

*Becoming Real with a Man.* There are still scores of women who believe that coquettish behavior will win a man over. Acting that way may get his attention, or stimulate his curiosity, but rarely will a meaningful relationship develop. Men tire of games a lot more quickly than most women realize. Men such as

Ben are basically looking for something more genuine with a woman; they've already played the games.

As we have said often in this book, breaking life-long patterns is difficult. It requires letting go of that which is known and certain, and trying that which is unknown and may not work. Even so, the act of trying to change is worth it. Naturally, all men can be tantalized in the beginning, but ultimately, a man wants a confidante, someone with whom he can be himself, without the pressure of performing.

## The Acceptor

It seemed that every other week, Janie had a new man to talk about when she came in for her weekly therapy session. At 33, she heads her own firm designing interiors for clothing shops and restaurants. She is exceptionally creative and intelligent, and is insightful both about herself and about other people. In the extremely competitive design field, it is Janie's excellent social skills—her ability to sell herself and her trademark offbeat ideas—that have earned her a large measure of her success.

Janie's social skills and perceptiveness didn't evaporate in her relationships with men. She demonstrated a good grasp of men's career drives and their need to be understood. With her terrific sense of humor and her ability to make men feel comfortable, Janie had no trouble attracting men. Each time she met a new man, she would talk enthusiastically about his accomplishments and what a wonderful time they'd had on a date. She would seem genuinely hopeful: "What do you know," she'd say, "maybe this one will work out."

But invariably, within several weeks, she'd say she had met someone new—"That last guy turned out to be boring," or "insecure" or "flaky"; or "I guess he met someone else—we didn't really click after all." Although Janie had said she truly wanted a permanent commitment with a man when she began therapy, it began to appear that either she wasn't genuinely interested in a sustained relationship—still wanted to play the field—or she was a perfectionist who was rejecting one man after another as not good enough for her. It was only after several months of intensive examination of her behavior with men that her self-defeating pattern emerged.

For all her stated interest in having a lasting relationship, Janie, it proved, was deeply cynical about men and love. She would draw a man to her, but stop at a certain point, afraid of being hurt or rejected. While her surface behavior was warm and accepting, her sense of humor would become cutting and sarcastic. Confused by these mixed messages, the man would pull away from her. Her overall effect on a man was intimidation; he could not trust her affection toward him.

Janie's hostility was so well disguised that even she didn't recognize it on a conscious level. It stemmed from a mixture of unresolved anger against her parents and resentment against men for wielding most of the power in the business world.

Janie's mother had been a romantic idealist whose desire to make their family life warm and affectionate had been slowly sabotaged by a husband who had become embittered and sarcastic as a result of repeated business failures. A tomboy as a child, Janie was determined from her teenage years to become a tough, savvy businesswoman, and had always fought her deep-seated romantic leanings. She didn't want to become a disappointed, victimized replica of her mother.

She eventually realized that her sharp sense of humor, cynicism, and sarcasm were her means of repressing her own romanticism and vulnerability. In effect, her wit was used as a shield to keep men at a certain distance.

She is now involved in a healthy relationship with Luke, a commercial illustrator who is as perceptive, intelligent, and creative as she is—she's not "settling" for less than an equal partner in her choice of Luke. Janie is just as funny and quick with Luke as she's ever been with a man. But today, much of the cynicism and sarcasm is absent.

How did she break her old patterns in this new relationship? Janie says she "tried to keep in mind from the very start that it wasn't a matter of maintaining the upper hand by putting him down, that it wasn't a matter of 'winning or losing' in some kind of battle against men, but that we would both lose out unless I was as kind and accepting and forgiving of him as I wanted him to be with me—the Golden Rule, 'Do unto others . . .' I had to accept his vulnerabilities and reveal mine to him, to let him in, not that that's always so easy to do."

"I value her insightfulness about me and about us as a couple," says Luke. "She knows men, and she knows me. She knows exactly what I am and what I'm not, but she loves me anyhow. Before, I always felt that women were either idealizing me so they could be romantic, or so realistic there was no romance. Now we've got some of both and we're accepting each other for what we are."

**Being Outspoken without the Sting.** Humor and perceptiveness can be used defensively, as a way to keep someone away, on the defensive. It can more positively be used to communicate understanding and caring. Janie learned to use her wit and insight in a kind and sensitive manner. Men such as Luke respond to women who are truthtellers, women who are not afraid to be challenging and outspoken.

Most men truly enjoy a woman who is direct and uncensored in her communication, as long as it doesn't carry along with it the stinging barb of judgment. This holds true even when she is commenting on some negative aspect of his behavior, if the criticism seems specific and not a blanket indictment of who he is. In fact, men are incredibly intrigued by the woman who is perceptive about them, particularly those who are unafraid of bringing their observations directly and humorously into the relationship. Most men secretly don't like to get away with things around a woman and when she "busts" them about their behavior, accurately but not judgmentally, they like it. This enjoyment comes from feeling known and accepted by the woman.

## Recognizing a Man's Need for Acceptance

Men frequently signal their wish for understanding and acceptance indirectly. They may feel embarrassed or uncomfortable putting this ubiquitous and deep desire into words because they feel it is not "manly." Some oblique indicators are, for example, a man's commenting admiringly on couples who have "revealing" talks, or he might enviously mention men whose wives "really understand them." He may confide in his brother, his sister, or his mother. He may seek out a woman friend to talk to, even a close friend of yours. These are all indications of a need for a fuller understanding that he is not finding with you. The truth of the matter is that he really would rather be sharing his confidences with the woman he loves but doesn't feel able to do so.

When we expose ourselves and are not understood, or are subtly depreciated or taken lightly, it can be devastating. It is to protect themselves from such hurt that men become indirect or turn to others. What are some of the desires, feelings, and fears a man wants to be able to confide in you? As we have discussed, perhaps the most vital subject men need to discuss is work. As repetitive as it may seem to you, men try to resolve problems in their work by talking about them—often boringly and sometimes endlessly. They need to be able to talk about their dreams and goals as well as their conflicts and frustrations. They need to feel they can reveal inner doubts and insecurities as much as they need to share their triumphs.

At some point in a man's life, he needs to discuss "what it's all about"—he needs to reveal the helplessness of feeling burned out and the frustration that accompanies not knowing what to do about it. Most men at one time or another sense a profound loss of interest in their work which fills them with anxiety and guilt. They may have wishes or fantasies about other things they might like to try. They may have anxieties about aging and physical decline, feelings of having "missed it," not achieving what they'd hoped. These concerns affect every man.

Another area that men may wish to discuss, but often don't know how, is sexuality. Men, just as women, may have doubts about the quality of their lovemaking and the general level of mutual satisfaction.

Yet another topic rarely brought up by men is friends. Sadly, most men have few male friends. Acquaintances, yes. Friends, no. Men have more trouble than women making friends as adults, because they're less comfortable with their emotions.

Men often experience some sadness when they think about the friends they wish they had, but they're uneasy revealing this, as if they shouldn't need friends, as if they should be more self-reliant.

The majority of men, furthermore, have strong needs for partnership and equality. They would like to stop clanking around in their suits of armor and feeling pressured to be a prince. The woman partner is a soulmate, a companion and ally through the inevitable struggles and heartaches of life. Every man wishes for the constancy of love and acceptance, the caring and compassionate friend who loves him and believes in his worth despite the mistakes he makes or the failures he suffers.

## Creating Trust

How do you foster a man's trust? Isn't it something that's either there or not? Is there really a way to get a man to feel freer and to open up to you with his feelings? Yes, you can help a man to become more expressive and open, if you choose. The key is the slow development of trust.

For all of us, men or women, the prerequisite for a real sense of trust is that we feel and believe that we are loved in spite of our flaws, quirks, and limitations. Ultimately, a man's hope is that your connection to him is not to a wishful fantasy of him but to the man himself.

Learning to let go of idealistic notions about men is a challenge for many women. Some women are afraid that if they give up these notions, they will experience a net loss; they will have "settled" somehow. Actually, it works in just the opposite way. Releasing a man from impossibly high standards allows him to become more fully himself. He hides neither his edges nor his softness, neither his fears nor his dreams, neither his weaknesses nor his strengths. What he brings to the relationship is more fully and completely his whole self, providing a richer experience for both partners.

There are some specific things a woman can do to encourage this if she wishes, but note that the growth of trust occurs over time—don't look for instant results.

Communicate your willingness to know more about how he feels and what he thinks about. Be receptive—which means having a consistently warm and inviting attitude. It does not mean it is your job to be on call or to watch vigilantly over him. Your being receptive cannot be conveyed in a few sentences, but words are often a first step. Let him know it is all right to confide in you, that you are interested in hearing more from him—what he thinks and feels but usually doesn't talk about. It helps to make time to talk when you're both relaxed and unpressured and will not be interrupted. Express your interest in his life plans, his dreams for the future and what obstacles he feels he must overcome. Let him know you understand there are probably many things he's never said, subjects you've never discussed with each other, and that you're interested in listening, in talking, and in knowing him more fully.

To feel understood is to feel loved. Acceptance that fosters trust and communication is the foundation of all fulfilling relationships.

# CHAPTER NINE

# Trusting a Man to Love Your Strength

Many women do not realize that a growing number of men today look to women not only for emotional support but also for inspiration. Whenever we tell women that men are attracted to strength in women, they look at us with a skeptical eye. The myth that the strong woman intimidates men and triggers hostility still lingers. But the fact is that men have always been in awe of the strong woman and cherished the fantasy of the earth mother.

The expression "Behind every successful man is a strong woman" is often quite accurate. History is filled with stories of women who were the primary guiding forces behind their husbands, the "power behind the throne." Then and now, this type of woman acts as an adviser, confidante, even a lie detector, understanding the man's real feelings and using her perceptiveness to help him avoid self-defeating illusions or behaviors.

In our psychotherapy practices, when we work with a man who is conflicted about a career dilemma, we always ask, "What does your wife or woman friend think about the issue? How does she feel about your boss or partner? How does she view this exciting but risky new venture you are considering?" We ask because we know she often has greater insight into the man's strengths and flaws than he does.

The bond between a man and the woman who leads and inspires him is, we believe, the most powerful and enduring bond of all. Such a woman engages a man, comforts him, and fascinates him at the same time.

## Men and the New Woman

Today, more than a decade after the beginning of the feminist movement, a new woman has emerged— strong and accomplished, she has made her mark in the world of commerce.

During much of the 1970s, as women struggled for equality, men were secretly resentful of and threatened by the new woman. Naively, men felt their exclusive domain had been invaded. They felt they no longer had a unique and valued position in the eyes of the women they loved. Then, in 1980, came the Great Recession, the most severe economic slump this country had experienced since the Great Depression of 1929. Its impact on men was profound. For the first time men talked openly about their financial anxieties and fear of failure. Many of these same men saw the obvious need for their wives to enter the work force in order to create a two-income family. Younger men, not yet married, found themselves viewing women in a different light. Instead of being threatened by the new career woman, they began to see her as a partner, a co-provider sharing the burden of making ends meet.

Men also began to view women not only as financial partners, but also as psychological partners. No longer was the world of work off-limits or mysterious to women. Women were out there too, with the same dreams, same goals, and same frustrations. Women knew what the game was all about. And men knew they knew.

Now, a new stage is beginning, one with vast potential. Women who are strong and successful are, in many instances, superior to men in terms of knowledge, financial capacity, and wisdom concerning the way the world works. Of course, much of this was true even in the past, but now women no longer feel they must keep their strengths a secret from men.

Men are also beginning to acknowledge women's intuitive powers and their value in the work arena. While men tend to be overly rational and logical, women are often better able to combine rational thinking with intuition and sensitivity both to people's body language and the subtext of what they say. This is a unique blend that can serve as a powerful supplement to men's more dichotomous—right/wrong, good/bad—way of thinking.

Many women today are very comfortable using both their intelligence and their intuitive skills to create, solve problems, negotiate deals, and manage employees. And they're expressing this uniquely feminine style of doing business in a direct way, rather than following the old model of success for women, which was "If you want to succeed in a man's world, you must assimilate into that world—you must dress like a man, think like a man, talk like a man, and act like a man." Most women discovered that they didn't feel comfortable imitating the male model, men didn't like women acting like a caricature of men, and most important, their actual performance wasn't enhanced at all.

Our observations apply not only to career women, but also to full-time homemakers and mothers. Regardless of the path they have chosen, homemakers may be as liberated psychologically as career women. They are aware, they are enlightened, they are unafraid to express their strengths. These women too are being seen by men in a new and dramatically favorable light.

Ten or even five years ago, we would not have been as confident of these observations as we are now. Because the emerging new woman is learning to balance her uncensored and direct expression of strength and competence with her capacity for caring and softness, men are finally trusting women to play an increasingly powerful role in their lives.

There are scores of men who admire and cherish the new woman. She can be indispensable in a man's life. She influences not only his personal and emotional life, but also his career.

## Men *Are* Receptive

If you told a man you just met you could help him become the man he hopes to be by inspiring him, he would very likely respond with skepticism. Most men have been conditioned to believe that they must retain the edge in a relationship in terms of power and money. Men received this message not only from our culture in general, but also, more specifically, from women's expectations. Men aren't blind to women's fantasies of the prince, and they know some women want to be the princess, not the queen.

In the past, men who had strong wives were often derided by other men as well as women. Such men were seen as "henpecked" or, worse, "castrated." The classic derogatory comment about such marriages was, "You know who wears the pants in that family!" Although these attitudes are changing, such deep-seated apprehensions are not easily dismissed even by so-called "liberated" men. This is why the phenomenon of loving the strong, even inspiring and motivating, woman is still not very openly discussed. Men who are drawn to such women are reluctant to broadcast their desires and attractions.

In order to understand men's concerns in this area, keep in mind how difficult it is for women to give up the romantic fantasy of Mr. Right. That fantasy can easily be dismissed on an intellectual level by women today, but the deeper emotional and psychological abandonment of the notion of the perfect man is still difficult. Similarly, it is difficult for men to set aside their stereotypical notions about appropriate "masculine" behavior in relation to a woman. With this in mind, it's easy to see why when a man meets a woman who possesses the dynamism, insight, and intelligence to function as a guide or mentor in his life, it is hard for him to "surrender" to her. And that is the appropriate word to use—"surrender"—for that is exactly what allowing a woman to lead feels like to a man.

We have all had the experience of feeling guarded and defensive when we give someone else the power to like us or approve of us. It's scary; it makes us anxious. Yet when we allow someone in, even when the person is going to teach us something that might make us feel foolish at first, or criticized, we feel relieved. It's never as bad as we think it's going to be. That is exactly what men struggle with when they allow a woman to assume a position of greater authority and leadership.

Men who learn this—and they are definitely growing in numbers—sense a net gain. They feel they are not alone. They not only have a woman who is understanding, accepting, and a pal, but they also have a real partner. They feel an exhilarating sense of relief because there is someone with whom they can share burdens, dreams, anxieties, and hopes. They feel larger, fuller, and stronger.

There is an interesting paradox here. Although men do have a deeply ingrained resistance to yielding power and authority to a woman, it is much easier for them to accept leadership from women than from other men, provided there is a sense of comfort and trust. A woman's accepting attitude allows a man's most vulnerable concerns to surface. With another man, unless he is an exceptionally close friend, such intimacy is blocked by a sense of competition or a fear of being put down. Men who have this kind of relationship with a woman feel that she knows them in a way no one else does. And they're usually correct in this assumption.

## *The Partner*

Kelly and Matt are celebrating their radio station's first month in the black. They purchased the mountain-region FM station just eight months ago. At the time, it was deeply in the red owing to poor management. Kelly and Matt changed the format to country music and have been steadily winning both listeners and advertisers.

Kelly, 36, began her career in radio news and eventually became a well-known television reporter in a large city. She was abruptly fired from the TV station two years ago after an ownership change. Matt, 34, was sales manager of the same station. They married just a few months after they met.

"Women who are well known for one reason or another often get a lot of attention from men, but most of them do not have the best motives," says Kelly. "They want to be seen with you or to be able to say they went to bed with the woman on Channel 9 news. Matt and I had a good understanding of each other right from the start. Being in the same business gives us a real advantage."

They had often talked about getting out of the urban rat race and moving to the country, and had attended several TV and radio conventions to research the ins and outs of station ownership. When Kelly was fired, they decided to realize their dream.

Kelly and Matt now work literally side by side at the tiny offices of the radio station. They each do shifts as deejays, and serve as cohosts on the Sunday talk and public-affairs shows. Matt heads the sales force of three, with Kelly counting as perhaps his most devoted salesperson. "Boy, do I rely on him for tips on how to sell," Kelly says with a smile.

"Of course, like any couple who decide to go into business together," says Matt, "we were worried about whether it might put too much of a strain on our marriage. But so far, we're having a ball. We're up here in the gorgeous mountains, making it financially, and running it almost as a mom-and-pop operation.

"I couldn't be happier, having someone who loves me as my business partner," Matt describes. "We're partners day and night. It's drawing us closer and closer, finding together what works and what doesn't work at the station. We're learning as we go how to advise and support each other, how to balance our strengths and weaknesses to be a good team. Her enthusiasm really inspires me. When I'm getting uptight, she sees that, gives me a hug, and we talk it out."

Says Kelly, "One piece of advice I'd give other couples who are thinking about going into business together is to make a deal not to talk business when you get home at night. Matt and I were getting burned out after the first few months, starting to get testy with each other. Now, we try to relax at home and get our minds off the station. Because if our free time doesn't replenish us and our marriage falls apart, this great life we have is going to be destroyed."

*Developing Mutual Support.* The partnership and mutuality that exist between Kelly and Matt have broadened their views regarding the rewards of relationship. Their marriage illustrates the way the elimination of sex-role differences or inequalities leads not to a colorless sameness, but instead to a richer and more vibrant union.

Their marriage depicts a new kind of marital team that seems more prevalent today. Whether it is a small radio station or a large hamburger stand, the fundamental issues are the same. In this entrepreneurial era, scores of men and women want to combine a love relationship with a career partnership. They believe the most exciting and stimulating relationship is one in which togetherness—at work and at home—enhances their love.

## The Achiever

Tracy, 28, is a woman who seems to live at double speed. Vibrant and enthusiastic, she is in constant motion. Tracy grew up in the midst of the hustle and bustle of New York City's garment district. Her mother was a seamstress in a clothing factory, and her father, who fled Poland during the war, made a modest living as a clothing wholesaler.

Tracy started work in the fashion industry while she was still in high school, designing inexpensive copies of designer clothing. When she was 24, her original designs won the backing of an investor. She launched, on a small scale, her own line of moderately priced career clothing for women. Her firm now employs twenty-five people and her salespeople have landed several large accounts with department store chains.

"I admit I was envious of Tracy's success and drive for a long time," confides Gordon, 25, her boyfriend of three years. "I would make little digs at her for being obsessed with making money and interrupt her when she started telling me about the latest deal she had made. I even gave her a lot of grief about the misdirected ambitions of the 'new career woman' her line of clothes is marketed for. It took me a long time to catch on to the fact that I was actually jealous of her phenomenal ease in the business world."

Until several years ago, Tracy felt insecure about her intelligence because she hadn't attended college. Over time, she overcame her insecurity and fear of people by learning how to talk and work with all kinds of men and women she encountered in the business world. She learned that self-esteem derives from action and deed, and she developed a positive, enthusiastic, direct style of doing business that, together with her stylish, well-made clothes, proved a terrific formula for success.

Tracy met Gordon when he came up to complain that her stereo was too loud—he was her new downstairs neighbor. She invited him in for a cup of tea and, seeing he was in a grouchy mood, asked him what, besides her loud music, was wrong. What was wrong, he said with a frustrated sigh, was that he was hassled at work.

In the next few months, they invited each other over for dinner occasionally, and their friendship slowly blossomed into a romance, although Gordon had moments of discomfort. "Here you are, head of your own company," Gordon would say a bit ruefully, "and I'm still trying to figure out what I want to do with my life."

Gordon was bright and his ideas in his job as a marketing associate in an advertising agency were creative, but he lacked the social skills, outgoing personality, and perceptiveness about people that make the kind of team player who prevails in a collaborative type of business such as marketing. In meetings, when he became frustrated trying to put across his ideas, he often got defensive, which invariably proved self-defeating. He would sense a decided distance growing between himself and his coworkers, but he didn't know how to reverse the process.

Soon after he met Tracy, he began taking business classes at night. "I knew he was trying to find himself, and that was fine by me," recalls Tracy. "My work is very narrow, and I loved hearing about all the interesting courses he was taking. He shared his books with me and took me to lectures at the university. For me, it was like getting some of the college experience I missed out on."

Tracy's relationship with Gordon could have been spoiled by jealousy and competition. Instead, Tracy smartly realized that Gordon was secretly envious of her business success, and decided she was confident enough in herself and what she was doing to not get thrown by his occasional digs.

"If I took his frustration personally, we could have fought all the time and broken up. I didn't give him any advice, because he didn't ask for it, not until much later." Nor did Tracy suppress her enthusiasm for her work simply because of Gordon's frustration in his own career. "I figure we're two very different people, and we both need to respect and accept each other for what we are. I set that model from the start, and more than anything else, that's what kept us together."

Over time, by being around Tracy, Gordon began to polish his own interpersonal skills. He began to ask her how she handled a difficult negotiation or a problem employee. Tracy's energy and belief in the possibility of success was infectious. Her love for him, the example she set as an unpretentious, direct businessperson, and her on-target advice to him about how to deal adeptly with office politics combined to bolster his confidence. Gordon renewed his commitment to his career, has been promoted, and, more important, is enjoying his work.

"Tracy was a real inspiration to me, when I think back over it," he says. "She set an example for me of how to play the game and still be yourself. Without my even realizing it, she was a sort of mentor to me. And that's the key thing—she never pushed me or criticized me."

*Breaking Old Patterns.* By sharing her experience, savvy, and enthusiasm, Tracy was a true and loving inspiration to Gordon. He experienced something unexpected with a woman—he found he could let go of the need to be the one with all the answers and, in the process, became stronger and more effective.

There are many bright and successful women today who are often reluctant to fully realize their capacity to encourage and even lead. Tracy was a mentor to Gordon, and he grew to truly cherish her.

If you find yourself in this kind of relationship, don't be shy about saying and doing what feels right for you. It is perfectly acceptable to break patterns and shatter old role expectations. Men don't always have to be the leaders.

## The Adviser

Angelo and Diane met three years ago at a charity event sponsored by a singles organization. Diane, 31, is an account executive for an advertising agency. Angelo, 30, is a partner in an executive search agency. They are planning to get married in the coming year. That they're together at all is "nothing short of a miracle," says Diane, "considering our problems at the beginning."

When they met, Angelo had just left a big executive search firm to go into partnership with another recruiter from the company. "I wanted to get out of that corporate mentality and do business my own way," recalls Angelo. "My boss was always on me trying to make me conform to the corporate style. I figured I would probably have to work longer hours running my own firm, but I could make my own rules and, of course, make a lot more money if we really hustled."

"I didn't take him seriously for the first few months," says Diane. "He was this cute, aggressive guy. He was fun to go to the movies with and took me places I'd never been, like to the racetrack for the first time, but he was so macho.

"He'd complain about the 'corporate jerks' he had to deal with all the time, but when I would make a suggestion about how to deal with the various people, he'd get really defensive. I could see why he had problems in his work—he's impulsive and can be too direct with people, abrupt, even rude, and that kind of behavior doesn't close deals. I know—I sell to all kinds of people. If you're in sales, you have to be extremely professional. You have to be sensitive to people's personalities and know how to handle their little quirks.

"Although he's got a great heart and can be very sweet and fun to be with, Angelo was caught up in being right all the time, even with me. He was also extremely jealous and possessive, which I couldn't understand. We were always arguing. He would try to pick fights with me if I couldn't see him because I had to work late or had other plans.

"I finally asked him why he was calling me all the time if he obviously wanted some kind of old-fashioned girlfriend he could control and dominate. What he said really surprised me. He said he was crazy about me because I was so smart and making it out there on my own in the business world. He said he admired and respected me, particularly for the way I got along so well with people. 'You make everybody feel good, Diane.'

"I told him I was willing to see if we could make it as a couple only if he would make a real effort to be less argumentative and controlling with me—that a relationship wasn't about winning, but about respecting each other's opinions and getting along together. Once I made a commitment to him, he made the effort."

Diane has become a powerful positive influence on Angelo. She is extremely perceptive about him and knows his weak points as well as his strengths. Diane is insightful, sensitive, and people-oriented, and in the last several years she has become an invaluable ally and adviser to Angelo, helping him develop people skills that not only boost his career success, but also have made him a more sensitive companion.

"Diane's done a lot for me," Angelo says. "She gives me wisdom and love combined with a lot of business smarts. She knows me like a book, and I've come to really trust her feedback. I used to be very combative, but she's helped me see that in the business we're in, I don't win unless everybody wins."

*Trusting Your Strengths.* Luckily, Angelo was able to appreciate the special qualities Diane possessed. Like so many men today, Angelo was more than willing to trade in outmoded and self-defeating beliefs about women for a more fulfilling relationship.

Whenever a woman presents herself in this way to a man, there is a strong likelihood of his being defensive in the beginning. It is not easy for men to shift roles, no matter how much they would like to. When a woman trusts herself and her own intentions, she will not come across as being negative or competitive. But when she is unsure of herself and questions her confidence, there is the danger that the man will think she is putting him down or trying to prove herself.

## Allowing Yourself to Lead

As we've described, men do not speak openly about their wish for or attraction to women who can inspire, motivate, and lead them. In the cases we have included, however, you can see the impact such women have on men and the sense of appreciation and gratitude they generate. But male receptivity to this kind of influence is, at best, subtle.

In order to stimulate this wish in men, you must

act on the assumption that it exists in all men. There are exceptions, but they are rare. Some men will accept your support and encouragement only sporadically. Others will appreciate it as an ongoing part of your shared experience. But remember first and foremost that men do want your ideas and inspiration.

Exploring the possibility of enhanced understanding and friendship between men and women requires the setting aside of relationship fantasies, as discussed in the previous chapter. It also requires you to risk the fullest expression of yourself, meaning that you don't pose, pretend, or hide your true strengths or insights. Even if a man doesn't ask, you can share them with him. This doesn't mean assaulting him with your knowledge and intuition if he's not receptive. It might be helpful to wait until there are warm, loving feelings between you before you tell him your ideas.

Often a woman is afraid to be so direct or straightforward with a man, for fear he'll be put off by her behavior. Be sensitive to timing and his receptivity, but be assertive. Take the initiative to learn more about the goals that drive him in his work life and the dreams and fantasies he may have about his life outside of a career. Take a sincere interest. What may seem boring initially will take on added interest when you see it from his point of view. So often in marriage concerns or issues keep coming up repeatedly, yet husbands and wives do not take the time to really learn what they are about. Don't fall into this trap. A sense of shared ambitions and partnership is a powerful adhesive in the best marriages. Working side by side to make your dreams a reality can be enriching for both of you.

As you begin striving together toward shared goals, and as you take the risk to give him guidance, you will discover new facets of each other's personalities. He will find in you a confidante and life mate who fulfills his secret hopes. You will find a new level of intimacy that is far deeper than you thought possible. As you give to each other, a synergy more vibrant than the sum of your separate selves will propel your union to greater levels of fulfillment.

# CHAPTER TEN

# Arousing a Man's Passion and Desire

Lust, chemistry, the intrigue of the romantic quest—these are the timeless ingredients of passion and desire. There are probably no more wonderfully complex yet potentially troublesome forces between men and women than those involving passion and desire. In their fullest expression, love and sexual desire fuse into a passionate bond. But passion is more than just sexual desire; it is also characterized by the release of the powerful emotions of love, hate, and rage, of lust, zeal, jealousy, possessiveness. Passion encompasses the myriad expressions of aliveness and intensity in a relationship.

When it is present, passion makes us feel more alive and vibrant. In its absence, we feel flat, bored, and uninterested. Passion is a way of responding to life, to ideas, to people, and, of course, to lovers. Passion always involves personal risk, revealing our feelings in as fervent and unrestricted a manner as possible. People who are passionate wish to like life to the fullest. They look for what is new, what is unexpected, and what is exciting and allow themselves to respond without inhibition.

As we grow older, we all become more cautious and conservative in how we act and react. But we retain vivid memories of those times in our lives when we felt less encumbered by expectations and restraints, when we were more childlike and spontaneous. We all secretly desire to reexperience feeling free and uninhibited. This is why romantic love is so alluring—for most of us it provides a context for aliveness, excitement, and passion. Indeed, most people, when they describe how they feel in the early weeks of a relationship, talk about how "alive" they feel. Actually, what they are experiencing is a resurgence of youthful emotions that lie dormant because as mature adults we tend to become more controlled and rational. Because it is so easy to lose our capacity for self-generating these wonderful states of being, we are drawn to those who can stimulate and free them in us. For this reason, women who arouse passion and desire are magnets for men.

Feeling alive comes about when we allow ourselves to feel peak emotions by letting go of restraints, inhibitions, prohibitions. As desirable as that sounds, there are men and women who are afraid of excitement and the intensity of passion both within themselves and within their mates. They fear it will result in a loss of control and even invite danger, for to experience passion is also to feel off-guard. This is why our mates, even though they love us, may at times inadvertently suppress our childlike enthusiasm, joy, and passion.

Most of us find passion and excitement in the realm of sexuality. It is in this domain that we can feel lust, desire, cravings, and the delicious anticipation of sexual union and release. But accompanying these delights are darker emotions that are frightening for so many of us—a fear which invariably blunts our capacity for passionate expressions. To love another person is also to experience moments of insecurity, anger, jealousy, and possessiveness. These are normal companions to the passionate bond.

Passion and sexual desire are present in the beginning of virtually all love affairs. The question that plagues most couples is whether the capacity to arouse and stimulate our mates to emotional heights can endure over time. Is it possible to maintain a sense of aliveness in a long-term relationship? In the beginning, novelty and freshness are sufficient to spark passion and desire in both partners. As they become familiar with each other, that spark must be replaced with the knowledge of how to consciously generate passionate feelings through certain attitudes and behaviors.

## The Passionate Woman

Down through the ages, men have foolishly suppressed and controlled the very qualities in women that they desire. The woman who was vital, sexual, and spontaneous and had a joyous sense of herself was viewed with caution by men. At some primitive level, men felt they could not control her—they wanted a more passive mate. But this is changing. Men are less threatened by giving up control and more inclined to relish women who are confident and uninhibited.

Today, more than ever, millions of women are exploring their capacity for passion, excitement, and desire in any area they choose. Women are finding passion at work, they are reaching a new level of uninhibited sexuality, and they are discovering the excitement inherent in any situation involving personal risk.

A common misconception about passion is that it

is only for the few that it is a lifelong way of being—it is only for "passionate people." Many people believe their basic personality is so fixed, so incapable of change, that it is almost impossible to create a dramatically enhanced relationship between themselves and their lovers. This is not true. It is one of the great myths of love that you can't do anything of any real significance to influence the expression, intensity, or longevity of passion and desire. Passion can be enhanced and rekindled—first by understanding how men and women differ in regard to love and desire, then by attuning your behavior to these natural laws.

## How Men Respond to Passion

Many women sincerely believe that the typical man is wary of the woman who is so comfortable with herself that she allows her emotions to emerge full-blown and uncensored. Regardless of how tentatively a man initially responds to a woman's intense and energetic expressions of enthusiasm, delight, and joy, rest assured he secretly loves it.

Men, especially driven career types, find that the woman who can share her passion with him provides more than just relief—she is rejuvenating and revitalizing. Popular wisdom has it that men want women who are docile and accommodating. They don't. The woman who is unafraid to be herself, to express her emotions, to assert her aliveness, is welcomed by men for a very particular reason. Most men are overly preoccupied with their work, or even burned out, and they need a counterbalance. As we have noted before, the antidote for such men is play rather than relaxation. This is what they seek with friends, and they also love to find it with the woman in their life. Men need and want to experience the aliveness that many women bring to a relationship.

Even the darker manifestations of passion, such as anger, jealousy, and possessiveness, serve to enliven relationships. It is one of the great myths of marriage that harmony and peace are always to be strived for. Sometimes the very opposite is what is needed for the relationship. When mild instability is the by-product of other powerful emotions, it can actually serve to revitalize a relationship. For example, jealousy, when unchecked, tends to be corrosive and even destructive between a man and a woman. However, one of the best antidotes to a taken-for-granted style of marriage may be small doses of jealousy. When a man or woman assumes their mate will be faithful regardless of the quality of the relationship, creating an element of doubt is often precisely what is needed to shock him or her into taking a fresh look. We are not suggesting that you set up contrived situations—we are merely noting small benefits from an emotion that is typically seen as negative.

Anger too may serve as a positive element at times. Discharging anger is often necessary as a prerequisite for the expression of warmth, love, and sexuality. That is why couples will often have very passionate lovemaking after a fight; it is as though a dam has been broken. Again, we are not suggesting you pick fights with a man, just that you not be so fearful of encounters that involve anger. Heated exchanges are often necessary and can evolve from a negative beginning to an intense and passionate conclusion.

## The Lover

Rhonda, 30, and Jeff, 32, have been married for just over two years. She is an administrative assistant in a mortgage firm, and he is an electrician. They met at a mutual friend's wedding and got married themselves four months later.

Rhonda describes their sex life today as "getting better all the time." It wasn't always so. Jeff was originally attracted to Rhonda because of her good-natured disposition and her easy, fun-loving attitude. She, in turn, was attracted to his boisterous personality, bedrock values, and attitude toward life, which is "work hard and play hard."

Rhonda had had only two lovers before she married Jeff; he had had a few casual relationships and a few serious ones. Rhonda had never felt particularly sexually desirable; she was insecure about her small breasts and wasn't comfortable being nude in front of Jeff. In addition, although she genuinely enjoyed sex, she was somewhat inhibited about expressing her passion. Her sexual style, overall, was affectionate but quiet and passive.

Jeff's sexual style was less inhibited—he was eager to experiment. But he sensed his wife's modesty and shyness, and this, in turn, inhibited him. She would change into her nightgown in the bathroom, and always insist on having the lights off when they made love. At first, when he tried to dispel her modesty by lightly teasing her about it, she would laugh too, and hug and kiss him affectionately as a way of reassuring him and changing the subject. But as time went on, unspoken resentment grew on both sides.

One night, he forced the issue by suddenly switching on the light when she pulled off her nightgown in bed as they began to make love. Their unspoken frustrations were finally put into words—an angry exchange of accusations about their sex life. Afterward, they lay in bed, not touching, not sleeping, staring at the ceiling feeling resentful and guilty, wondering, "Is this the way it's always going to be?"

In the months afterward, their lovemaking fell into a predictable routine accompanied at times by a sense of strain and tension. They both remember the moment at a friend's party when somebody told a dirty joke and they stood there, unable to laugh along with everyone else, unable to look at each other. Their sex life had become so infused with conflict and disappointment that even the mention of sex made them uncomfortable.

After so many months of estrangement, they both decided a vacation might help. Coming back from a warm and close evening out, Rhonda decided to try to break her own behavior pattern. "I believed Jeff loved me, was loyal and faithful even during this rough period. I guess I knew I had to take some kind of chance, to do something different." Late that night they took a dip in the Jacuzzi together and Rhonda began to caress him in ways she had never tried before. Afterward, in their room, Rhonda finally allowed herself to let go of her inhibitions and enjoy the best lovemaking they had ever had.

Happily, over time, as Rhonda grew to trust in Jeff's love for her, his desire for her, and his appreciation of her slender body, she became interested in making that aspect of their marriage as fulfilling and rewarding as all its other aspects. She began reading articles on sex in women's magazines and purchased several books on sexual techniques, then began trying out those techniques on her husband, to his delight.

Whereas in the early days of their marriage she had looked at sex as an expression of her affection for her husband, she now began to view it as a uniquely enjoyable advantage of being married, not overburdening it with meaning. She took equal responsibility for making sure they didn't fall into boring routines, seducing him at unexpected times and places, even one memorable day on a hike through a secluded meadow. She enjoys setting the stage for sex, with playful physical affection, music, even necking in the living room as they watch television.

Very wisely, Rhonda doesn't view sex as a validation of her worth or as a duty—she lets her husband know when she's really not interested, but allows him to take turns seducing her in the role of active lover. Rhonda has blossomed sexually as a result of her courage to take risks as well as Jeff's patience and love. His reward is that the woman he loves has become a passionate sexual partner.

## *The Seductress*

After ten years of marriage, Brenda, 31, felt a growing secret resentment against her husband, Brian, 34. The problem was their sex life. "He peaked sexually before our first child was born, it seems. I know that I often put him off when our two kids were babies—I was too exhausted or distracted most of the time. But now that the kids are five and six, it seems I'm very interested in sex again, but he isn't. If he turns to me once a week to make love, it's a lot, and even then, it's over with very quickly and not exciting. And we used to be such great lovers."

Brenda possesses a lively and warm personality. She has continued to work as a high school administrator throughout their marriage. Brian is co-owner of a drugstore. Overall, they're an involved and successful two-income family, sharing household and child-care responsibilities flexibly and equally. But Brenda was starting to question the friendship and partnership that she and her husband had worked so hard to develop within their marriage.

"Maybe that's why our sex life is so dead—we've become best friends, and that's killed the passion. I don't want to walk away from what we have, but giving up on sex seems too high a price to pay for staying married."

In listening to Brenda, it became clear that she was blaming Brian for not initiating sex more often and for not giving her the exciting sex life she was interested in now that their children were no longer infants. She had fallen into a passive attitude and, what's more, a resentful, blaming one.

Although she had not communicated her dissatisfaction to him in words, she no doubt was doing so with her body language, moods, and frustrated sighs before, during, and after their sexual interactions. Her husband had come to interpret her signals as a decided lack of desire for him. Put off by what he sensed as rejection and as disappointment in him as a lover, he initiated sex infrequently and reached orgasm as quickly as possible. She believed he had lost his desire and skills as a lover; he felt she didn't desire him, so he didn't try to be a good lover. They were in a stalemate.

Brenda felt she shouldn't have to make the first move to put the sexual passion back into her marriage. "I am not going to become one of those women who greets her husband at the door dressed in a negligee—that's really not me." But she did come to understand that in order to break the stalemate between her and her husband and dissolve the inhibitions that had developed between them, she had to stop blaming him, set aside her resentment, and begin showing him her interest and receptivity. If she wanted to effect change, it was she who had to set change in motion.

Brenda began by showing Brian more physical affection—massaging his neck, holding his hand as they sat at the dinner table after supper, kissing him lightly at unexpected moments. She followed this with increased physical closeness in bed, lying close to him and stroking his body affectionately. And she began to initiate sex more often, beginning with affectionate kissing, embracing, and stroking, and followed with encouraging, tender lovemaking.

As she communicated her interest, appreciation, and passion to Brian, he began to trust in her desire for him, and responded with increasing enthusiasm. Over a period of months, their sex life became better than either of them had imagined it could be, with a high level of invention. Now Brenda says, "I can be in the middle of a meeting at work and suddenly think about what we did in bed the night before and get chills down my spine. We're trying new things with each other, not just positions but different moods, styles, and attitudes, even to the point of playing out some of our fantasies in little dramas."

Their revitalized sexual life has had a delightful and unexpected effect on the rest of their marriage. They've rediscovered a sense of playfulness, humor, and aliveness that has increased their joy in each other.

## Stimulating Desire in Men

Nothing shuts down romantic and sexual desire in a man more quickly or dramatically than performance anxieties. The woman who is overly graphic and explicit in describing what she wants sexually or who too aggressively initiates sexual contact with a man may run the risk of arousing anxiety, not passion. Men are drawn to women who express interest and receptivity, yet men still feel some need to be in control. Men need to experience a sense of relaxation and confidence, and they often find this when they make that first move.

Creating relaxation in a man is related to a sensitivity to timing and to specific demands or pressures. Men won't tell you they need this sensitivity, for they either aren't fully conscious of the need or are ashamed to admit it.

There certainly is nothing wrong with a woman's being bold or assertive. You, obviously, have every right to express and go after what you want. The problem, however, is that there may be some negative consequences if you overlook the possibility that a man may have doubts about his ability to perform. Remember, for men relaxation is an essential prerequisite to a man's erection and always precedes a state of sexual excitement. Although you are not responsible for his state of well-being, your sensitivity to his ease and comfort will be rewarded by his feeling free and sexy.

When do men get turned on? Why does it occur at seemingly odd times? Have you ever been busy and preoccupied when a man unexpectedly becomes amorous? Let a woman be getting dressed, be reading, or be otherwise occupied, and all of a sudden, as if some alarm has been triggered, the man seems compelled to move toward her in a tactile and sexy way. Sound familiar? No, he is not trying his best to be terminally annoying. Rather, he senses a woman's momentary lack of interest, which creates an atmosphere in which he feels comfortable because he is in control as he attempts to seduce.

Conversely, if a man is given too much sex for too long a time, he gradually will tend to become complacent, lose contact with his feelings of passion, even take the woman's desire for him for granted. It's not that he doesn't appreciate or value this gift of love, it's just that when it's given too much, the man loses the excitement attached to it and comes simply to expect it.

The antidote to this neutral state of affairs requires a specific course of remedial action. And it is here that many women make a fundamental mistake. They move toward the man too assertively rather than behaving in a way that causes him to move toward her.

Women who have rich and rewarding sexual relationships with men understand the need never to be totally constant with a man. Unfortunately, "wanting" or "longing" is much more intense a feeling than "having," and men need to be put in touch with such feelings occasionally to arouse their passion.

Don't be afraid to create a little suspense and intrigue. Don't hang on his every whim or try to please him all the time. This gets boring to men. Don't be available all the time. Let him wonder about your love and desire for him occasionally. This won't endanger your relationship, it will cause him to be more respectful, attentive, and interested. Don't be overly romantic or always pushing him to be—it's the quickest way to kill a man's romantic wishes. You may get the flowers but you certainly won't get the feelings. Remember, by creating reminders of your separate identity and desires, you will maintain the psychological space that will motivate him to move toward you.

Some of you may be saying, "Well, all of this sounds like game-playing, and I don't want to have to do that." You are right—it *is* a game, and, when played with sensitivity, a delightful one for both women and men. But "game" does not mean manipulation. While understanding, partnership, and friendship are dimensions of a relationship that do not involve strategy, passion is and always has been a game. Arousing and sustaining romance and passion in a man requires understanding how men operate and being willing to put your knowledge into action. You may choose not to play that game, but you will be missing out on a lot of enjoyment and fulfillment.

Women who can periodically ration their needs for romance and learn how to build and sustain mild levels of uncertainty, distance, and tension in a man get much more from men in the long run. Subtle behavior changes will result in a man's becoming more loving, attentive, and passionate.

Stimulating desire in a man is not a verbal process. Don't announce what you are doing—just do it. Being assertive and adventuresome in this way is not a threat to your love but rather an exhilarating dance that enhances the love relationship.

## Becoming a Sexual Person

First, you need to assign prominence and priority to sexuality in your life. In order to experience passion and desire, you have to learn how to set aside daily troubles and anxieties.

Sexuality has to be a source of real pleasure for you, not merely a way to validate your worth and desirability or to take care of his needs so he won't stray. Too many women and men look upon their sexual relationship only as a way to affirm their love or to assure themselves of their mates' fidelity. Concerns such as these, while understandable, do not lend themselves to actions that stimulate desire or playfulness.

You need to enjoy sex, and your enjoyment has to be communicated to your partner. While it's true that men can be cautious with women who are overly aggressive, in general they desire women who are passionate and sexual. Ask yourself whether you really like sex, or whether there are areas of subtle sexual discomfort or disinterest. Search within and get in touch with the various aspects of your unique sexuality. Often, merely acknowledging areas of shyness or discomfort will enable you to experiment and overcome such inhibitions.

What about the timing of sexual overtures? Neither men nor women are always in the mood. Just as you may find it annoying if a man approaches you when you are busy, he feels the same way when he is busy. Unfortunately, many couples allow the logistics and demands of day-to-day life to dominate their time and think of sex only when everything else has been taken care of. This is just when they're likely to be exhausted or worn out. Women are most responsive to sex when they are relaxed, and so too are men. And like women, men want some anticipation, teasing, or seduction. They may not say they want it, but it's what works!

How do we find out what a mate likes sexually? Couples tend to fall into predictable sexual routines and tired assumptions. Too often men and women do what they think is sexy and tantalizing, rather than finding out, by trial and error, what really turns their lover on. Are you aware of what your mate feels and likes? Are you observant and sensitive to his cues as to what he enjoys? Do you let him know with words or your body language what stimulates your passion, or do you fall into the trap of thinking he should be able to read your mind?

## How Men Feel About Romance

Imagine for a moment a familiar scenario. A woman and man meet. Both feel strong interest and attraction. He makes the initial move and begins pursuing her. In spite of fearing he may be revealing his desire for her too soon, he brings her flowers for that first wonderful lazy day they spend together having a picnic in the country.

He phones nearly every day and makes it clear he wants to spend a lot of time with her. He tries not to call too frequently or appear too needy and thus risk pushing her away with his strongly felt interest. He becomes moody when he is at her house and she gets a phone call and talks cheerfully and animatedly—he is sure she's talking to another man. He feels vaguely jealous, possessive, and, he knows, inappropriately territorial. He cannot help himself—he wants her and pushes on, determined to win her love.

It may be unclear to him, perhaps because of his own insecurities, that she is also beginning to feel loving toward him. She thinks his slight awkwardness and signs of shy insecurity are endearing and refreshing. She loves their quiet walks at dusk along the beach, the intimate dinners he cooks for her, and all his sweet beguiling gestures that let her know he cares.

Finally, she tells him she cares for him, too. She whispers "I love you" for the first time in an especially passionate peak of lovemaking. Over breakfast the next day, she tells him she meant what she said the night before: "I love you." But instead of joy on his part, this marks the onset of what seems to her his slow withdrawal.

As you will remember, a man feels romantic desire and expresses it most openly when he is actively striving to capture a woman's heart—when he is pulling her toward attachment. As long as she is distant, he will pursue: his desire to secure their bond is what motivates his chase. Then she acknowledges her love at the height of his pursuit. She believes that her commitment and the reassurance it conveys will free him to even greater heights of passion and desire. But it is at precisely this juncture that his romantic fervor may begin to wane. Oddly, he may cease the very behavior that won her love. Why?

When a woman affirms her love, she closes the distance between herself and her lover. He feels that he has won her love—they are united, bonded. He feels relieved, secure. His romantic chase has succeeded and he no longer feels a need to try to win her love—she has confirmed that he has won it. His seeming to take her love for granted makes her feel confused, disappointed, and angry, for she believes his romantic behavior should not only continue but reach new levels of intensity, since she has become so willing and eager to give to him.

At this point you may be wondering, "So what about enduring romantic passion in a man? Is there any hope, or are we just supposed to relish those early weeks or months, then resign ourselves to a union that is devoid of those magical feelings of romantic love?" Not only is there hope, but, in many ways, men are much more predictable and more receptive to influence than you might imagine. The secret is in understanding men and being willing to turn that knowledge into action.

Remember, for a woman, romance and an expression of her passions are often associated with trusting a man and feeling close to him. In this state she feels the least amount of psychological tension and conflict, making her freer and more relaxed. Men operate on a different dynamic. Their feelings of romantic passion are linked, at some level, to the tantalizing effect of uncertainty as to whether she truly cares for him.

As you will remember from our discussion of the Polarity Factor and how it explains men in love relationships, a man is most actively attentive when he is moving toward the woman and attempting to form an attachment with her. As he gets closer and more certain of her love, his chase begins to slow down.

What we are saying is that men respond positively to unlimited amounts of trust, friendship, understanding, and partnership, but they can handle romance only sporadically. They become uncomfortable with expressions of romance when they are too frequent or intense. It is as though they become satiated. But after a period of no romance, a yearning for it will build up within the man, once again reviving his interest in it.

Are we suggesting that you become manipulative and act hard to get in order to arouse a man to greater heights of passion? No. We simply want you to understand how men really are, and realize that a little distance is good for a relationship. When you occasionally want to do things by yourself, don't worry about the effect your not being available will have on him. When you take care of your own needs and desires, you will, as a side benefit, probably stimulate romantic behavior in him.

## A Passion for Life

You may believe that the ability to be passionate is a personality trait you're either born with or not; the fact is, passion can be learned. It is not something in and of itself, it is a fuller, enhanced expression of the emotions we all possess. We are all capable of feeling passion and having a passionate response to the world around us.

Everyone is capable of aliveness, which, of course, is what passion is all about. It is uninhibitedly experiencing and expressing our feelings in their fullest intensity. As we have noted, the emotions involved in passion originate in childhood. Passionate individuals are those who either have not allowed adult prohibitions to overly constrict them or have taken stock of the ways in which they have been contained and then chosen to do something about it.

## The Free Spirit

Laura and Max have been married for seven years. Max, 35, is a dentist. Laura, 33, has a master's degree in nursing and has worked in nuclear medicine for years. Their marriage had been good and they had a small circle of friends, mostly neighbors or people they knew from work. They had enjoyed renovating the rambling old house they'd purchased and looked forward to their twice-yearly vacations, when they'd load camping gear into their car and head off to a national park in a state they'd never been to before.

Then, two years ago, Laura began to feel stagnated, both in her career and in her life in general. She had gone right from college to graduate school and then to work. She had always been very achievement-oriented, anxious to build a career and a secure financial base. For years she had worked long, hard hours at the hospital, on the typical nursing schedule that rotates constantly, so that she could not sign up for classes or join groups in her free time. She found herself becoming restless to try new things, to have a life that involved more than just working and her marriage. She decided to take the chance.

With her husband's encouragement, Laura cut back her nursing schedule to two days a week, transferring to a research project that guaranteed a regular swing-shift schedule. Laura is now searching to find her passion in life. She is in flux and uncertain of the direction she's going, but is energized rather than depressed by her search. Always interested in art, she is working on various projects—writing and illustrating a children's book, sketching designs for furniture, and investigating various ideas for going into business for herself.

At this point, Laura is experimenting and researching—she's taking a vacation from her many years of income- and achievement-oriented activities. "I have to remind myself often that I don't have to prove myself or push myself into a new career right away. Sometimes I worry that I'm just being a dilettante right now, but that's okay, too. In fact, my days are wonderfully exciting. I've met so many new, interesting people and am constantly getting energized by them."

Laura's new zest for life has been contagious. Says her husband, "Laura's passion and enthusiasm, her willingness to try new things and take risks, has opened up our life incredibly. She's always bringing home interesting people to dinner. We've gotten active in the art scene, going to openings and collecting art in a small way, and we have a very stimulating new circle of friends.

"Our home is buzzing and alive all the time with people, music, and ideas. It's a very open, encouraging environment for us all. Laura's vibrance and unpredictability make her a continuing and intriguing challenge to me."

# Becoming Passionate

We conceal passion and desire for two basic reasons. The first has to do with vulnerability. Our feelings are private, while our words and behavior are more public. When we are emotionally open we may feel naked, even dangerously exposed. If we have concerns about being "seen" by our mates, we may hide our passion to prevent feeling quite so vulnerable.

The second reason we may hide passion and desire concerns intensity. Some people interpret high levels of emotional intensity as dangerous whether the feelings are positive or negative. We all have comfort zones defining which emotions are acceptable and which are not. Anything outside a comfortable range of intensity can, for some, trigger anxiety and fear over loss of control. The solution is to dampen and hide passion, for such feelings typically arouse a sense of danger.

If there are difficulties in a relationship, passion is the first thing to vanish and the last to come back even after the problem has been solved. More specifically, passion may be hidden when:

We are hurt.
We are disappointed.
We are feeling angry and punitive.
We accumulate hidden resentments.
We don't trust our mate's love.
We are unsure of how attractive we are to our mate.
We feel guilty.
We are anxious and unsure of ourselves and hence are not relaxed.

These feelings can have a cumulative negative effect that ultimately erodes comfort and trust in a relationship. How then do you learn to become aware of and let go of these destructive forces? Here are some suggestions.

**LETTING GO OF OLD ATTITUDES.** Some people carry old, largely unconscious attitudes with them into current relationships. These attitudes vividly color their intimate dealings with another person and set the limits of passion in the relationship. For example, if expressing anger was not a comfortable part of your childhood and was associated in your mind with feeling out of control, you probably find it difficult to reveal negative emotions to your mate.

Old attitudes about sex also affect how passions are expressed. Was sex dirty, wrong, bad in the past? If so, there are probably vestiges of such feelings that may still be operative. Were you taught that if you liked sex a lot you were probably "oversexed"? Or that it is wrong to give a man any sort of sexual encouragement because you are then responsible for his arousal and must carry through with the act? Perhaps you were led to believe "normal" women have lots of orgasms very easily or that "passionate" women are always in the mood irrespective of fatigue, children, or other preoccupations.

Take a look at your old notions and see how they influence your comfort in passionate expression. Recognize that some may be anachronistic and totally unrelated to who you are and how you feel today.

**RELEASING HIDDEN RESENTMENT.** Unexpressed anger always constricts passion. A good rule of thumb is that if it is important enough, get angry. Stick up for yourself; get it out in the open and keep it that way until it is resolved. If the anger is from the past, try to finish it. If it's related to an ongoing situation, let your feelings be known clearly and come up with some specific solutions to the problem.

If the annoyance or irritation is not important enough to get angry about, then let it go. Releasing anger is not a coward's way out, for in any relationship there are countless minor conflicts that we must learn simply to pass off, for there is nothing constructive we can do about them. To stay mad about the little things is destructive and self-defeating, for it only results in our feeling less alive and less loving toward our partner.

**ENHANCING SELF-ESTEEM.** We hide things about ourselves we believe to be dangerous and expose things we feel are safe and will be accepted and approved. Look for judgments you've made about yourself that you've assumed your mate would make too, even though you haven't ever clearly checked them out. Being more "alive" is simply being more yourself. It is showing more of your feelings, and more directly. It is trusting and expressing your thoughts and observations. In short, it is assuming that you are worth being loved.

First of all, how do you present yourself to your mate? Are you hiding, wearing disguises? How much of yourself do you really allow him to see? Most of us have secret fears and doubts about our sexual desirability.

When we feel inhibited or self-conscious, it's usually because we feel we're not enough—not attractive enough, not free enough, not lovable enough. Don't let negative self-doubts become facts. Don't allow yourself to hide behind shyness or self-consciousness. When people hide behind their shyness they come across as dead or invisible. The first step in overcoming this is to let yourself feel the shyness. It's perfectly all right. Nervousness and discomfort mean you are alive. The important thing is to decide to reveal and express other emotions that you usually keep hidden under this cloak of inhibition.

In order to reveal more of yourself, you must revise some notions about shame and embarrassment. Whenever we try something new, such as learning to dance or play tennis, we feel silly and awkward. That's natural. Similarly, learning to be less inhibited and more expressive and passionate than you have been previously involves the chance of feeling foolish—but that's good; you're taking risks. Not allowing yourself to be dominated by self-consciousness will make you feel more powerful and more alive. Women who are at ease with themselves, who arouse passion and desire in their men, are able to let their inner feelings emerge relatively uncensored.

Remember, becoming passionate follows some period of risking the expression of feelings. You don't start out being passionate; it is a quality that becomes part of you only after conscious intention and action. If you act on your wish to be passionate, you will come to feel that way. For example, if you wish to be sexy with a man, at first you will likely feel self-conscious, as you would in any new activity or behavior. Trust that you will move through that period of awkwardness and your behavior gradually will become more natural. Feelings dictate how we behave, but how we behave also changes how we feel. Men respond not only to how women feel, but also to how they act, and how you act is under your control.

We find the visualization technique to be very helpful in learning to release new feelings. None of us can do anything unless we can visualize ourselves doing it, and this certainly holds true for becoming less inhibited. Try to imagine yourself acting in a more passionate or sexual fashion. Close your eyes and picture it. Throw caution to the winds. Imagine saying and doing things that are not typical of the way you usually conduct yourself. Imagining and visualizing yourself as less inhibited and restrained will prepare you to be this way with your mate.

The woman who arouses passion and desire in a man reaps tremendous rewards. We have concentrated on what you can do to stimulate and influence a man, but the reciprocal process your actions trigger is no less enriching. The man who is stimulated in this fashion will not only be attracted to you and form a close bond with you, he will also be more loving, romantic, and comfortable with returning the gifts you give him.

# CHAPTER ELEVEN

# Deepening Love Through Friendship

Michael, 33, describes an experience that enabled him to understand what he really needed in a woman. "After my wife left me, I felt angry and heartbroken for the first couple of months, then got back on my feet, ran around, and even started having some fun. Six months after the separation, I went on a vacation to Europe by myself. In Rome, I visited the Vatican to see Michelangelo's ceiling of the Sistine Chapel. As I looked up at that majestic work of art, I was suddenly overcome with the most profound loneliness I had ever known. I remembered how much my ex and I had always wanted to tour Europe, and how enthralled we used to be when we visited museums together.

"The rest of my vacation was pretty gloomy. I just dragged through it with the constant realization that I had lost my best friend. The loss of her as my lover, the ego wounds—all of that I could survive. But the loss of that special friendship was unbearable."

If you have ever heard either men or women express the feeling that their mate is their "best friend," you know from the way they say it how fortunate they feel. While some people believe the epitome of success in a relationship is reached with passionate and romantic highs, others feel blessed when they find someone who's a friend and companion—and this is particularly true for men.

Before the sexual revolution, the idea of men and women being true friends in the context of marriage was considered improbable, given their very separate role definitions as well as complex tensions collectively known as the "battle of the sexes." It was as though this simple bond could not coexist with intricate sexual, familial, and economic interdependencies.

Men, women, and our society as a whole have changed greatly as a result of the women's moment. Men and women are much more alike today—they're both out in the working world. Men are participating more in household and childrearing responsibilities. And after much examination and experimentation focused on what is feminine and what is masculine, both men and women feel more comfortable expressing both the masculine and feminine aspects of their personalities. At this point, men and women are also in what without question is a continuing evolution of sex roles and behavior, and they are more understanding, accepting, and appreciative of the innate differences between the sexes. After a long period of adversarial tension and mistrust followed by exciting and positive change, we have entered a new era of equality and respect. Thanks to this truce, perhaps for the first time in history, men and women are exploring what it's like to be close to each other in a nonsexual fashion.

This move toward reconciliation and platonic relationships has been speeded along by the demise of the sexual revolution, and also by health concerns. Men and women who, if they had met in 1968 or

1975, would likely have had casual sexual encounters are today more likely to spend time together as platonic friends. While some people may miss that dizzying era of sexual promiscuity, deemphasizing sex has actually served to create new opportunities for friendship between men and women.

Another factor aiding men and women in exploring the possibility of genuine friendship has been the blurring of sex-role definitions. The more equal, the more similar, our ambitions, struggles, and experiences, the greater the probability that we can relate to each other more as we do to like-sexed friends. Differences may facilitate attraction, but similarities tend to make us feel more trusting of and, importantly, more interesting to each other. When we find we have a lot in common with someone, we are typically delighted with this discovery and want to spend time together.

We advocate the enduring, nourishing bond of friendship between men and women and are less approving of fleeting romantic intensity that has more to do with fantasy than reality. Remember the three stages of love: in the course of a rich and mature relationship, romance and infatuation evolve into a more durable, and for many a more satisfying, state of companionship. Not that passion becomes only a memory; passion can and should be continually rekindled. But friendship is essential and fundamental. It creates the experience of being kindred spirits. It is, in fact, one of the strongest ties, especially for men.

## The Nature of Friendship

The psychologist Erich Fromm said, "The deepest need of man is to overcome his separateness." Friendship is about achieving that. It is the antidote to the human dilemma we all face at one time or another in our lives—loneliness. As you undoubtedly know, getting married or being in a relationship doesn't mean that you'll never experience loneliness. Friendship does, however, diminish our separateness. But, of course, it's more than just a respite from feeling alone. Its rewards are among the best we can experience.

All friendships share certain qualities. First of all, there is a sense of trust. We know the other person cares about us—we are liked, even cherished, for who we are and what we contribute to the other person. There is the sharing of common interests and values. There is a sense of goodwill and fidelity toward one another—we trust that the other person has our best interests at heart, will not betray us, and is a loyal ally.

As the friendship endures, it is strengthened by the knowledge that we have so much invested and it has rewarded us. There is also the joy of shared history, of nostalgic reminiscences about or experiences together. The future is also part of each friendship—plans, dreams, anticipations, and the comfort of knowing our friend will be there to share those with us as well.

As children and adolescents, we find friendships easier to establish than we do as adults. Girls especially form tight bonds with other girls—they share clothes, get their mothers to buy them identical outfits, and wear friendship rings. Boys too form relationships with other boys who become their pals and buddies.

The expression "my best friend" starts in childhood and holds special meaning. Sadly, as we grow up, our skills at establishing these critical relationships are not as polished. Many adults are wise enough to retain old friends, but terribly clumsy at making new ones. As we get older, we unfortunately develop more false pride. We lose sight of the simple invitations we could extend as children—"You want to play with me?" We become more guarded, less receptive, even though our need for such close ties has not diminished. It is as though we're not supposed to need them anymore.

In our therapy practices, we deal with this kind of false pride almost every day. Men and women who are smart in every other area of their lives become dense when it comes to reaching out to other people. They secretly believe that old high school notion that popular people don't have to work at making friends, that it just happens. If only that were true!

As adults, most of us do manage to stick our necks out enough now and again to form new friendships. And, unlike children, we learn the complexities as well as the rewards that are involved. Adult friends are expected to make demands on each other in times of difficulty. We need them then. By their presence, they let us know we are cared about, loved. They always know when we are hurting, often merely by the sound of our voice.

We all need support, and close friends provide us with it. For a woman, the expression "She's there for me" captures the feeling that she can rely on her woman friend, no matter what. Men use the term "a stand-up guy" to indicate a friend who won't let them down, who can be called upon in time of need.

Friendships can get rocky. We may argue, offend each other, let each other down, have falling-outs, even go through times when, busy with other people or endeavors, we'll be in less frequent or no contact. Yet there is still the feeling we will one day reconnect, because otherwise we lose too much. Indeed, as we grow older, the value of longtime friendships is heightened. We're acutely aware that it is too late to develop the deep, knowing, and sustaining ties that can only be formed by years, even decades, of sharing life's sorrows and joys.

It is because of the years invested that friends are able to put us in touch with happy times in the past. Indeed, it is with our best friends that we often regain contact with the child within us and find ways to play again.

Friendship between lovers and between husbands and wives is similar to other kinds of friendship, yet it is often more profound and meaningful because of the added complexities of romance. Marital partners who are good friends have the capacity to blend sexuality and passion with tenderness and companionship.

## Men and "Opening Up"

Men are often described as having trouble "opening up," being verbally expressive and allowing themselves to be emotionally vulnerable. As a result of this contained psychological style, men are more susceptible to numerous stress-related illnesses. They are portrayed as being unable or unwilling to communicate openly with their wives or to establish anything but the most superficial relationships with male friends.

To some degree, these dire assessments are accurate. It's correct, lamentably, that men don't bond with other men as often as they would like to think they do. It is also true that some men do not have intimate dialogues as often as their wives. And finally, men who refuse to acknowledge inner fears do tend to suffer from stress more than those who deal with their feelings more openly. But it has also become clear from our firsthand observations of contemporary male behavior that the solution is not simple: it is not just that men should "open up" more.

For example, men who complain about their career-related anxieties without developing specific skills to cope with them tend to suffer even more stress. In fact, the coping strategies recommended most often to deal with job-related stress emphasize learning to be "tougher" and more effective, not "softer" or more verbally expressive.

Men have no difficulty with the expression of feelings in general. What is hard for them is the expression of certain feelings—those exposing tenderness or vulnerability. Men can be passionate and extremely open even with these feelings, provided the context is viewed by them as "heroic" in some sense. This is why athletes and soldiers can allow themselves to cry openly, for they feel they are in a "heroic" context in which issues of courage and honor prevail.

Women may believe they want men to express the whole range of their emotions. But our experience with men, women, and couples has demonstrated to us that what women really want is for men to be more open and expressive of loving feelings toward them—not the entire spectrum of feelings. A woman is likely to be quite unnerved if a man becomes too open, too vulnerable. Exposed male vulnerability and pain trigger strong anxiety in most women. She feels as if the man has suddenly violated a trust, broken an unspoken agreement, revealed weakness, and, worse yet, as if she is supposed to fix it. Women know that you can't have both emotional expressiveness and dynamic, action-oriented behavior in abundance in one man. It is a bit of a trade-off.

Men are not very interested in being emotional and vulnerable as a general way of being. But many men today are beginning to allow themselves to be more revealing and open, selectively. They are learning that it enriches them to allow their mates into their inner thoughts and feelings, and, too, that their children benefit from seeing their father as a real person rather than a two-dimensional figure. In addition, men are beginning to learn that in the world of work, fears that are kept bottled up become toxic and damaging.

Men, overwhelmingly, prefer action to emotional expression. This does not mean that men will continue to be silent strangers to the women who love them. It does suggest, though, that women can help men to open up when they understand what "opening up" means to them. Women who understand and accept the forces that dictate men's choices regarding expressiveness are tremendously valued by men.

## Sexuality as a Disguise for Closeness

Because it is still difficult for men to express their emotions and needs in a direct fashion, they may be communicated in a disguised way. Sexuality has traditionally been a means of expression for men and also an avenue that enables them to make contact. So often what passes for a man's passion, lust, and sexuality is really an attempt by the man to get close to a woman.

Prior to the sexual revolution, it was an ironclad belief that men had a more powerful sexual drive than women, and were slaves of their raging testosterone. Men's "obsession with sex" was explained as a normal, healthy, biological fact of life—men simply needed more sex than women. We know better now—when it comes to libido, men and women are pretty much equal. Furthermore, even in the past, male sexual drive was not what it seemed to be. Going back many centuries, the male's apparent hunger for sexual conquest hid a deeper desire—the wish for physical and emotional contact—intimacy. The reasons go back to the ways in which boys form attitudes about emotional expression in childhood. Although boys do cry, have tender feelings, and experience times when they are reduced to utterly uncontrolled emotionality, unlike girls, they pay a price for those expressions—embarrassment and shame. Boys are taught from an early age to hide their emotions as part of male self-control and self-containment.

Physical expressions of feelings, too, are more open and acceptable for girls. More comfortable with closeness, girls are freer to explore and fulfill their needs for physical contact and affection. Boys have equal needs for closeness, but the channels for their expression become narrower with age. Every mother has seen her son pull away from an affectionate kiss on the cheek, fearing someone will think he's a "baby" or "sissy." And many a father has felt his son recoil from a playful hug, letting Dad know he's "too old for that."

The physical contact a boy gets in the allowable, aggressive context of sports or fighting, therefore, may be the only contact he gets for years. Little wonder he's so enthusiastic when he reaches the age of sexual experimentation! Sex affirms men's masculinity while at the same time allowing them to satisfy their hunger for closeness. The stereotypical female fear that "he's only interested in my body" is often fairly accurate. A man's stored-up need for physical affection often does take this form. But a man's aggressive sensuality does not necessarily mean all he wants is sex. Expressions of sexual desire are frequently a disguised wish for greater intimacy.

While some men look to sex to satisfy their need for intimacy, others are fearful of the emotional hungers and dependency needs that may be stirred up during the act. Some avoid sex altogether because of their fears, and others exhibit sudden indifference to their partners after what may have been passionate, highly emotional lovemaking. This abrupt turnabout only appears unfeeling; in fact, it is a concerted attempt *not* to feel. It is a reaction triggered by emotions that are too intense and uncomfortable. Men who quickly turn away from a woman after making love are not necessarily cold or insensitive—they may be trying to hide or push down the inner conflict which has been stirred up in them by the closeness they just experienced.

Mark, 36, is unusual in that he is very much aware of this inner turmoil. "Whenever I used to be sexually involved with a woman I would get complaints about going to sleep right afterward. Only recently have I been able to explain that to myself. When I make love, it really is lovemaking—I feel tender, wanting to please, even loving. It's as if it's okay to feel all that at the height of passion, okay to lose myself, to even feel like crying. But right afterward, the enormity of what I felt is too much—I feel as if I'll have to get married—as if the wonderfulness of the act demands nothing less than a commitment. So I cope with all those mixed feelings by going to sleep." Mark cannot fairly be characterized as insensitive, even though his overt behavior certainly makes him appear to be. It's the Polarity Factor—too much closeness for Mark is a clear signal for retreat back to separateness.

Other men who have a fear of intense attachment deny their fear by indulging in obsessive sexual conquest. For these men, sexual conquest has, at its core, a wish for closeness and connection to a woman. The seeming insatiable sexual appetite is really a love-starved man's disguise! Because this need is unrecognized, never admitted, never expressed, the so-called Don Juan rarely does feel loved or fulfilled. That is why he feels so empty as he relentlessly seduces, then flees from, woman after woman. What the Don Juan wants and desperately needs is emotional contact with a woman, but his fears surrounding these desires are so great he can't allow himself to recognize them.

Typically, the Don Juan had a mother who was inconsistent in her loving—sometimes warm, even seductive, other times cold and aloof. Because of the combination of yearning and fear that characterized his relationship with his mother, his emotional needs for a woman are associated with a heightened sense of anxiety, a palpable threat of danger. His longing for warmth and attachment, set in motion by his mother's undelivered promise, propels him to defy the threat of danger and frantically seek out women. Fearful of allowing himself to love fully and need a woman, he limits his interactions to sexual conquest —it allows him to be seemingly close to a woman without being intimate.

Fortunately, as both men and women are evolving, there is less of a need to hide fundamental human feelings such as the desire for warmth and for being cared for. Moreover, as men are more aware of the ways their sexuality can disguise other motivations, they are more likely to seek friendship with a woman, directly and honestly.

# How Men Respond to Friendship

Men and women are strikingly different in the ways they behave with friends. Female friendships are characterized by physical affection and emotional expressiveness. Men's ties are more indirect. Women phone each other just to talk; men phone each other to set up activities. Women share intimacies in conversations; men are more likely to exchange factual information.

However, just because men's conversations seem to be about stereotypical activities such as poker games, racquetball, or a fishing trip, don't think there isn't meaningful communication going on. Men communicate in a kind of language that may seem indirect to women but is revealing and understood by other men. For example, men typically discuss life concerns, dreams, even apprehensions in disguised terms; they report how well they are playing the game or philosophize on what it's all about. Their desire to experience sharing and intimacy is there and is being expressed, albeit disguised somewhat behind bantering or even what appears on the surface to be competitiveness.

Regardless of how many male friends he may have, every man, however secretly, wants a wife who is also his best friend. Without that, there is a kind of loneliness that, even though it may feel familiar, leads to an ache that all too many men know. In spite of man-to-man bonding, which partly serves as a way for men to communicate deeper feelings, there are many men who don't participate at all in this form of intimacy, nor do they have other close friends, even female ones. Sadly, surveys on this subject indicate that the majority of men do not have a close or best friend.

When in trouble, men typically do not reach out to their male friends in the same way women do to their women friends. As therapists, we often see a man whose marriage is in trouble or who is suffering fear of failure in his work who typically has no one but us to talk to. Undoubtedly you have known a man who waited till the last minute to tell a buddy that his marriage was unraveling, whereas his wife's friends had known for a long time. Men's fear of competition is used as a standard excuse, but the truth is most men aren't as competitive in a friendship as people think.

As a result of their inhibitions and concerns about looking weak, for many men male bonding isn't enough. They want a more intimate and trusting relationship in which they can open up in an uncensored fashion. They seek this with women. Men want and need friendship with their mates even more than women do. Because they hold back from other men, a tremendous hunger builds up in them. For men who have been divorced or widowed, the loneliness can be agonizing, which is why these men often remarry as soon as they can. They want to recapture the friendship that was lost.

Men respond to true friendship with gratitude and loyalty. They feel closer, less alone, more trusting. They feel they have a life companion, someone who is by their side sharing life's adventures. A woman who understands this can become a soul mate to a man, someone who knows and understands him.

## The Pal

Stuart, 30, had had only one fairly long relationship, lasting one year. Since then, he had dated a number of women on a casual basis. Although Stuart said he felt ready to get married and wanted to have children, he had a pattern of pursuing women chosen primarily for their looks. His taste ran to tall, thin, gorgeous women he invariably stopped phoning after a few dates because he felt they were self-centered or shallow.

One day he announced in therapy, "I've found the woman I'm going to marry—if she'll have me." Instead of describing the woman's legs and hair and how pretty and sexy she was, as he usually did, Stuart said, "She makes me feel as if I've found a best friend!"

Nikki and Stuart had met on a daylong bicycle ride sponsored by a biking magazine. Pedaling next to each other up a steep hill, they joked about the tough incline and started talking. At lunch, they sat at the same table. "No matter what I said, Nikki picked up on it right away—we talked about bicycles, hikes we'd been on, places we wanted to go on vacation—we had even read some of the same books and agreed on what we liked and didn't like about them. The next afternoon, she took me to a bluegrass music festival. It's easy to be with her. We just spent time together, like buddies."

Seven months later, Stuart and Nikki now have a close relationship. While he has mentioned a couple of problems—he's not crazy about her roommate, and she has asked him to be more reliable about phoning her when he says he will, which he now is doing—he is hopeful they'll continue to get closer, and eventually marry. What Stuart found in Nikki is a pal, a buddy, a woman who enjoys the activities he likes and can be a friend without male-female power struggles or conflicts.

Because of Stuart's old pattern of choosing tall, slim, very pretty women, we asked him what Nikki looked like, and he pulled out a snapshot of her taken on one of their weekend trips to the mountains. She has a friendly, open face and is attractive, but not pretty in a classical sense. Five foot two, she has short, muscular legs and is the opposite of his former type.

*Discovering What* Really *Attracts Men.* The reason we mention Nikki's appearance is that we feel this case history vividly illustrates our belief that a woman's attitude, personality, and behavior and the emotional response these trigger in a man are much more powerful determinants of male attraction and bonding than her looks, no matter how definite a man's physical type seems to be. The warm, comfortable feeling of friendship that Stuart has with Nikki is what has made him cherish her and want to marry her.

Bonnie is also a Pal. Today Ray finds her to be a warm and trusting companion. But these feelings are in sharp contrast to some of his earlier impressions of her.

"When I walked in on you and your girlfriends and heard you really taking men apart, talking about what jerks and 'rough drafts' we were, I knew that we were not going to make it as a couple. I need a woman who's going to be my friend—we're obviously not suited to each other."

Ray had been in another room at the party when he came into the kitchen and overheard Bonnie and her women friends having a "bitch session." When he told her on the drive home that he wanted to break up, and why, she tried to laugh off his comments. "C'mon, that's just the way women talk. Anyway, I'm not your buddy, I'm your lover."

She was surprised at the anger this last remark triggered in Ray. "That's exactly it, Bonnie! And I'm

tired of the stupid romance act you put on with me.
Save your lingerie and champagne for a guy who's
Neanderthal enough to want that as a steady diet!"

Enraged by what he'd said, Bonnie jumped out of
his car and slammed the door when he pulled up in
front of her apartment building. "And I hope you'll
find the fishing buddy who'll make you happy! Too
bad you can't marry Ernest Hemingway."

An outside salesperson for a drafting firm, Bonnie, 35, was extremely competitive and aggressive in
her career. During work hours, she dressed conser-
vatively and was the consummate business professional, determined to outdo men in a field very
much dominated by them. After hours, she became
a different person. She traded her dress-for-success
suits for slinky dresses and high heels. She also
traded her efficient career persona for that of a flirtatious bombshell.

She prided herself on being able to attract almost
any man she wanted. But at the same time, she
looked down on men for taking the bait. "Men are
so easy—put on a short skirt and watch them come
running." She was also aware that while men were
initially drawn to the sexiness she projected, her
relationships rarely lasted more than a few months.

A veteran of many brief affairs, usually with unre-
liable or elusive but exciting "rats," she had developed an us/them mentality, a conviction that men
and women were fundamentally at war, a war she
was determined to win. She and her girlfriends talked
for hours each week, laughingly exchanging the latest gossip on their affairs. It was one of these sessions that Ray had walked in on.

She had met him at a party, asked him for his
number, and phoned him the following week. They
had been seeing each other for two months, mostly
for movies and art openings or dinners at the chic

restaurants at which she was a regular. Several times he had asked her to go for drives in the country, to a baseball game, or on a fishing trip. "I want to show you this magical lake I found way back in the mountains—it's so serene there," he'd said more than once. She had always refused to share in these activities, kissing him and saying, "Those are men things—take one of your men friends."

After their fight, she had gotten on the phone to one of her friends and told her what had happened. She was shocked to hear her girlfriend say, "Oh, God, Bonnie! He was so nice! He's the best man I've ever seen you with—you could have married him!"

During the next few days, Bonnie found herself crying in her car on the way to and from sales appointments. Ray's and her girlfriend's remarks kept repeating in her mind. She admitted to herself, for the first time in years, that she wanted a serious relationship, even marriage.

She phoned Ray and asked if he'd meet her at a coffee shop that evening. They talked for hours, honestly, like friends. Bonnie found she felt delightfully easy and comfortable just being herself with him. As they got ready to leave, she said, "If I buy the tickets, will you take me to a Dodger game?"

Bonnie is discovering she sincerely enjoys many of the activities she disdained before. She has been frightened and scarred by numerous affairs that ended badly, but her deep-seated fear of intimacy is gradually being replaced by trust and respect for Ray. She is slowly revealing more of herself to him.

For his part, Ray is becoming freer and much more open with her. Before, he had felt subtly resentful of her, feeling that she only wanted him as an attractive escort. Because his appetite for nightlife and exaggerated romance was limited, he hadn't wanted to see her more than one or two times a week. As they began to share a broader range of activities, Ray began to feel that he could be more himself with Bonnie, and began to want to spend more and more time with her.

*Becoming a Friend to a Lover.* One of the most common fears of men and women is that the development of real friendship in the relationship heralds a dangerous loss of excitement and eroticism. The culture tends to underscore that fear by making unfortunately sharp distinctions between what is friendly and what is sexy. Most of us have a tendency to buy into that false distinction, while the truth is that lovers can be friends and vice versa.

Becoming a friend to your lover doesn't mean the loss of passion; it adds an important dimension to the relationship. Passion dies most frequently because of a slow accumulation of hurt and resentment. The ease of communication and feeling of commonality that occur in a close friendship are an effective antidote to that misunderstanding and pain. When people are friends, they understand each other more. When lovers are also good friends, they have the potential to use their understanding in ways that can actually broaden passion rather than diminishing it. Lovers who are friends have something to talk about after making love. And they have the mutual openness and acceptance that leads them to want to make love.

## The Initiator

Janet and Gene have been seeing each other for nine months now. For the last month, he's been dropping phrases like "when we're an old married couple" and "on our honeymoon," but hasn't come right out and formally proposed. Janet, 34, has had to stop herself from asking him several times, but she's determined to wait for him to propose to her. "After all, I've taken a lot of the risks and done a lot of the proposing of things in this relationship. I'm going to let him do the marriage proposal all by himself."

In fact, if Janet hadn't taken a lot of the initiative after she met Gene, 35, it's doubtful that they would ever have gotten to know each other. It was Janet's turnabout two years before that radically changed her attitude toward men and behavior in relationships.

"I was at a party. I'd come with a girlfriend, and was looking around at all the couples talking to each other, the men going up to women and starting conversations, the women introducing themselves to men. I was really envious of the women I saw doing the approaching. I had spent the last week feeling bitter and victimized, cursing this guy I'd gone out with a couple of times for not phoning to ask me out again, wondering what I'd done to turn him off.

"I had stayed home that Friday evening, feeling sorry for myself for not having a date. And I thought back on all the times I had waited for men to call me, resenting them. Watching the people at the party, I realized that I rarely ever took any initiative with men. That I waited for men to approach me at parties, and went home depressed when the 'right one' didn't talk to me. I had also expected the man to have all the plans together, to be a real take-charge guy who'd make the decisions where we'd go to dinner and even when he'd see me next. I realized that I was resenting men for making me feel like a victim, when I was, in fact, making myself a victim by being so passive."

Janet began making some of the moves herself. And it wasn't always fun. "I found out real fast what men have to go through. Going up to a man at, say, my health club and striking up a conversation, or saying 'Let's exchange phone numbers and see if we can get together for a movie next week,' was really hard sometimes, and I would feel terrible when I sensed there was no interest on his part. But then I did meet and go out with some interesting men because I made the first move. And I felt more power, more balance.''

Gene was in a creative-writing class Janet was taking at the universty. ''I was very attracted to him the first time I saw him, and when he read one of his stories in class, I felt we shared some of the same ideas and feelings about life. I went up and introduced myself during the break and told him I loved his story. I asked him if he'd like to go for coffee at the university coffee house after class and felt like a jerk when he said he had to meet somebody—I thought he had a girlfriend, or a wife.

''As the class went on, and we both read our writing in class, we exchanged looks and a few words, and I really felt something when our eyes met. When there were only two more classes to go before the course was over, I decided to risk being rejected—if I didn't make a move, we might never see each other after the class ended. So I asked him again if he'd like to go for coffee after class. He said no! Long pause, and then, 'I have to give my brother a ride home—we share a place together.' I just went ahead and pushed it. 'Are you married?' I said. 'No,' he said, 'I don't even have a girlfriend.' 'Well,' I said, 'give me your number—I'll invite you and your brother to a dinner party I'm having next week.' ''

Gene was attracted to Janet right from their first writing class, but was, and is, a shy person. He was greatly relieved when she took the first step to let him know she was interested in him. The warm interest and friendliness she displayed by inviting him to the dinner party and subsequently suggesting things to do and showing both him and his brother around town reassured him, encouraged him to lose his shyness with her, and allowed him to more quickly and more easily trust her growing caring for him.

Her willingness to risk by taking the initiative buoyed his confidence and freed him to reveal more of his personality to her. She set a model as a friend, which had a very positive effect on their relationship.

*Taking the Initiative.* Whether it's in our neighborhood, the places we shop, the classes we attend, the groups we belong to, or even in our jobs, each of us has a large number of people in our lives whom we see on a regular enough basis to recognize their faces, but to whom we don't speak. We haven't been introduced or we haven't had a specific reason to talk to them, so we don't. We may nod or smile or even say hello, but that's as far as it goes. The person, whether male or female, who takes the chance to initiate a connection greatly increases his or her social possibilities.

You may find you have nothing in common. You may make a business contact or casual acquaintance. You may talk to that person just once and learn something or hear something you need to hear at that moment. And you may meet that someone special. It sounds somewhat crass to our ears, but we've often heard it said that "it's a numbers game—the more men you meet or date, the better your chances of finding that someone you truly click with." We've also heard it said that the woman who sits home waiting by the phone may wait a long time.

Taking the initiative puts you in a more active, powerful position. It gets you out of the passive posture of waiting to be approached or asked out by men who might not interest you at all. But whether it's making that first move of introducing yourself to someone and striking up a conversation or the bigger risk of asking a man to go out with you for coffee or lunch or to a movie or to a cultural event, you are taking responsibility for your own experience, taking action.

How do men respond? Almost always, they like it. Men hate having to be the one to make the first move all the time and risk the rejection. When a woman takes the initiative, it is both flattering and a great relief. Moreover, while aggressive men or men who are womanizers have no trouble introducing themselves to women—men you'd probably rather not meet!—in the case of many very worthwhile but reserved or shy men, your taking the initiative may be the only way you'll meet them.

Evelyn is an Initiator too. She and Larry have been married for six years. They're both in their mid-forties and are childless. "If I thought we'd come home from work every night, have dinner, and just sit in front of the television set, I might never have gone on our second date! I'm so bored with our life. Larry's getting a paunch, and is starting to work late a lot at the office, and I just walk around sighing. He's a good man, and I love him, but I don't know what to do."

Evelyn and Larry are at a crisis point in their marriage. She feels bored and envious of other couples, even single women, for leading more exciting lives. She feels that Larry has reached a premature middle age. He's no longer the dashing, adventuresome man who used to take her to jazz clubs at midnight or away for the weekend to funky, offbeat resorts in the mountains. The problem with their marriage is that Evelyn has been passively waiting for Larry to deliver excitement to it as he had during their courtship and the first few years of their marriage. She expected him to come up with things to do, to take her places, to get tickets for interesting events.

In fact, Larry did make an effort to suggest activities, but over the years he had become discouraged by Evelyn's increasingly hard-to-please attitude. "Why bother?" was the way Larry had come to feel.

Having lunch one day with an old friend whose marriage Evelyn envied, Evelyn was once again complaining about how bored she was with her marriage. "You and Jim are always taking a class or going off to a ranch for the weekend or getting involved in some community activity—I wish Larry would come up with even one idea like that for ten of Jim's!"

"You think my husband initiates any of that?" her girlfriend asked, astonished.

Evelyn decided to make a commitment to behave in a more positive, affectionate, and loving manner toward Larry. Although he was initially unresponsive, she continued, knowing that their marriage wouldn't heal overnight. She also decided to be less passive and stop expecting Larry to be her knight in shining armor. She arranged for them to go out with several other couples to casual dinners and a concert at a jazz club that had recently opened nearby. Warm feelings began to reawaken between them. They began to talk again, and she told him how sad she felt that they had grown so far apart and said that she was committed to reversing the process.

When Evelyn began taking the initiative and suggesting new activities for them to do together, she was delighted to find that Larry enjoyed it. His response was one of relief—it was a burden lifted: he no longer had to be the one who was automatically expected to initiate plans and activities. The new, equal dynamic greatly reduced the resentment on both their parts.

"All of this has brought us close again," Larry says, "and worked magic on our sex life. I was feeling for a while that it was all over for us, that I was becoming like an old man—but the way we're going, they may be right that life begins at forty. I give Evelyn a lot of credit for turning us back in a positive direction."

*Assuming Responsibility for Change.* Every friendship, every marriage, needs to evolve continually. As Woody Allen says to Diane Keaton in the movie *Annie Hall*, "A relationship is like a shark—it has to keep moving or it dies." Both individuals are responsible for investing the requisite energy to keep a relationship active, alive, moving forward. Both must participate in new experiences that generate shared feelings, something to talk about, things to plan and dream about. This is particularly true for couples who are either childless or whose children are grown and so provide less of a focus for interaction.

If the truth be known, most of us would like certain changes in our lives and relationships. All too frequently, our mates are held at fault when these changes do not happen. They don't need our suggestions, they don't hear our complaints, they aren't moved by our pleas, they don't even read our minds. If change is to occur, we must stop asking our mates to provide it and start assuming the responsibility for initiating it ourselves.

Basically, the person who wants a change is the one who is responsible for making it happen. It is not only infuriating but utterly futile to wait around for someone else to make our lives better. When we wait, we feel passive and, worse, at the mercy of the sensitivity or generosity of our mates. When we become responsible we don't wait, we are not passive, and, instead of allowing ourselves to be victims of the fates, we move things in the direction of our choice.

One reason some people resist taking this more active and effective road to change has to do with pride—or more accurately, false pride. "If he doesn't take the initiative, doesn't think of it himself, or doesn't do something without my prompting, it's no good. An experience is only good when he does it because he wants to—asking ruins it!" All these feelings have to do with false pride and not love. Sometimes it is actually more loving when we initiate than when a mate does so from habit. When a mate responds and adjusts to something new that we do, it is a reflection of love, because he or she is doing something that is not natural.

It is important to act rather than wait. When we act we automatically feel less resentful and boost the possibility of enriching our lives in ways we would like.

## A Loving Provider

"When I first met Michael, I sensed that in some way he was uneasy about going out with a businesswoman," recalls Janine, an advertising saleswoman. "His friends are artistic types—writers, poets, and artists. And from what he told me, before me he had always been involved with very intense, rather crazy actresses and artists. He phoned me six times a day, but I knew he had doubts about us as a couple, and I did too. There was no way I was going to be the mature, practical one in the relationship so he could be the crazed creative artist. I told him from the start that there had to be a good balance between us, with both us being responsible adults as well as creative people."

Janine, 36, met Michael, 34, a playwright and freelance journalist, two years after the breakup of her eight-year marriage. Following her divorce, Janine had moved to another city. In her evenings, she took classes in film, creative writing, and theater arts. It was on her first volunteer job doing publicity for a play that she met Michael, who had written the play.

"He is an incredibly talented writer and a very warm, giving person," Janine says. "At first I was intimidated by his friends, and I think he didn't know how I would fit in and wondered if I was too 'straight'—but we worked all of that out. I really enjoy the ideas and passion of the theater and art worlds that he's introduced me to. There are some pretentious frauds and snobs, but you find that anywhere—I can hold my own. And he's learned to appreciate the business world and the 'art' of what I do. He even had a minor hit with a play based on the sales game, with the lead character modeled after me.

"Money was a thorny issue for us at first. I make in the high five figures and he was living in a cheap studio, earning $500 to $1,000 for free-lance magazine articles, just enough to pay the rent so he could write his plays. He'd refuse to go to expensive restaurants even if I asked him as my treat, because he couldn't reciprocate.

"It wasn't until we'd been seeing a lot of each other for a few months and really fell in love and began to trust each other on a deeper level that we were able to even start talking about our future and the economics of being together. I told him I love my work and the money it brings in, and at the same time I believe in him as a writer and don't want him to become a stockbroker or mogul just so he'll make a lot of money, too—I'd already had one competitive, materialistic marriage. On the other hand, I didn't want to live a bohemian, financially insecure existence.

"After a lot of long discussions, we decided to get married. We pool our incomes and have enough money for a comfortable, while not extravagant, lifestyle. I handle the bills and finances and negotiated the deal for our house, because I'm good at it and enjoy it. He cooks and shops more than I do, but he's happy with that—he only writes in the mornings anyway. I'm trying to get pregnant now, which we're both very excited about. I'll continue working and he'll be more of a househusband."

"Some people might think our marriage is somewhat of a role reversal," says Michael. "Janine makes five times what I do, but we both work very hard at what we enjoy doing. Her belief in me as a writer genuinely helps keep me going, and after many intense relationships with women who were as crazy as I used to be, I am extremely grateful to be married to a woman who's stable and sane and as loving and supportive as Janine. We complement each other very well, I think. Many writers burn out very young, and can't afford to have a family. My life could have been very lonely and unstable, but she's making a family possible for us—I consider myself a very lucky man to have found her."

## Men's Wish for Companionship

As you can see from these cases, men do want friendship with the women in their lives even though this wish may not be obvious to their mates or even to themselves.

Many women fail to recognize or act on this male desire not only because it is often unexpressed or expressed indirectly, but also because a man's wish for closeness may be threatening to a woman. Many women are wary of men's neediness. A woman may fear being drained, may fear that her own needs will go neglected, may be afraid she'll lose some of her independence if the man is too possessive or becomes a best friend. Both traditionally and today, many women are quite satisfied to have women friends as their best friends and compatriots and don't see a man as a likely candidate; whether consciously or unconsciously, many women want men to fit into the stereotypic male role of being strong and self-reliant.

More often, however, it is the man who fails to signal his desire to transform a romantic relationship into one that has friendship as a central component. Remember, though, that all men have deep desires, however hidden, for companionship. Do not assume a man is different, regardless of how self-contained or self-reliant he may appear.

To help you recognize this need in a man, ask yourself, does he talk about his career or his dreams with you? Does he complain about not doing more things together? When you do take the initiative, is he delighted, even pleased? Has he talked to you about your involvement in or knowledge of what he does? Does he ever want to spend time with you with no particular agenda other than just being together? These are questions you can ask yourself as a way of detecting his unexpressed wish for more friendship between the two of you. But even if he doesn't show a wish for friendship, rest assured, it is there. Every man craves it, but many don't even realize it is possible.

## Becoming Friends with a Man

The first step in moving toward friendship with a man is, for many women, the hardest one. It requires the giving up of some romantic wishes. A friend is not mysterious, not elusive. Friendships are based on understanding, acceptance, and knowledge.

The second major step in creating friendship with the man in your life is to move from thinking to behavior, from intention to action. Friendships are based on deeds rather than thoughts. When queried, most men and women will readily acknowledge that they would like to feel more companionship with their loved ones. But those who succeed are the ones who translate that goodwill into their daily conduct. With that in mind, the following are some ideas to consider and perhaps put into action if you wish to enhance this facet of your relationship.

We suggest you begin talking to him in the same easy and uncensored way you talk to your woman friends. We cannot stress this too much. If you begin acting as though you're friends, he will become more relaxed and trusting with you. Become a model for openness and ease of relating.

Take the initiative. Women who do so find they create a new sense of vitality. There are scores of men who may be dynamic leaders in their work, but who grow weary of having to continue that same posture in their home life. Men love women who sense this wish for equality and partnership.

Let him know that you want to share common interests and involvements. Let him know that you care about the things you do together. If your relationship has few shared interests or activities, develop them. Whenever we work with couples, we find this advice is generally accepted but less frequently put into actual practice. It's not something you talk about, it's something you do together—for example, take classes together, develop hobbies and mutual cultural concerns, read the same book and discuss it, learn more about his business and tell him about your work, and so on.

An important tip: don't wait to initiate until you find yourself highly motivated and bursting with enthusiasm. Real excitement and genuine interest typically come only after you participate in an activity. Prior to that, we all tend to be somewhat passive, even lethargic. Most of us dream or plan; few of us actually implement those plans. We usually wait for the other person, and then we have someone to blame when the old patterns are not broken!

If you sincerely want to inspire a sense of friendship with a man, then talk with him about your common dreams, plan the future, both long-range as well as the coming week. Couples who work, play, and dream together form a powerful, enduring, and fulfilling bond.

# CHAPTER TWELVE

# The Rules for Staying in Love

Keeping a relationship alive is an ongoing task, but its rewards are clearly worth the effort. Men and women are equally responsible for what they do and for what they fail to do. In our work with couples, we have found that there are predictable pitfalls as well as guidelines for what works. For most couples, good intentions and loving hopes are necessary but not sufficient to ensure vitality, commitment, and a love that grows and matures with the years. More is needed. Specifically, it is critical to have an awareness of the subtle beliefs, actions, and personal attitudes that enable one to breathe life, joy, and vitality into a love relationship.

## Rule #1
## Relationships Don't Just Happen
## We Create Them

Most of us grow up believing in the magic of "chemistry" between lovers. Love feels exquisite, inexplicable, and ultimately beyond our control. We "fall" in love. We do not consciously decide to become lovers, it is something that seems simply to happen, that we observe with delight and amazement.

The truth of the matter is that while love's rewards can be priceless, it costs something to achieve them. Good relationships do not just happen, they are the result of conscious effort and work. Good intentions are not enough. For a rich and fulfilling love relationship to develop, a more active posture is needed. Love requires an awareness of what is needed to make our loved one happy and fulfilled. It demands honesty with ourselves about what we truly feel and genuinely wish to give. Perhaps most critically, it requires us to be comfortable with action. Without action, there is at best only talk, and at worst there are complaints, blame, and the gradual growth of destructive attitudes and feelings.

The course of a relationship is never determined by luck or fate, it is the result of ongoing decisions for which each partner is responsible. Even when both the man and the woman are unaware of the impact of what they do or fail to do, these actions and inactions mold and alter the bond between them. A relationship is the sum total of how we conduct ourselves.

We are all conscious of how we are in the beginning of a relationship. But despite our best intentions, many of us become lazy along the way and less sensitive about the impact of our actions. Yet, relationships are never static, they are either growing or in some subtle form of decline. We continue throughout a relationship to be responsible, as a result of our conduct, for love's ongoing quality of aliveness and warmth.

Understanding and accepting this rule will not make you feel burdened or frustrated—rather you will feel empowered. When you are aware that the course of love is up to you, that you can shape your own destiny, you will feel hopeful, even optimistic. Instead of being a passive observer, you will be a participant in your quest for and achievement of love.

## Rule #2
## Love May Be Dormant,
## But It Never Dies

Anyone who is married secretly fears that stagnation might be the ultimate fate of the relationship. Because sustaining a bond with another person can be so arduous and divorce is so prevalent, we often fear that love will wither and die. Such scary speculations are often engendered by myths about the magic of love—if it can appear mysteriously, then its demise may be equally puzzling. Many people are convinced they can fall out of love as easily as they fall into it.

Yet, in spite of these fears, love rarely dies. True, when people divorce they make sure there are no more embers glowing in order to feel at peace with the decision. But when love seems absent in a relationship, what happens is that something else has eclipsed it. Negative feelings tend to mask or mute positive ones. When we are angry, frustrated, or disappointed, we allow these feelings to predominate over love, yearning, and need. Emotional indifference becomes a mask protecting us from revealing hurt and anger. Emotional numbness becomes a way of defending ourselves against the risk of caring again. So when love becomes dormant, it is only this negative facet that is revealed to us. Bitterness hides the sweetness of a love that was once quite evident—

hence the origin of the idea that love and hate are closely related. Actually, expressing anger and verbally lashing out at our mate is not just evidence of wounded love, it may in fact be a wish for contact, a wish that comes out in a distorted fashion.

When bad things happen in a marriage, we feel a need to protect ourselves. We fear hurt and rejection, pull into ourselves, and become convinced that love has died. But it hasn't. And it can be revived. Understanding that deep, positive feelings may be dormant rather than nonexistent opens new pathways for revitalizing and enlivening a relationship. You can put this rule into action by first separating what you feel now from what you felt at the beginning of a relationship. Remember, the love you felt in the past was real and it is now a measure of the potential that still exists.

Love can be revived, but beware of the deadening effects of false pride and stubbornness. People who need to be right, who seek vengeance or revenge, never learn how to revive the warmth and richness that once existed. First, the sources of anger and sadness must be identified clearly. Having done that, there must be a full expression of feelings followed by forgiveness and acceptance. Remembering the love you once felt, retrieving the memories and images of the caring and desire that once existed, is mandatory for finding the motivation to do what is necessary. When the negative factors that paralyze love are isolated and then dispelled or set aside, the positive feelings can then be uncovered.

# Rule #3
## A Mate Is Not a Solution

The rewards of being in a relationship are so highly praised that we come to believe that love is the antidote for all that ails us. There is the promise that life will be complete, wonderful, richly gratifying. We become convinced that old wounds will be closed and insecurities healed.

Each of us has areas of vulnerability, and at some level we all nurse old hurts. It is true that love is a special process of connection, intense concern, and giving, but it is not a solution to internal problems. Love may be one of life's greatest experiences, but it is not life itself. Feeling you are one with your lover is wonderful, but never literally true. No matter how tight, loving, or intense your relationship or marriage, you are still individuals as well as a couple.

Unfortunately, we all grow up being influenced by cultural and societal forces to embrace strategies to bolster our self-esteem. Many of these strategies are of dubious worth, and others are actually dangerous and self-defeating. For example, traditionally men were sold on the belief that money and financial success would make them feel worthy, and women on the belief that being loved and married guaranteed limitless benefits. While both money and marriage are undoubtedly desirable, they are not antidotes for the pain of old wounds or disappointments. It is important to understand that you are responsible for healing yourself. Mates can provide support and are certainly a cure for the ache of a lonely heart, but they cannot erase past experiences that may have led to feelings of doubt and inadequacy.

When we burden a mate with excessive expectations, we invariably feel disappointed and our loved one feels resentful. Such hopes are self-defeating fantasies and rarely result in our feeling relieved. Moreover, even when an association with our partner seems to make us feel better about ourselves, the good feelings must be incorporated within ourselves in order to be lasting. If these positive feelings and attitudes are not internalized, then we have merely invested our mate with tremendous power, and if that person leaves, we are left alone and bereft of a healthy self-image. Ultimately, we must find the capacity and courage to regard ourselves in a positive light. We must learn to first love ourselves or we will never feel truly worthy or be able to really love another.

## Rule #4
## Love Is About Acceptance, Not Change

Too often we foolishly believe that love and marriage are a license to remake someone. We think that it is all right to smooth out the rough spots in the person we love, even though in so doing we may diminish those very qualities that endear that person to us.

In the name of communication and the sharing of feelings, many people today believe that it is perfectly acceptable to request change or modifications in our mate. While it is important to air complaints and dissatisfactions, many of us go too far. In the guise of being candid and honest, we are often attempting to remake our mate's personality. It won't work. Even when a mate seems compliant, he or she will unconsciously resist.

Marriage carries with it a common myth: that all issues can be brought to the family bargaining table and haggled over. Nothing could be further from the truth. There are many issues that arise between women and men that are not negotiable. There is nothing wrong with this, and it doesn't reflect a lack of love or diminished sensitivity toward one's mate. We all have facets of our personal identity and personality that are our own, not destructive or hurtful, and not subject to change.

True, some things can and should be negotiated if they are intolerable. However, it may be worthwhile for you to reconsider the meaning of "for better or worse." That phrase in the traditional wedding ceremony was meant to remind us that we all have flaws and shortcomings. Moreover, as we come to know each other better, the flaws become increasingly obvious to us. It is at that time that real love and acceptance must come into play.

Often even in the initial throes of love, we begin to try to change our beloved. Many of us are attracted to differences, but then set out to systematically eradicate those unique qualities to which we were first drawn. Differences can be emotionally threatening. It is as though we take them personally, as though they imply a rejection or negation of who we are and what we value.

The reality is that love is about accepting someone's flaws and cherishing that which is special and lovable. Even change or modification that is in someone's best interest may not be seen that way by him or her. Often, attempts to force change implicitly depreciate the other person. Change, even when it is justifiable and possible, comes about only when the person who changes does so because he or she wishes to. Further, that wish is always preceded by a sense of being loved and accepted.

# Rule #5
## Lovers Are Not Mind Readers

One of the fantasies of love is that our mate knows us in a way we have never been known before, that he or she is somehow tuned in to our innermost thoughts and dreams. It is the wish to be so intimately known that fuels many of our romantic quests. We crave not only love but also a feeling that we are not alone, that we are recognized and visible. Whenever men and women speak of chemistry, one thing they mean is that there is a sense of recognition, an awareness that they are alike, are "soul mates." This is why we assume our mate knows us, understands us, and can anticipate what we will think and feel. And when our mate doesn't, we may feel sad, disappointed, even betrayed.

But as much as we might desire it, a mate is never a mind reader. We cannot assume that a mate always knows our wishes, hopes, and hurts. Ultimately, we are responsible for making ourselves known to those we love. People who need to be understood yet do not make an attempt to make that happen are only setting themselves up to feel like victims. For some, there is the feeling that if they have to tell their mate what they need, it is somehow spoiled even though they get what they wanted. Men and women who feel this way think the measure of a loving gift is how sensitive and intuitive it is, when in fact the opposite is more accurate. When you tell a man what you need and he responds to your request, that is really an indication of his love for you. Anticipation of your desires, mind reading, is a fantasy; a mate who cares enough to listen and respond lovingly is a treasure.

Men and women who are understood by those

they love achieve this by communicating who they are. They do not passively await a magical kind of intuition from their beloved. In the absence of honest sharing and disclosures there is only the possibility of misinterpretations, insensitivity, and hurt.

## Rule #6
## It's Not What You Say,
## It's What You Do

Conventional wisdom has it that relationships are always enriched by communication and tend to run aground when there is meager dialogue between a man and a woman. We are led to believe that confusions are cleared up when lovers engage in open and honest dialogues. It certainly seems to be true that in disturbed and conflicted marriages we are most struck by an atmosphere of coldness and silence. But while it is often accurate to isolate communication problems as contributing to relationship conflicts, it is not so clear that more communication is needed.

Sometimes people talk too much—they say one thing while really meaning another, or they say things to each other for reasons other than to impart information or express feelings. Quite often, communication is used to manipulate, induce guilt, or place blame even though it is presented as positive and loving. Communication can be, and very often is, a weapon. In some relationships, talking is not a way of imparting information but a subtle form of coercion or manipulation whose goal is to change the other party.

In the final analysis, a relationship is measured and evaluated by the conduct of both parties and not just by what is said. Actions do speak louder than words. How often have you heard people note that their mate may promise a lot but fails to deliver? Words may convey intentions, but how we back up those words is what ultimately has an impact. If you wish to have an alive and caring relationship, it is best to communicate that by acts of loving, caring, and sensitivity. Asking yourself what you have done lately for your beloved is better than telling that person what you would like to do.

## Rule #7
## Stable Relationships
## Are Always Changing

Most of us are taught that stability grows out of equilibrium, constancy, and permanence. We learn that change may be dangerous and therefore should be avoided, that emotional upheaval should be minimized at all cost, for it threatens the integrity and continuity of a relationship. We are told that the stable relationship is one that goes on from year to year impregnable to the treacherous forces that would seek to change it and alter its course.

The truth is that relationships are always changing, for we as individuals are constantly in a state of growth and flux as we move through our lives. And the capacity to deal with change in a positive fashion is a basic necessity in a strong, loving relationship. Couples who encounter difficulties are those who stubbornly resist change for fear that their love may not be strong and sustaining enough to accommodate the unpredictable effects of change. Enduring relationships have the flexibility to greet change not with fear but with acceptance and a positive attitude.

A marriage is forever evolving and changing over time. In the beginning, the wonderful and exhilarating feeling of falling in love is closely tied to newness and the slow process of getting to know someone intimately. Initially, we don't fear change, for we are much too busy enjoying the discovery of yet another new and interesting facet of our lover. Then something curious happens. We get to a point where things seem absolutely perfect and we don't want anything to be different. When the newness begins to wear off we can even feel we are falling out of love. But we can enjoy a continual sense of novelty if we have a receptive attitude toward change.

We must learn to deal with two kinds of change: our own changes as individuals and the changes we see in our mate. What is important is not being fearful of either one's own or one's mate's personal change. Take a chance and assume your mate can handle your growth, that his love is strong enough and his trust great enough that he will not be devastated by your growth. And give him the same respect, latitude, and room to grow in return.

While the emotional flux that is a necessary by-product of personal change is often uncomfortable, it is also a wonderful antidote to the moments of staleness and boredom that occur in any long-term relationship. Having "bad times" doesn't mean the relationship is bad or seriously troubled. All good relationships have occasional difficult times. It is important to understand that those bad times don't mean the relationship is deficient but rather signal some new change that the couple must address in a positive and flexible way.

## Rule #8
## Love Is Always Poisoned by Infidelity

In the last two decades, we have seen a rising level of both sophistication and cynicism in this country. Birth control and the ensuing sexual revolution brought widespread experimentation and a slow but steady erosion of the value of fidelity. Sadly, we have become accustomed to infidelity as affairs have become increasingly commonplace. Once, men were far more likely than women to engage in extramarital activity; today men and women enter into affairs with equal frequency.

Part of the thinking was that affairs weren't particularly hurtful. "What they don't know can't hurt them" became the flimsy rationale. "Affairs may even be good for a relationship" was the wishful excuse. People were lulled into believing that infidelity was relatively benign—if everyone is doing it, it must be all right. Wrong! Although infidelity doesn't lead to divorce as frequently as it did in the past, it does permanently damage the bond of love.

An affair is not a solution, it is a symptom of a problem. Men and women who are unfaithful are attempting to resolve internal dilemmas by seeking momentary refuge in another partner. Taking that avenue is rarely effective as a solution, and even if it feels all right, something destructive has happened that cannot be undone even if the other person never finds out. There has been a violation of one's commitment, which has profound implications.

When we respect and honor the marital commitment, we feel comfortable and at peace with our conduct. We don't have to hide anything or worry about covering our tracks. Deception is a destructive and dishonest act which never leads to a positive outcome. Moreover, when we act in a dishonest way, we secretly know it and feel devoid of honor and character.

Honor and loyalty are critical to any strong and loving relationship. Honor is not merely some lofty, abstract concept; it is always part of our daily conduct. Loyalty too is something that is to be practiced as well as espoused; otherwise love is weakened and trust diminished. Traditional values were developed for sound reasons. They were not constructed simply to sanctify the marriage or as moralistic dos and don'ts to limit personal freedoms. Rather, they were created empirically over time and reflect behaviors that are love-sustaining, not love-depleting.

## Rule #9
## Blame Is Irresponsible

When we are alone, it is impossible to hold someone else responsible for our happiness. If we feel good and content within ourselves, we know it is our own doing. If we feel bad, we also suspect the reasons for that will ultimately lead back to us. We may shake our fists angrily at the fates or mull over the less than perfect treatment we received as children, but we don't have someone specific to pin our disappointment, frustration, and hurt upon. But marriage changes all that! We all enter marriage with hopes flying high, ready to try and eager to give our love. And what do we find? Marital bliss soon transforms into marital imperfection as we find with amazement and dismay that it doesn't fulfill all our needs and even creates a new set of problems and issues which we must deal with and handle.

Marriage creates the perfect medium to breed blame and accusation. When we are single, the explanation for discontentedness is "If I'm unhappy, it's because of me." In marriage, this lament quite easily transforms into "If I'm unhappy, it's because of you." Marriage partners are the most convenient of scapegoats.

Critical self-appraisal is always a whole lot harder than blame. It's much less threatening to find fault with what "they" are doing or not doing and more painful to come to grips with what "we" may be doing. Blame is cut-and-dried: it is *your* fault, plain and simple. When we hurl an accusation it always feels so much simpler than figuring out what we are doing that feeds into the source of our unhappiness. It is easier to hold someone else responsible for our misery and to feel sorry for ourselves than to assume the responsibility for our own state of being.

Blame is always self-defeating. It reinforces personal passivity and makes us feel victimized and at the mercy of another's treatment of us. The goal of blame, however vaguely defined, has to do with some sort of change we want to happen. But it always makes the fulfillment of *our* wish contingent upon *someone else's* action. Blame is typically repetitive, is intended to induce guilt and to plant a stinging barb in our partner. The harvest one reaps from repeated blame is rarely positive change but rather a building resentment and slow alienation of affection.

Don't allow yourself to fall into the trap of blaming, for it simply doesn't work. Assume a more affirmative posture. Be clear and specific about what you want and how you plan to go about making that happen. The more personal responsibility we assume for the quality of our lives, the less we need to blame others and, most important, the happier we become.

# Rule #10
## Giving Is Contagious

Love requires moments of real unselfishness and giving. Love in the absense of mutuality is more a clinging dependency than a loving respect and caring for one another. While adult man/woman love requires a balance between giving and receiving, moments of unselfishness are the essence of love.

The 1960s taught us to appreciate and get in touch with our feelings. They also provided a license for self-involvement that made personal happiness the centerpiece of the love relationship. Even marriage vows were modified to reflect the emphasis upon self: "till death do us part" was changed to "as long as we meet each other's needs." Although the 1960s have come and gone, traces of the legacy of the "me" generation remain. We are gradually moving away from an era when marriages were casually discarded and divorce thought to be an interesting adventure, but what persists is a dogged focus on self and on personal gratification. Staying in love takes more than that.

Real love at times requires putting our own needs on hold and responding to the needs of our mate—not endlessly, not unilaterally, but sometimes. The strongest and most dramatic way we have of experiencing the bond of love is through giving to our mate unselfishly. That act connects us directly to the very heart of love. In fact, we feel much more "in love" when we are actively giving to our partner than when we are receiving.

Giving in a love relationship is contagious. It provides a model of generosity and concern that encourages reciprocity. Don't give to get, for that is unloving. Neither should you allow yourself to give unendingly in a vacuum. A good rule of thumb for all of us to follow is: give 70 percent and demand 30.

## Rule #11
## Love Doesn't Punish, It Forgives

Everyone makes mistakes. Everyone hurts and disappoints his or her mate at times. We are all occasionally insufferable and annoying. One of two things then happens: we either develop the capacity to forgive and go on, or we gradually accumulate resentment.

There are two forms of forgiveness. First, it is important to learn how to forgive yourself. None of us is perfect; we will all inflict pain from time to time on our lovers. Forgiving oneself is not excusing or justifying the hurtful actions, it is simply forgiving—letting go of the negative feelings attached to what we've done to bring hurt to our mate. Self-forgiveness is not to be taken lightly, for if it does not occur there is inevitably a buildup of destructive feelings of guilt and self-recrimination.

Second, it is critical to learn to forgive your mate fully. The wish to hurt, to retaliate, to be proved right, even to extract a confession of wrongdoing from a mate is normal. All but the angels among us have these rather self-righteous and base urgings. But ultimately when the anger begins to cool, the final step in restoring love and harmony is forgiveness. Forgiving unblocks love. No matter how hurt or angry you are, irrespective of how right you may feel, and regardless of how much you may blame or want to strike back, you can't love again in a positive way until you choose to forgive.

What exactly is forgiving? First, it is an intentional act that is a choice. It cannot be coerced or forced out of a person. "I said I accepted your apology" is not enough. Forgiving is not something one says, it is not a verbal process. Rather, it is an internal act that releases anger and hurt. Forgiving is not forgetting. Simply because we shelve something temporarily or put it out of our minds, we have not necessarily forgiven it. Forgiving is not excusing, and it doesn't involve rationalizing or explaining away hurt feelings. Forgiving is getting to the point where we are willing to let go of painful negative feelings. This active and intentional choice is necessary in order for the relationship to move on in a warm and loving fashion.

These are the guidelines we have found to be effective in enabling couples to create an environment in which love flourishes. If you put these rules to work along with an awareness of what really goes on between men and women, we are certain that you will discover a level of satisfaction and happiness that makes all of the necessary work well worth the effort.

Our purpose in this book has been to show how staying in love is possible, and that making a relationship work need not be the exercise in disappointment and frustration that it seems to be for so many people today. Though we have focused more closely on the ways in which men respond to love, we hope you are left with our most basic message: only those acts which enhance our own self-worth, dignity, and personal integrity are worth engaging in with the person we love. Feeling good about ourselves leads to an air of confidence and ease that makes love happen and keeps it most alive.

# APPENDIX

# Quizzes:
# Styles of Loving

The following series of quizzes are designed to measure different styles of relating. As you will notice, each quiz is keyed to a relevant chapter in the book. Their purpose is to help you better understand how your unique attitudes, feelings, and behaviors toward men affect the quality of your relationships.

We believe it is helpful if you take each quiz in order to evaluate potential problem areas in how you relate to men. After scoring each quiz, you may wish to refer back to the specific chapter in order to deepen your understanding about your feelings concerning particular attitudes or behaviors.

## CHAPTER TWO: WOMEN WHO UNKNOWINGLY FEAR INTIMACY

1. I can't imagine being as open with a man as I am with a woman.                    T F
2. I feel that the man in my life is also a very close friend.                          T F
3. I'm aware of having a strong need for privacy.                                       T F

4. I feel closest to a man when I also feel most vulnerable with him.          T F

5. I often feel my barriers go up when I'm with a man.          T F

6. I'm more comfortable with my women friends than with my men friends.          T F

7. I hate the silences when I take a long drive with a man.          T F

8. I enjoy long walks and holding hands with a man I care for.          T F

9. I am uncomfortable when I see a man cry.          T F

10. When a man gets emotional I wonder if he is weak.          T F

11. I enjoy being with a man most when there is at least some distraction—friends, children, or some sort of structured activity.          T F

12. When it comes to men, I really like the self-contained, strong-and-silent type.          T F

13. I'm afraid if I really let a man get to know me he won't like me.          T F

14. I must admit I don't trust men all that much.          T F

15. I don't like to bare my soul to a man any more than I like him to bare his soul to me.          T F

16. The more of me that I reveal to a man, the better I feel.          T F

17. After sexual contact, I feel best being held close and quietly by a man.          T F

18. There are things about my past that I could never tell a man.          T F

19. I have serious doubts about myself and feelings of inadequacy.          T F

20. Revealing my inner feelings to a man is very difficult for me to do.          T F

21. I'm aware that I don't allow myself to get too close so that it won't hurt so much if I lose a man I care about.          T F

22. If I let myself go with a man I'm afraid he will want and expect too much.          T F

23. I really don't enjoy men who discuss their work problems with me.  T F

24. The more contact I have with a man, the better I feel.  T F

25. In my relationships I prefer not to do a lot of talking about inner feelings.  T F

## Scoring

Score one point for any of the following marked T: 1, 3, 5, 6, 7, 9, 10, 11, 12, 13, 14, 15, 18, 19, 20, 21, 22, 23, 25.

Score one point for any of the following marked F: 2, 4, 8, 16, 17, 24.

Add up your score.

## Interpretation

O–4: A score within this range signifies a consistent feeling of personal comfort, an ease and willingness to be yourself with a man, and a wish to foster feelings of closeness. Moreover, it also reflects your basic acceptance of men and the pleasure you take in allowing them to be open with you and move closer toward you. Your confidence and self-esteem will promote and help sustain an intimate bond.

5–7: Men will generally feel open and at ease with you, although a score within this range does suggest the presence of subtle barriers that may prevent real and ongoing closeness with a man. Such boundaries may result from personal questions relating to self-worth or to unclear and ambivalent reactions to the more vulnerable aspects of men's feelings and behavior.

8–11: Scoring within this range reflects the existence of certain blocks to closeness with a man. Such blocks are not caused by whatever discomfort men may have with intimacy but rather by your own fear of emotional closeness. It may be important for you to address issues of self-worth and trust.

12 and above: A score in this range indicates that you have significant difficulties with intimacy. These conflicts reflect underlying feelings of inadequacy and a fear of exposure. Men will feel uncomfortable being open with you, for they detect your anxiety whenever the communication of real feelings occurs. It may be helpful for you to explore just how much you accept yourself and whether you can really tolerate a man's knowing who you really are.

## CHAPTER THREE: HOW INNOCENT EXPECTATIONS BECOME DANGEROUS

1. In a love relationship I don't expect a man to feel as romantic about me as I do about him.                                                        T  F
2. I'm disappointed when a man stops doing those thoughtful little things that reflect real caring.                                                   T  F
3. I don't feel good with a man unless he has a better education and makes more money than I do.                                                     T  F
4. I rarely lose respect for a man who isn't strong and confident with me.                           T  F
5. When a man isn't as interested in making a commitment as I am, I feel rejected.                  T  F
6. It doesn't bother me when a man I care about isn't very protective of me.                         T  F
7. I can't stand being with a man who lets someone push him around or take advantage of him.                                                      T  F
8. I don't like it when I sense fear in a man.      T  F

9. It usually doesn't upset me when I'm the one who always has to suggest an intimate dinner or a quiet weekend away with a man.   T F

10. I'm much more tolerant about a show of emotion in my women friends than I am in a man.   T F

11. In general I don't think a lot of a man who isn't more accomplished than I am.   T F

12. I never push too hard in a relationship.   T F

13. Most men I know are stronger than I am.   T F

14. I must admit I feel a little uncomfortable with an emotionally sensitive man.   T F

15. I don't resent it when a man seems to need his friends as much as he needs me.   T F

16. Basically, I think men like to string women along.   T F

17. It annoys me when a man has no fashion sense and doesn't know how to dress himself.   T F

18. I'm not at all uncomfortable when a man shows signs of insecurity.   T F

19. I expect no more from a man than I do from a woman.   T F

20. Generally, I like a man to be stronger and more skilled than I am.   T F

21. I have no particular expectations that a man should know how to take care of himself in a dangerous or difficult situation.   T F

22. I prefer the stronger, more self-contained type of man.   T F

23. As a relationship goes on I tend to feel somewhat disillusioned with my mate—I wish he would change and be more responsive to what I need.   T F

24. I don't really expect the man in my life to see things the way I do, and I'm rarely disappointed when he doesn't.   T F

25. My father was strong, capable, and successful—he gave me everything I ever wanted.   T F

## Scoring

Score one point for any of the following marked T: 2, 3, 5, 7, 8, 10, 11, 13, 14, 16, 17, 20, 22, 23, 25.

Score one point for any of the following marked F: 1, 4, 6, 9, 12, 15, 18, 19, 21, 24.

Add up your score.

## Interpretation

0–4: A score of 0–4 reflects a well-established sense of personal identity. You are secure enough within yourself to view men clearly and relate to them without unrealistic expectations. Men no doubt feel comfortable being themselves with you and enjoy your fundamental acceptance of them.

5–7: A score of 5–7 suggests a recognition of the basic realities of men's behavior but also a hint of disappointment and resentment. It is possible that your need for men to meet your wishes and expectations may lead to gradual disillusionment.

8–11: Scores of 8–11 are indicative of a good deal of illusion about men and disappointment in them. Expectations you bring to relationships run a real risk of creating feelings of pressure and discomfort in men. Your attitudes toward men, fueled by inner feelings of insecurity, may make trust in and closeness with men difficult to attain. Your expectations are experienced by men as demands.

12 and above: Scores of 12 and above reflect serious interferences caused by misperceptions about men. Men will not feel comfortable with you, and as your attitudes are gradually expressed and recognized by them, they will become increasingly wary, distrusting, and resentful. It would be helpful for you to explore in detail your heightened expecta-

tions of men if you want a man to feel at ease with you.

## CHAPTER FOUR: WOMEN WHO SECRETLY FEEL CONTEMPT FOR MEN

1. The thought of needing a man is not frightening to me.   T F
2. I find myself feeling angry at men without knowing exactly why.   T F
3. Most men tend to be either bullies or weaklings.   T F
4. I respect and value men as much as I do women.   T F
5. I never want to care about a man so much that losing him would be devastating.   T F
6. I enjoy a man who can share his personal problems as well as his triumphs with me.   T F
7. The only things men really get emotional about are sports and work troubles.   T F
8. Outside of work and beyond earshot of their friends, men tend to be big babies.   T F
9. When a man seems "needy," I tend to lose some respect for him.   T F
10. I'm not worried that giving a man what he needs will deprive me of the time or energy to take care of myself.   T F
11. I'm afraid that I could lose myself in a relationship, and I've fought too hard to ever allow that to happen.   T F
12. Men may say they want to get close, but what they really want is to possess a woman.   T F
13. I feel that there is a healthy balance of dependency between my mate and me.   T F
14. I enjoy a man's vulnerability—it lets me know he is human and I trust him more.   T F
15. I feel as good when I'm able to give the man what he needs as I do when he's sensitive to what I need.   T F

16. I know I need a man in my life, but I really don't like men in general all that much.     T   F

17. If a man can't handle my being aggressive sexually then I think that's his problem.     T   F

18. I generally tend to give my trust to a man fairly easily.     T   F

19. I think most men are basically fairly secure.     T   F

20. I feel as good around a man when I'm being active and assertive as I do when I'm being soft and receptive.     T   F

21. I enjoy it when I can really show up a man.     T   F

22. It's hard for me to respond sexually to a man unless I'm the initiator.     T   F

23. I secretly expect a man always to be ready sexually even though I know I'm not.     T   F

24. I think all men are basically alike.     T   F

25. I was uncomfortable around my father.     T   F

## Scoring

Score one point for any of the following marked T: 2, 3, 4, 5, 7, 8, 9, 11, 12, 16, 17, 21, 22, 23, 24, 25.

Score one point for any of the following marked F: 1, 6, 10, 13, 14, 15, 18, 19, 20.

Add up your score.

## Interpretation

0–4: You easily balance the emotional demands of a relationship with your wish for independent activity or work. Your score is indicative of a high level of personal comfort and a feeling of ease around men. While you may be quite strong and accomplished, your strength and competence are not expressed in a manner that indicates an angry or competitive attitude toward men. Whatever hurts you have experienced in the past with men have been resolved and worked out sufficiently so that current relationships are not poisoned by them. Essentially, you are perceptive with men and nonjudgmentally sensitive to their vulnerabilities.

5–7: While you feel relatively comfortable with an interdependent relationship with a man, sometimes you fear that giving more to him will result in less available for you—you fear he will be too demanding. Your responses indicate a slight tendency toward either ignoring or discounting certain areas of relating; you may find that men are a bit cautious and hesitant with you.

8–11: You tend to overlook or deny a man's emotional requirements. Scores within this range indicate that all but the most confident and self-assured of men may react to you with guardedness and anxiety. A man may not be open with you for fear of being seen as "less" by you. Men may view your strengths not simply as wonderful and interesting assets but rather as potential weapons. It is likely that your unresolved hurts from the past color current relationships, creating discomfort and alienation in the man. You need to feel more relaxed and at ease with who you are.

12 and above: Your discomfort with a man's dependency and your fear of being drained or exploited by him cause you to withdraw from him emotionally. You may not intend to be intimidating to a man, but men will clearly respond to you as intimidating. You bring an edge to your relationships that is sure to create anxiety in men. It may be helpful for you to explore your own comfort levels with personal strengths and to try to come to peace with old angry feelings toward men that continue to surface in new relationships.

# CHAPTER FIVE: HOW THE NEED
# TO CONTROL BACKFIRES

1. I think men's interest in sports is a bit excessive and may reflect immaturity.    T F
2. Men are basically tall little boys much of the time.    T F
3. It's not particularly important to have most things in a relationship go my way.    T F
4. Most men need to do some growing up.    T F
5. My way of doing things is usually a lot better than anyone else's.    T F
6. I'm not afraid to fly in airplanes.    T F
7. I don't mind crowded or close places where I can't get out easily.    T F
8. I don't like a man to need me for anything maternal.    T F
9. Most men are capable of monogamy in a long-term relationship.    T F
10. I feel most secure when I know that a man needs me.    T F
11. I tend to be suspicious even if a man doesn't give me reason to be.    T F
12. It doesn't bother me when my mate goes on trips alone.    T F
13. If you are not vigilant, most men will play around on you.    T F
14. Most men need a good woman to polish the rough edges.    T F
15. It's good to let a man think he's making the decisions.    T F
16. I feel comfortable in a relationship even if I don't know where the man is or who he's with most of the time.    T F
17. If a man allows it, I tend to take over and assume the more dominant position.    T F
18. Most men are capable of having women friends and keeping it platonic.    T F
19. Sex happens only when I'm in the mood.    T F
20. It's no harder for me to receive criticism from a man than it is to give it out.    T F

21. In relationships, I have never tended to be
    a bit bossy.                                      T F
22. I'm not possessive and jealous with a man.        T F
23. I find it vaguely disturbing when I'm not
    totally aware of my mate's activities.            T F
24. I have a strong need for order and organi-
    zation and for things to be done in a par-
    ticular way.                                       T F
25. I tend to get upset when I can't reach some-
    one on the phone.                                  T F

## Scoring

Score one point for any of the following marked T:
1, 2, 4, 5, 8, 10, 11, 13, 14, 15, 17, 19, 23, 24, 25.

Score one point for any of the following marked F:
3, 6, 7, 9, 12, 16, 18, 20, 21, 22.

Add up your score.

## Interpretation

0–4: Scores of 0–4 are indicative of a general sense
of well-being and a trusting, easy going manner
with men. Because you like yourself you have no
need to control or direct your mate's feelings and
actions. While it is possible that you may err on the
side of letting a man you care for have his way too
much, you certainly will not be overcontrolling with
him and will not make him feel uncomfortable or
resentful.

5–7: Scoring within the 5–7 range means that control may be an underlying problem for you, however
well disguised its manifestations may be with men.
Men may be a bit cautious with you, questioning
whether you like and trust them. They sense your
need to be in control as a way of feeling more secure.

8–11: A score between 8 and 11 means that control is definitely an important issue with you and one that affects your relationships with men. It is difficult for you to like, trust and accept men the way they are, which probably leads you to want to change them in certain ways. The forces that such feelings set in motion are likely to prevent a man from being at ease with you.

12 and above: Scores this high reflect strong needs for control and the power role in a relationship. Past disappointments and hurts lead you to try to protect yourself through the various manifestations of control —endless proofs of love, suspicion, and the use of threat, and the fear that if you are not powerful you will become powerless. Your persistent need to be in charge, which creates a hurt-before-you-get-hurt attitude, will alienate men, particularly those you value most.

# CHAPTER SIX: WOMEN WHO GIVE TOO FREELY

1. I'm afraid that my just "being" isn't good enough for a man—that I have to "do" for him and keep doing in order to hold his interest.                                          T  F
2. I usually have to do most of the work in a relationship.                                        T  F
3. I feel I'm really lovable to a man.              T  F
4. The more I care about a man the less afraid I am of being abandoned.                         T  F
5. It's never hard for me to stand up for what I want and need in a relationship with a man.                                                   T  F
6. I usually feel more comfortable giving to a man than receiving from him.                     T  F
7. I give too much to a man because I need too much.                                             T  F

8. I find myself drawn to men with personal problems and seem to always end up trying to solve them.    T F

9. I don't enjoy taking care of a man.    T F

10. I'm aware of needing constant reassurance of a man's love.    T F

11. I feel that my father never really loved me.    T F

12. I used to go out of my way to try to get my father to approve of me.    T F

13. I can't remember feeling bad about the way my mother treated my father.    T F

14. Neither of my parents abused alcohol or drugs.    T F

15. I never seem to truly believe it when a man tells me he loves me.    T F

16. When it comes to men, I'm aware that I have low self-esteem.    T F

17. I usually don't get involved with a man too quickly or too intensely.    T F

18. Even though I care about a man I typically don't put his needs ahead of mine.    T F

19. I'm inclined to defer to a man even when I feel that I'm basically right.    T F

20. I would rather sacrifice my needs in a relationship with a man than take the chance of being wrong or coming across as demanding.    T F

21. I rarely end up taking care of a man, particularly in those areas where I know he is perfectly capable of taking care of himself.    T F

22. I haven't felt exploited by the men in my life.    T F

23. My worst fear in a relationship is of being abandoned.    T F

24. I would like mutuality in a relationship, but I don't demand it.    T F

25. I only rarely have the feeling that I'm being taken for granted.    T F

## Scoring

Score one point for any of the following marked T: 1, 2, 6, 7, 8, 10, 11, 12, 15, 16, 19, 20, 23, 24.

Score one point for any of the following marked F: 3, 4, 5, 9, 13, 14, 17, 18, 21, 22, 25.

Add up your score.

## Interpretation

0–4: A score of 0–4 reflects a well-established level of confidence and self-esteem. You undoubtedly trust your feelings and sense of what is appropriate, and consequently you don't fall prey to self-sacrificing behavior. You feel lovable and you expect a reasonable degree of mutuality, and men tend to like and respect you.

5–7: A score in this range suggests that to some degree you doubt your own worth and the sincerity of a man's love, and you may allow yourself to be taken a bit for granted. You may be overly attentive to his needs and neglect your own.

8–11: Scoring in this range reflects important and long-standing self-doubt. You expect too much of yourself and far too little in the way of sensitivity and reciprocity from the man. You are in danger of being easily neglected by men because you are afraid to stand up for those rights in a relationship that are both realistic and appropriate.

12 and above: Scores this high indicate a serious danger of being at the mercy of men and even victimized by them. You tend to be self-effacing and self-sacrificing. Rather than endearing you to a man, these qualities instead create a serious likelihood of your being exploited, neglected, and even abused. It is important for you to focus more on learning to care for and accept yourself and less on pleasing the man.

## CHAPTER EIGHT: GIVING UP THE PRINCE AND FINDING THE MAN

1. Men may be all right in a work context, but they are pretty backward when it comes to love and relationships.   T F
2. I can find something of interest or something I like in many men I know.   T F
3. Women have changed a lot in recent years; now I think it's men's turn, and they have a good deal of changing to do.   T F
4. I don't think I really understand men.   T F
5. I must admit I'm afraid of men and cautious with them.   T F
6. I think I've given up most wishful illusions about men, and I find I enjoy them anyway.   T F
7. I've never really been able to maintain a strong platonic friendship with a man.   T F
8. It's hard for me to truly forgive a man when he has let me down or hurt me.   T F
9. I'm no more demanding or critical of others than I am of myself.   T F
10. At heart I'm basically an idealist.   T F
11. There is a right way and a wrong way of doing things.   T F
12. I've been told that I'm somewhat of a perfectionist.   T F
13. Men tend to open up about themselves around me.   T F
14. I had a brother I liked as a child.   T F
15. In spite of their not being perfect I like and enjoy men.   T F
16. I find that most men have some pretty serious deficiencies.   T F
17. Most men have a needy or vulnerable side that I find endearing.   T F
18. Most of my interactions with men are at a superficial or flirtatious level.   T F
19. I like sharing confidences with men.   T F
20. I've always found it difficult and uncomfortable to talk with my father.   T F

21. When I am in a relationship I am mono-
    gamous.                                          T F
22. In a relationship my mate feels secure in
    my love for him.                                 T F
23. I like men pretty much the way they are.        T F
24. The man in my life seems to confide more
    in his friends than he does in me.               T F
25. I'm basically approving and supportive of
    my mate's relationships with his friends.        T F

## Scoring

Score one point for any of the following marked T:
2, 6, 9, 13, 14, 15, 17, 19, 21, 22, 23, 25.

Score one point for any of the following marked F:
1, 3, 4, 5, 7, 8, 10, 11, 12, 16, 18, 20, 24.

Add up your score.

## Interpretation

21–25: You genuinely enjoy the company of men.
You like to know them without preconceptions or
expectations of how they should be, and as a result
men seek you out and allow themselves to get close
to you, knowing they will be accepted.

17–20: You feel generally accepting of men, yet
there are moments when old feelings of distrust
emerge, causing you to be somewhat self-protective.
While men may not be put off by this they may tend
to be cautious with you and slower to commit
themselves.

13–16: You are ill at ease with men and more
concerned with receiving understanding than with
giving it. Your need to over-simplify a man's needs
and your failure to take into account who a man
really is may make men distrustful of you.

12 or less: Because of past hurts and disappoint-

ments, you distrust men and have difficulty feeling any genuine warmth toward them. Men will likely be guarded in your presence, perhaps even subtly hostile, for they may not realize that your facade is really a means of avoiding hurt. Most men will not remain in a relationship with so little warmth and acceptance.

## CHAPTER NINE: TRUSTING A MAN TO LOVE YOUR STRENGTH

1. I feel uncomfortable being in positions of leadership. T F
2. I'm not hesitant to express my feelings or voice my opinions. T F
3. I believe that I am a good judge of people and I trust my perceptions. T F
4. I have few illusions about men and can see their strengths and weaknesses pretty clearly. T F
5. I am not particularly career-oriented myself and I have little personal knowledge or understanding of the kinds of work experiences men have. T F
6. Men respect me and what I know and can do in the world. T F
7. I don't feel I'm really treated as a peer by the men I know and care about. T F
8. I'm not able to give to a man without somehow losing a bit of respect for him. T F
9. Men I care about value my observations and opinions. T F
10. Men I'm interested in see me as strong but are not intimidated by me. T F
11. I understand and can see through my mate's blind spots. T F
12. I'm often overly critical or judgmental. T F

13. The man in my life usually sees me as an equal partner.    T F

14. Most of the time I'm more dependent upon a man than he is upon me.    T F

15. Men tend to be threatened or a little intimidated by my strengths and capabilities rather than seeing them as assets.    T F

16. I don't lose respect for a man even though we both know I'm better than he is at certain things.    T F

17. It's very hard for me to use my strengths constructively rather than competitively in a relationship.    T F

18. I have not had close and mutually revealing relationships with men.    T F

19. Being in a leadership role or position with a man I care for doesn't diminish my feelings for him.    T F

20. Men tend to be patronizing and talk down to me in subtly disrespectful ways.    T F

21. A man values his partnership with me in much the same way I value it.    T F

22. You have to be careful with men and treat them as if they have fragile egos.    T F

23. I like men and have enjoyed strong friendships with them.    T F

24. I don't look to a man for any more support or protection than I'm willing to give him.    T F

25. When I'm with a man I sometimes conceal my competence or intelligence.    T F

### Scoring

Score one point for any of the following marked T: 2, 3, 4, 6, 9, 10, 11, 13, 16, 19, 21, 23, 24.

Score one point for any of the following marked F: 1, 5, 7, 8, 12, 14, 15, 17, 18, 20, 22, 25.

Add up your score.

### Interpretation

**21–25:** Your sense of independence and wish to experience life's challenges are contagious and evoke a powerful feeling of attraction in men. Because you trust your strengths and feel comfortable with them, men will trust you emotionally as well as value your intelligence and enthusiasm.

**17–20:** You believe in your strengths and find taking the initiative acceptable most of the time. You feel free to express who you are, though there are times when you secretly wish the man in your life were more of a leader, more dominant, or more the initiator of shared experiences.

**13–16:** Whenever you do find yourself in a position where the responsibilities are equal in a relationship, you feel uncomfortable. One of your primary wishes in a relationship is the fantasy that it is possible to shift life's responsibilities from yourself onto another. Your secret belief is that the man is the one who does the "mastering" in life, which prevents you from exploring and expanding your own sense of confidence and competence.

**12 or less:** You want the man to be the strong one. You insist on hanging on to outmoded notions of the nature of men and are still basically in search of the strong decisive male who will protect you. Most men, sensing this secret wish, will feel resentful and burdened. Sadly, your insistence on traditional ways of relating robs you of new experiences that would enhance your self-esteem.

## CHAPTER TEN: AROUSING A MAN'S PASSION AND DESIRE

1. I see myself as fundamentally cautious and
   conservative.                                    T  F

2. I feel things a lot more intensely than I am able to show and let other people see.     T F

3. There are few constraints I place upon myself when I'm with someone I really care about.     T F

4. I believe that people see me as spontaneous and a bit unpredictable.     T F

5. I sometimes experience long periods of boredom and apathy.     T F

6. At times, people who are childlike or youthful tend to annoy me.     T F

7. People seem to think I have a good sense of humor.     T F

8. I really enjoy being silly and playful at times.     T F

9. I tend to take myself too seriously.     T F

10. I can't seem to overcome feelings of shyness and inhibition even when I'm around someone who cares and whom I trust.     T F

11. I wish I could feel more alive and excited than I do.     T F

12. Staying in control is very important to me.     T F

13. Strong sexual feelings sometimes make me nervous.     T F

14. At times I can get very jealous and angry.     T F

15. I can express my feelings of insecurity as openly as I can express feelings of desire.     T F

16. I feel nervous and unsure of myself most of the time.     T F

17. I don't look to a man for approval and validation.     T F

18. I'm more comfortable and open around women than I am around men.     T F

19. I enjoy my individuality.     T F

20. When I'm with a man, somehow I feel I lose part of myself.     T F

21. My mother and father were openly affectionate with each other.     T F

22. As a child I was most often obedient and very rarely rebellious.     T F

23. I rarely use profanity or "dirty" language.  T F
24. I'm comfortable with my body and uninhibited in bed.  T F
25. I prefer making love with the lights out.  T F

## Scoring

Score one point for any of the following marked T: 3, 4, 7, 8, 15, 17, 19, 21, 24.

Score one point for any of the following marked F: 1, 2, 5, 6, 9, 10, 11, 12, 13, 14, 16, 18, 20, 22, 23, 25.

Add up your score.

## Interpretation

21–25: You have a zest and enthusiasm for meeting life head on. This ability to trust your own instincts and feel comfortable with your physical being will stimulate very passionate interest from men. Men are excited by you and drawn to your promise of intense and alive experiences.

17–20: You are reasonably comfortable in expressing yourself and being open, yet you feel a lingering sense of caution often enough so that your comfort level may suffer, especially in the sexual area. Men are drawn to you but also tend to alternate between a sense of trust and feelings of reserve, just as you do.

13–16: You rarely express sexual feelings and emotions in general with any spontaneity. Unfortunately, this fear of being too revealing and exposed may block intimacy between you and men. Without knowing why, men will drift away from you as a sexual partner.

12 or less: Your conflicts over sexual expressions and emotional release prevent you from

feeling relaxed and comfortable with men. Your inhibitions are invariably sensed by a man, regardless of whether he actually comments on it, making this an area of conflict for the two of you. Regardless of your past experiences with men, you are depriving yourself of a life fully lived—your caution is clearly excessive.

## CHAPTER ELEVEN: DEEPENING LOVE THROUGH FRIENDSHIP

1. As an adult I've never been able to sustain a platonic friendship with a man who was important to me.   T F
2. I have a sense of commonality and shared experiences with men.   T F
3. I could never have a man as a best friend.   T F
4. I don't believe that men can handle friendships with a woman; they always want more.   T F
5. My mate is also my close friend.   T F
6. While I am discriminating, I tend to like and trust men.   T F
7. I like knowing and being known by a man in a relationship.   T F
8. I don't worry that a deeper friendship will erode the feelings of passion in my relationship with a man.   T F
9. I fundamentally like who my mate is even though I'm aware of his flaws.   T F
10. The man in my life sees me as supportive.   T F
11. With my mate, sex can be as playful and silly at times as it is passionate.   T F
12. My communication with men occurs at a variety of levels—from playful to very moving and mutually revealing conversations.   T F
13. It's easier for me to become friends with a man with whom I'm not romantically involved.   T F

14. I can't really picture being friends with a man because most of them seem so focused on things that are uninteresting to me.     T  F

15. My mate would never be able to handle or understand my having a simple, nonthreatening friendship with another man.     T  F

16. I could never trust the man I'm involved with to have a friendship with a woman and spend time with her when I wasn't around.     T  F

17. If you really get to be "buddies" with a man he will lose interest and start looking around for another woman.     T  F

18. I like the feelings of trust and comfort that I have with a man when he becomes my friend.     T  F

19. Most men are a whole lot more interested in what a woman looks like than in what kind of real friend she can be.     T  F

20. If you are too nice to a man he will take you for granted and start treating you badly.     T  F

21. Men stay with women who are mean to them because they basically like getting punished.     T  F

22. I don't wait for a man to take the lead—I present myself in a friendly way, often initiating contact and expressing interest.     T  F

23. I will ask a man to go out or to do something with me when I'm interested in him.     T  F

24. I don't believe men place much importance on companionship in a relationship.     T  F

25. The feeling of independence and partnership I get from being an income provider in my relationship is very important.     T  F

## Scoring

Score one point for any of the following marked T: 2, 5, 6, 7, 8, 9, 10, 11, 12, 18, 22, 23, 25.

Score one point for any of the following marked F:
1, 3, 4, 13, 14, 15, 16, 17, 19, 20, 21, 24.
Add up your score.

### Interpretation

**21–25:** Your desire to feel close to a man and establish a sense of partnership is communicated in a warm, inviting fashion. This ability to establish an atmosphere of trust allows you to have rich and fulfilling relationships with men.

**17–20:** You enjoy feelings of closeness and companionship with men, but there are times when old romantic expectations may block you from experiencing genuine equality. A man who needs a real sense of equality might feel a vague discomfort with you.

**13–16:** You rarely feel sufficiently trusting to be genuine friends with a man, though you may hide your distrust enough for there to be an absence of conflict over this issue. Nevertheless, men who want a sense of sharing, equality, and person-to-person loyalty will not feel totally relaxed or fulfilled around you.

**12 or less:** You are unwilling to let go of romantic and other unrealistic expectations and rarely feel any real trust in a man. You don't believe openness and equality are possible between men and women. For you the "battle of the sexes" is never over. Even if you do develop a relationship, you will continue to remain somewhat apart and estranged from your partner.

There are good men out there—and here's how to find them

# Smart WOMEN Foolish CHOICES

## DR. CONNELL COWAN & DR. MELVYN KINDER

Why is it that so many women have everything going for them—except satisfying personal relationships? Clinical psychologists Dr. Connell Cowan and Dr. Melvin Kinder reveal the startling answers. Find out why smart women are almost magnetically drawn to the wrong men and how they can change their love-defeating attitudes to open up new opportunities for romantic happiness. Find out what really makes men fall in love—and stay that way. "A fascinating, helpful book."—*Los Angeles Times*

---